D0627174

THE GREAT AMBASSADOR

THE GREAT AMBASSADOR

A Study of the Diplomatic Career of the
Right Honourable Stratford Canning, K.G., G.C.B.,
Viscount Stratford de Redcliffe,
and the Epoch during Which He Served as the
British Ambassador to the Sublime Porte of the
Ottoman Sultan

By Leo Gerald Byrne

Ohio State University Press

PREFACE

SOME years ago I chanced upon the record of Stratford
Canning. The discovery was made during the process of
gathering material for a novel on the period of the Crimean
War. The more I read of this man and his work the further
I was led in my search, and so great did my fascination
become that I felt impelled, eventually, to share with others
what I had learned about him.

For a substantial part of the first half of the nineteenth
century Stratford Canning was Her Brittannic Majesty's
Ambassador to the Ottoman Sultan. In this role he played a
significant part in the drama of high-level diplomacy and
exercised a singular influence on the intertwined history of
Europe and the Near East. He had, according to Winston
Churchill, "a wider knowledge of Turkey than any other
Englishman of his day," and he was hailed by Tennyson as
"the voice of England in the East." To the Turks he was
Buyuk Elchi—the Great Ambassador.

In spite of these accolades he is today virtually unknown to otherwise well-informed laymen. When one considers, by way of contrast, the notoriety accorded many far less influential personages of the Victorian era, his disappearance from history, so to speak, assumes almost the proportion of a mystery. If for no other reason than to do him justice it seemed worthwhile to me to attempt this book. My motives go beyond that simple goal, however, for I consider it nearly impossible to achieve a good understanding of nineteenth-century European history and its relevance for our own day without specific reference to Stratford Canning, his ideas and his work.

I have written this study primarily for the intelligent layman who likes to be informed as much as is reasonably possible. The sweep of history encompassed by the terminal points of Stratford Canning's career is so vast that I have elected to offer a substantive account of his work rather than to construct a formal and detailed personal biography. With that end in view I have tried to avoid, without sacrificing historical authenticity, the obscurantism and picayune concerns one sometimes finds in the professional monograph. The bones of historical evidence in this area have already been cleanly picked, but much of the intellectual nutrients are stored in warehouses not readily accessible to the layman. I have tried to present a fare chosen from among the products of recognized scholarship. Where there are sufficient variants of opinion I have tried to justify in my notes the particular flavor I have chosen.

Beyond the particulars of Stratford Canning's life but through the medium of his career I hope to reveal a chain of ideas and events which have had a permanent bearing on human history. In that process I hope, also, to indicate the role of skilled diplomacy in human affairs; especially do I wish to demonstrate the necessity of what is often suspiciously referred to as "secret" diplomacy. There is no argument over the fundamental premise that in a democratic society the people as a whole must exercise ultimate control over foreign policy, even if only through a parliamentary medium. There are, nevertheless, a host of intermediate prudential decisions which should be left to competent statesmen to work out, and these workings should be free from the glare of journalistic or parliamentary publicity, no matter how well-intentioned such publicity might be. Failure to observe this rule of practical wisdom has more than once involved humanity in great tragedy. Tentative opinions openly reported too easily become irretraceable postures of national pride. When this occurs reason seldom holds her sway among the nations.

In preparing this study I have depended heavily on certain sources which deserve special mention. Chief among these is the monumental biography of Stratford Canning written by one of the great archivists of the nineteenth century, Stanley Lane-Poole, in 1888. This work, printed in two volumes totaling nearly one thousand tightly packed pages, is a major source for the history of Stratford Canning and his times chiefly because Lane-Poole had access to the unpublished manuscript memoirs written by Canning after his retirement from public life. From these manuscript memoirs Lane-Poole excerpted hundreds of lengthy citations, and, in addition, he copied a host of private letters from Canning to his mother, sister, brothers, and friends. By 1930, when E. E. Malcolm-Smith began to restudy the life of Stratford Canning, she found that the complete manuscript memoirs as well as many of the private letters had disappeared. By diligent cross-checking, however, with private papers of other individuals and the official archives of the British Museum, the Public Record Office, and the British Foreign Office as well as with official archives in Vienna, Paris, and elsewhere, she concluded that Lane-Poole had copied faithfully and well. Hence, all references in this study to the memoirs are to the manuscript memoirs of Canning as recorded in Lane-Poole's *Life of the Right Honourable Stratford Canning.* In 1933 Miss Malcolm-Smith published her *Life of Stratford Canning,* which was shorter but had the benefit of more research into documents made public long after Lane-Poole's work. Both of these biographies are long out of print, however, and each of them labors under the burden of having been written for English readers and presumes a familiarity on the part of the audience with details of English domestic politics as well as with usages and mores which may be unclear to the modern American student. On the political background of the Crimean War, Professor Harold Temperley's *Britain and the Near East: The Crimea* has achieved an aura of almost scriptural authority, but even this work is now past the quarter-century mark and was written before the staggering events of the Second World War, to say nothing of the cold war of the fifties and sixties. With the help of all this scholarship I have attempted to look back at Stratford Canning's world from a perspective that is now longer and wider.

I am indebted to many people for whatever degree of success I have achieved. I owe a special debt of gratitude to Adeline Corrigan of the Cleveland Public Library for the initial encouragement to pursue this goal and for the acquisition of my first research material. I am also obligated to Sydney N. Fisher, Professor of History at the Ohio State University, for professional encouragement and advice and for his efforts in interesting the Ohio State University Press in my work. James Hafer, of the Newark, Ohio, Public Library was always at my command in procuring material from the Library of Congress and elsewhere, as was Mrs. John Gibney, of the staff of the Denison University Library in Granville, Ohio. T. Edwyn Dickerson, of Newark, Ohio, deserves special mention for his invaluable help in checking not only literary error but unwarranted deductions from historical evidence at hand.

The officers of the Ohio State University Press have exhibited unusual patience and understanding, and I trust that these virtues will be duly rewarded.

More than anyone else, of course, my wife, Antoinette, is responsible for the completion of this work. Without her complete and unselfish co-operation it could never have come into being. Only those who have been through similar experiences will know the full extent of this debt.

Finally, all shortcomings in this book are matters of personal responsibility alone.

LEO GERALD BYRNE

THE GREAT AMBASSADOR

I

STRATFORD CANNING belongs to the group of individuals who might properly be described as catalysts of history. These are persons who, though they did not rule nations nor lead mighty armies nor crystallize in their own being the evolution of epochal social or religious movements, just as surely helped to shape their own times and influence the future. It is quite true that the history of the nineteenth century can be written without reference to Stratford Canning; it is equally true that the story will be incomplete without him. The details of much of the change wrought in that era would have been far different from what they were had he not been on the scene. The opinion might even be hazarded, furthermore, that the substance of many changes would have been other than it proved to be. The final judgment as to the extent of his influence is probably beyond historical competence, but whatever that judgment might be there is little doubt but that he left the mark of his character and personality on Europe and the Near East.

Stratford Canning sprang from a family stock that had long combined what were to be the dominant traits of nineteenth century England—mercantile interests and government service. One of his forebears, Sir William Canynges, is listed as being a bailiff of Bristol in the middle of the fourteenth century. Another was Lord Mayor of London in the fifteenth century. In the seventeenth century one branch of the family was rewarded by James I with a manorial seat in Ireland, and the stock was invigorated with the blood of Derry and Wicklow. It was from this Wicklow strain, and from the Stratfords of Baltinglass (his great-grandfather had married one Abigail Stratford in 1662), that Stratford Canning took his direct root and bore his given name.

Originally the Cannings had been wool merchants in the west country, but the move to Ireland had tended to remove them from the channels of trade to banking and factorage and later to law. This ancestry notwithstanding, an observer of Stratford Canning's infancy and boyhood would have had dismal forecasts for his future. There had been an abrupt decline in the family fortunes by the time of his birth.

His grandfather, the first Stratford Canning, must have been a most stern and tyrannical patriarch. Two of his three sons rebelled and were disowned in early manhood. Thus disinherited, these two young men gravitated back to the land of their progenitors and there, in England, attempted to establish themselves as best they could. The older of the two was a counsellor, but he died penniless in 1771, leaving behind him an infant son, George—the future Prime Minister. The younger, the second Stratford Canning, married the daughter of a Dublin merchant, Mehitabel Patrick, and was able to secure a partnership in a small London banking firm which became known as French, Burroughs, and Canning.

Stratford and Mehitabel Canning were scarcely settled in their own London home when they were constrained to take over the parental responsibility for their baby nephew, George. His mother had turned to the companionship of a reprobate actor after the death of her husband and abandoned him. In spite of their own struggles with a growing family the uncle and aunt were able to send this boy to Eton and thus start him on the road that was to lead to Parliament and the Prime Ministry. It was a debt that George Canning never forgot and one which he had an early opportunity to repay, for the second Stratford Canning died in 1787, a bare six months after the birth of his fifth child, and just when his business was beginning to prosper.

This fifth child of Stratford and Mehitabel Canning was a boy, and he was also named Stratford Canning. He was born in the family house in St. Clement's Lane on the fourth of November, 1786. His prospects were bleak, as his father had never been able to amass a fortune to provide an inherit- ance for his sons, and the family was never far removed from poverty. Mehitabel Canning was a resourceful woman, however, and kept her children—four sons and one daughter—together. She was able to eke out a respectable living from her husband's business and thus maintain a pleasant home.

The infant son, Stratford, soon became the special responsibility of Cousin George, although the latter was but a youth himself. Even when the young widow was forced to give up the London house and move to Wanstead in Essex, at the outskirts of Epping Forest, George Canning was a constant guest.

It was not only his sense of responsibility that made George Canning a constant visitor. It was a pleasant place to come to, for in spite of the rigors of her life Mehitabel Canning kept a lively household; and George's friends were always welcome as well. Young Stratford's earliest recollections included memories of the brilliant conversation of Charles Fox and Sheridan and Hookham Frere among others who frequented the house, all of a type to make the young Stratford Canning dream of things far beyond the confines of his own home.

Babyhood was not unduly prolonged in those days, and at the age of four he had already been enrolled in a neighborhood dame school where he received the rudiments of formal instruction. Then at six he was, in his own words, removed to "the sterner discipline" of Mr. Newcome's school for boys at Hackney. Here he remained for three more years until Cousin George thought it time for him to be entered at Eton.

The occasion was a memorable one for Stratford Canning. The twenty-five-year-old member of Parliament brought his nine-year-old protégé straight to the provost's lodge lest the academic authorities have the slightest doubt as to the identity and quality of the young scholar being entrusted to them. The rising star of George Canning assured his little cousin the privilege of sitting to table at the provost's that first night and a warm introduction to the headmaster of the lower school on the next morning. Upon his patron's departure, however, Stratford was quickly relegated to the lowest depths of public school life. He was forced, like all beginners at Eton, to endure the near servitude to the "upper formers" while he struggled to conform, at the same time, to the strict classicism of the scholastic regimen. In later life he was to observe that while the system had its obvious advantages in producing strong-minded and self-disciplined scholars, the excesses to which the procedure was often carried could destroy all the good effected.

Nevertheless, the ten years he spent at Eton prepared him, as similar years did many others, for the arduous tasks of later life. They provided him with the mental tools he was to use for fifty years of service on the world scene. They gave him, too, his means of private recreation, the writing of poetry, which would carry him through many a lonely and desperate hour. Here, too, he saw much of the great and near great, as Eton was a favorite spot for George III and its students were welcome guests at Windsor on Sunday afternoons.

Even more attractive for the youthful Stratford Canning were the visits to Parliament where he could watch his idols, Pitt and Fox, and Cousin George, in action. These were exciting men in exciting times. Revolution had gripped France and its tumult echoed in the Houses of Parliament in the form of angry debate over what course England should follow. There were defenders of rank and privilege who argued that England should rush to the aid of the discredited French aristocracy. Pitt, the Prime Minister, resisted the tide again and again, and it was not until the French Republic reached out over the borders of France and attempted to seize the Low Countries that he bowed to the demands for war. The resulting conflict brought strain and fear as the stature of Napoleon Bonaparte seemed to grow with each passing month. So while the young student at Eton explored the world of knowledge, he was more captivated by the world outside, and the most vivid memory he took with him from these days was the picture of the great hero, Nelson, with Lady Hamilton at his side, strolling about the grounds of the school and smiling at the scholars.

When Stratford Canning was admitted to King's College at Cambridge in the summer of 1806, Nelson was gone, Fox was gone, and so, too, was Pitt. The armies of Napoleon marched across the continent from Gibraltar to the Elbe, from the North Sea to the heel of the Italian boot. The Peninsula Campaign was but a germ in the mind of Sir Arthur Welles- ley, and England stood virtually alone. From his throne in Paris the Emperor had begun to bestow their respective kingdoms on his brothers; the Spaniards cowered in fear; Austria had been humbled along with Prussia; and Alexander of Russia waited nervously for the blow to fall upon him.

For a brief period after the death of Pitt the Tories were out of office and the country was administered by a rough coalition dominated by the Whigs under Lord Grenville. It did not long survive, however, and early in 1807 the Tories reorganized the government and formed a Cabinet in which George Canning was named Foreign Secretary. It is not surprising that the young Cambridge scholar Stratford Canning was given part-time employment as a précis writer at the Foreign Office.

The relative freedom enjoyed by scholars matriculating at the great English universities offered no obstacle to the pursuit of such work, but the young man was soon to be faced with a choice that would greatly affect his future career. That future, he had already decided, would be spent in Parliament and, he hoped, would culminate in a ministerial post, after the example of his now famous cousin. That cousin, he was certain, would inevitably head a government as Prime Minister, and it can be surmised that Stratford Canning secretly dreamt of sharing governmental responsibility under such leadership. It would have been the normal dream of any alert, intelligent young man reared in the circumstances and surroundings that had been his.

In consequence of these aspirations it was with some hesitation that Stratford Canning faced up to a suggestion from George in the summer of 1807 that he accept appointment as second secretary to a British embassy to the Danish court in Copenhagen. He acceded to his cousin's urgings only upon assurance that the assignment would be brief. Ostensibly Stratford Canning wondered about absenting himself from the university for such a period of time, but in reality he debated the possibility that such an engagement might serve to divert him from the course he had already charted for himself, or that it might be construed as a willingness to be diverted. These fears George Canning countered with arguments that must have been sufficiently compelling, for Stratford agreed to go, at any rate. In spite of his announced fears he then left the university without bothering to go through the formalities of making arrangements for his absence. This departure really marked the end of his formal education even though he managed to get back for another term or two. Years later Cambridge finally saw fit to reward him with a degree in return for his services to the Crown.

The mission to Copenhagen was one necessitated by the lengths to which England was driven in order to counter the intrigues of Bonaparte. Relations between England and Denmark had been severely strained because of a bold and unprecedented action against the neutral Danes that George

Canning had been forced to resort to in the spring of 1807, almost immediately after his entry into the Foreign Office. Intelligence reports from the continent had indicated that Napoleon was about to seize the sizable Danish fleet in an effort to break the British blockade of the Continent. George Canning had thereupon spurred the Cabinet into ordering the British admirals to enter the Baltic and secure the surrender of this fleet or, failing that, to destroy it. The Danes, of course, with Napoleon at their back, had not seen fit to acquiesce without a show of resistance. The resulting action had led not only to a seizure of the fleet but to an occupation of Copenhagen by British forces. It had been a purely practical action against a neutral nation without a shred of legality, yet it had proved to be a master stroke in the maneuvering between the two mighty antagonists. Subsequent revelations show that even before the British fleet had reached the Baltic Napoleon had informed the hapless Danes they would soon have to choose between himself and his enemy across the Channel.[1]

Now that the deed was done George Canning hoped to convince the Danes to save themselves by a formal alliance with England, and he sent a mission to Copenhagen to propose that course to them. The chances for success were not great, but, on the other hand, a failure to accomplish the objective would cause no additional difficulty.

This was the first excursion into the world of diplomacy for Stratford Canning. He had not yet reached his twenty-first birthday when the mission sailed at the beginning of October,

1807. His role was, of course, completely subordinate, but it was in this period that he began to write what would prove to be an almost countless number of notes, letters, and essays. They were articulate and descriptive, with rare insight into people and events. They were written to his mother, his sister, his brother William, an Anglican vicar (later to be Canon of Windsor), and to several friends of his days at Eton and Cambridge, including Henry Wellesley, the son of the Marquis of that name and nephew of Sir Arthur, the future Duke of Wellington. Important and revealing, too, are those written to Joseph Planta and David Morier, young colleagues at the Foreign Office and collaborators of future days.

Throughout these early letters Canning returns constantly to the theme that this is but a passing phase in his life, but a taste of England's burden in the outer world, so to speak, and that he will soon be back at loftier pursuits. Yet one can almost read in them an effort to convince himself that this is not the life he seeks; only an intense interest in and awareness of what was going on around him could have dictated those letters. To quote from them here is beyond the scope of this work, since he makes no pretense of discussing great issues or events, preferring rather to describe cities, houses, and palaces, kings, governors, and princes, and to compare courtly modes and social customs. They are observations neither pretentious nor assuming.

The embassy of Mr. Merry to the Danes was as unsuccessful as it promised to be; indeed, it was never officially received, and its members saw more of the Swedish court at Halsingborg and Stockholm than they saw of Denmark. But for Stratford Canning it was the seed that started a long and great career, even if, at the time, it seemed neither romantic nor exciting.

By the end of the year he was back in England. "The next six months," he wrote in his memoirs, "were spent either in London or at Cambridge; in London for the performance of my official duties at the Foreign Office; at Cambridge in keeping terms, attending lectures, drinking milk-punch, which was then in fashion at all the colleges, and exercising my unfledged wings at a spouting club for eventual flights in oratory."

Idyllic as such a life may sound, it would probably have not satisfied him for very long. Fortunately, he had little time in which to grow bored, for he continued in the same passage: "Before we had reached midsummer a new prospect opened for me abroad—one so alluring for youth and its natural aspirations that I looked to it with eagerness and delight, though not quite forgetful of my late miseries at sea, nor by any means inclined to relinquish permanently the more congenial position I had obtained at home." [2]

The new prospect was another suggestion from his cousin that he go abroad on a second temporary assignment, that of secretary to Robert Adair, the newly posted Minister to the Sublime Porte in Constantinople. "We reckoned" Canning reminisced years later, " . . . on being free to return after a few months, and I was, therefore, allowed to retain my office at home, though, of course, without receiving the salary assigned to it. I had also to keep a good half of my terms at the University." [3]

1. Winston Churchill, *A History of the English-Speaking Peoples* (4 vols.; New York: Dodd, Mead and Co., 1957), III, 315.

2. Stanley Lane-Poole, *The Life of the Right Honourable Stratford Canning* (2 vols.; London: Longmans, Green, and Co., 1888), I, 36-37.

3. *Ibid.*, p. 39.

II

BRITISH foreign policy during the Napoleonic Wars was based on the nation's stark need to survive in face of the overwhelming power amassed by her enemy on the Continent. Unable to come to grips with the French military machine on land and, indeed, lacking the trained manpower to do so through much of the period, Britain was forced to use her maritime supremacy to guard the perimeters of the Continent and throttle as best she could the further expansion of the Bonapartist empire. Additionally, Pitt and his successors sought every opportunity to harry the enemy within the borders of his greatly expanded dominion. Whenever Napoleon rested from his campaigns and turned his attention to domestic matters British agents on the Continent were ready to seize upon each sign of restiveness or rebellion in the conquered provinces. Coalitions or alliances, based on the promise of English help, were formed almost haphazardly with any country or faction showing even the faintest hope of emerging as a real threat to French overlordship.

More often than not these "revolts" would die a-borning before more than a token of English aid had arrived. Again and again the ally of yesterday would be forced to declare itself the enemy of today. Thus, for example, the Dutch, who had sought help in 1794 only to see British troops thrown from their soil, found themselves waging a naval war against England by 1797. When the French Royalists seized Toulon in 1793, they saw their hopes smashed by the departure of an English fleet which had no troops to land. Spain, destined to be rescued finally by Wellington, sent her fleet to battle Nelson at Cape St. Vincent. Austria and Russia, after a brief league with England, were soundly beaten at Austerlitz and made to declare themselves to be in a state of hostility with their former friend.

The sequence of alliance and misalliance, moreover, had a double-pronged effect. On the one hand, it eventually caused London to doubt the real intention of the rebelling power. On the other, it created a fear, on the Continent, that a British alliance was tantamount to a kiss of death. By the mid-point of the long struggle the possibility of viable partnerships had become extremely slim.

The uncertainty and confusion of the times were never more strikingly illustrated than in the case of the tripartite relations between England, Russia, and the Porte in the years 1806-9. Russia had been England's best and surest ally during most of the conflict. Toward the end of the year 1807, however, even she had been humbled, and the Peace of Tilsit had bound her to the Napoleonic cause. The English ambassador had been dismissed from St. Petersburg in December of that year and relations between the former allies had been broken.

Unfortunately, at Russian behest, England had previously lent the force of its fleet to the perennial struggle of the czars against the Turks. Hostilities between the Czar Alexander I and the Sultan Selim III had arisen over a dispute regarding the Danubian principalities of Moldavia and Wallachia. These provinces were under the suzerainty of the Ottoman Sultan, but by earlier treaty arrangements between Russia and the Porte the Czar had certain rights respecting their administration. In 1806, as Napoleon was maneuvering against the Russians, he had prevailed upon the Sultan to abrogate the existing arrangements. His machinations had the desired effect of drawing off Russian troops to occupy the provinces in question, thereby weakening the forces facing him in the field. England, in a desperate counterstroke to bolster her beleaguered Russian ally, had sent her Mediterranean fleet to Constantinople and had demanded that the Sultan adhere to the original treaty stipulations. The Turks, however, casting a wary eye at the obvious imbalance of power, had chosen to ignore the British gesture and to heed, instead, the more immediate threat from France. As a result, normal relations between London and the Porte had ceased, and the British ambassador had departed from Constantinople in 1807. After the Peace of Tilsit, then, England found herself in the paradoxical situation of being in a state of hostility both with Russia and with Turkey while they were in conflict with each other. Had it not been for the terrible consequences at stake the confusion might have been comical.

The inanity of this position, and the uprising against the French on the Iberian peninsula with its promise of eventual land operations against Napoleon, spurred London into attempting a rapprochement with the Turks. With this end in view George Canning dispatched an able diplomat, Robert Adair, to Constantinople in mid-1808. Stratford Canning was sent along as secretary to Adair.

The purpose of the Adair mission was to restore normal relations between the two countries, not only as an end desirable in its own right, but as a means of future security for the Turks as well. As the English Cabinet read the portents they felt certain that Napoleon's dreams of world empire did not countenance the continued existence of the Ottoman Empire once the rest of Europe was brought to heel. This concept Adair was instructed to impress upon the Porte with all possible vigor.

By force of circumstance the journey to Constantinople was one of leisurely pace. Overland travel was, of course, completely interdicted; and the sea passage was a distance of almost three thousand miles. The voyage was subject, not only to the ordinary delays of weather and provisioning, but also to the necessity of awaiting naval protection. Although Napolean had no fleet in being, privateering was rampant, and the Mediterranean was swarming with seaborne scavengers of all types. More than that, all available English seapower was concentrating in the harbors of Portugal and southern Spain. The British admirals were understandably loathe to spare the necessary convoy required for safe passage to the Bosporus. In spite of all the obstacles, however, the embassy set sail from Portsmouth early in July on board a thirty-gun frigate and made fair progress down the Atlantic.

At Cadiz and again at Gibraltar they dallied for a time and listened to the rapidly unfolding plans for operations on the Peninsula, operations whose romance and glamor appealed to all the younger minds aboard and evoked in many a desire to stay and fight alongside their martial brothers. Stratford Canning was not immune to these emotions and was sorely tempted to quit the foolishness of Turkish diplomacy in favor of more direct participation in the struggle, but he had given his word and he stifled the temptation.

The diplomats were delayed for another month at Palermo, and although the inaction was painful it was compensated for by new sights and wonders. No one so steeped in the classics as an old Etonian could fail to be moved by seeing with his own eyes the glories of Agrigento and Segesta, the temple of Minerva at Colonna, and a host of other places hallowed by lines of Virgil and Horace. Canning's letters home at this time are filled with literary and mythological allusions and bear eloquent testimony to his great joy. They reflect what were to be the last carefree days of his youth.

Not until the latter part of October did the little fleet of a frigate and two brigs reach Tenedos and the approaches of the Dardanelles. There they learned of the initial victory of British arms in Portugal and, slight though it was, they celebrated the news lustily, as Canning reported in a letter to his friend, Wellesley: " . . . we are indebted to your gallant uncle for them [the victories] . . . Our little fleet . . . did honour to the occasion by making as much noise as their guns would permit, and so much was my patriotic ardour inflamed that I volunteered, in spite of wind, rain, thunder and lightning, to go up to the Dardanelles and put the Pasha there in mind of our conquests in Egypt by telling him how the French, all terrible as they are, had been drubbed in Portugal." [1]

However, he had to postpone his gloating, for he had not yet learned the manner in which the Turks dealt with the infidels from the West. This initial approach to Ottoman officialdom got him no further than a meeting with the Pasha's Greek dragoman, or interpreter, whom he first described as a "secretary." This individual's appalling ignorance of the world situation so irritated Canning that in the rash and intemperate exuberance of youth he informed the hapless fellow, upon failing to arouse his interest with the report of the victory over the French, that the British had undoubtedly bottled up the Russian fleet in the Tagus as well! Only then did he succeed in making the dragoman's eyes light up—tragic testimony, in Canning's mind, to the brute level of existence in the Sultan's domains. "Yes, the animal, insensible as he was," he observed in the same letter to Wellesley, "hated the Russians, because his masters the Turks hated them, . . . and though there was nobody, as usual, standing by ready to bastinado him if his supple face did not exactly express what his master expected, yet so strong was the force of habit that he could not even in absence move a muscle otherwise than he would have done at the feet of the Pasha."

The Turkey to which the Adair mission had come was, so far as law and administration were concerned, basically the same empire that had struck terror into the heart of Medieval and Renaissance Europe. It lacked only the virility and grandeur of that empire of Suleiman the Magnificent which had reached from Belgrade to the Persian Gulf, from Mesopotamia to Tunis and Algiers. In the centuries following that zenith of glory the sultans had kept too close to the confines of the palace and the harem. By this time the vassals of the Sultan had become unruly and rebellious, his army almost nonexistent, and the administration corrupt. The lifeblood of the Empire was running out, and that it continued to exist at all was merely an accident of the times: the preoccupation of the European Powers with their own conflicts and their consequent inability to agree on its dissolution and partition. The hard core of former Ottoman power, the Corps of Janissaries, was now nothing more than a praetorian guard, self-seeking and dedicated to its own preservation, with no concern for the borders and frontiers of the Empire.

The reigning Sultan, Mahmud II, held his throne only at the sufferance of these Janissaries. They had recently murdered his Grand Vezir, and he himself had come to the throne by violence shortly before that. Even during the time the Adair mission was proceeding to its destination, there had been violence and bloodshed in the streets and environs of Constantinople. A palace revolt had destroyed the would-be reformer, Selim III, in May of 1807, and the Janissaries had placed the victim's cousin in power as Mustapha IV. Then an anti-Janissary coalition had, in turn, deposed Mustapha in July of 1808 in favor of his brother, Mahmud. The leader of this coalition had assumed the office of Grand Vezir and had attempted to resume the modernizing work of Selim III. A late resurgence of Janissary power ended in the death of the Vezir, however, and had there been another surviving male of the Ottoman dynasty Mahmud II would undoubtedly have lost his life as well. As things stood, the new Sultan had learned a vivid lesson of the dangers of reform or attempted reform.[2]

In view of the turmoil and fear surrounding the throne and affecting all those near it, the British negotiators had no easy time making contact with the Porte. Haliki Pasha, the governor of the Dardanelles, eventually received the embassy because he needed the services of a European doctor, but for weeks they were refused permission to enter the Straits while Haliki listened and procrastinated as only a Turk could. Everything had to be referred to the capital, but no word ever returned. Only when the patience of the British emissaries was perceptibly near an end were they allowed to proceed some distance up the Straits where they were assigned a ramshackle, deserted villa of sorts as a residence. It appeared, however, that all the preliminaries they had gone through outside the Straits were about to begin all over again in an attempt either to wear down their patience or to extract further concessions from them. Adair had decided, by this time, that the period for patience had come to an end. He was firmly convinced that the Turks wished to talk but were hoping that the British desire for negotiations would lead to greater than usual promises. This was the Porte's traditional method of bargaining: to vacillate until there was no hope of further concession. Over and above this barrier, the French envoy at the Porte was throwing every possible obstacle in the path of successful discussions. The French recognized full well the import of the mission.

At length Adair sent a message to the Porte which stated that if no more progress were made he was under instructions to terminate his mission and withdraw. To back up the force of his words he ordered the captain of the ship to trim the vessel for sea. The sight of the British ship with sails unfurled and anchor drawn did the work of "twenty conferences," as Adair put it, and brought the Turkish plenipotentiaries to serious talk. Finally, on the fifth of January, 1809, the Treaty of the Dardanelles was signed. It restored peace between England and the Ottoman Empire. England recognized the inviolability of the Straits, and Turkey, for her part, withdrew the restrictions against British commerce, thus driving a wedge in Napoleon's continental embargo against England.

This was Stratford Canning's first experience in dealing with the diseased Empire of the Sultan. From it he learned a first principle of Ottoman diplomacy, namely, that the Turks would delay decision for as long as the other party would tolerate delay, and that they respected people dealing from a position of strength far more than they respected those imbued with tolerance and good will.

His first impressions of the Turks were, accordingly, hardly calculated to engender feelings of sympathy toward their lot: a sickness which he ascribed to their own faults. In a summary of his views which he wrote to George Canning in the spring of 1809, he paid tribute to the personal qualities of the people as a whole. As for the leadership, he wrote, "But the government is radically bad, and its members, who are all alive to its defects, have neither the wisdom nor the courage to reform it. The few who have courage equal to the task know not how to reconcile reformation with the prejudices of the people. And without this nothing can be affected." And his prophecy follows: "Destruction will not come upon this empire either *from the north or from the south;* it is rotten at the heart; the seat of corruption is in the government itself." [3]

It was the perceptiveness revealed in letters such as this, combined with the fine reports of his superior, that was thwarting his ambition for public service at home. The Foreign Office did not have an endless reservoir of people well-equipped for diplomatic service, nor was it a simple matter to move them about when they were available—as witnessed by the slow progress to Constantinople of the Adair embassy. A young man who showed ability and alertness was not going to be ignored by George Canning, especially not one to whom he felt a close personal tie. Stratford Canning was being marked for service.

Immediately after mutual ratification of the treaty Adair was formally accredited as the Ambassador to the Sublime Porte, and Stratford Canning was certified as Secretary of the Embassy. Along with this certification came a latent commission as Minister Plenipotentiary which was to take effect upon any prolonged absence of the Ambassador. In a private letter of July 30, 1809, accompanying this commission, George Canning made it abundantly clear that this was a merited reward and not in any way to be construed as a process of nepotism: "I have great pleasure in sending you your appointment of minister plenipotentiary; although I hope you may not soon have occasion to make use of it. . . . I feel myself justified on public grounds in doing, what, on private grounds *alone,* you know me well enough to know I would *not* do, in your favour . . . . "[4]

The Foreign Secretary's expressed hope that his young cousin would not be too soon thrust into a position of severe responsibility must be taken at face value, but it is not presuming too much to suppose that he did see that the probability of such an event was close at hand. The Court of Vienna was beginning to show signs of restiveness under the French yoke, and Adair was already in secret contact with agents in Vienna to ascertain the true nature of the stirrings. Were they to erupt with any real promise immediate liaison would be in order, and Adair was the only diplomat of standing who could fill the demands of such immediacy. He would have to transfer to Vienna.

If this pattern of the future was merely a probability in the view of George Canning, it had become a foregone conclusion to Adair himself. He had actually broached the matter to Stratford Canning as early as February or March before his formal accreditation as Ambassador to the Porte had taken effect. The Ambassador had apparently paid no heed to Canning's clear desire not to receive the appointment, for it was on Adair's recommendation, rather than George Canning's preference, that the arrangement was made. Canning's reluctance was based on the grounds that such a development would needlessly delay his own return home.

Once the plan of succession, so to speak, was put into effect Canning had little choice but to acquiesce in the judgment of his cousin and the constant urging of his immediate superior. Nor, once the *fait accompli* was accepted, is it surprising that his reluctance over the agreement gradually changed to a feeling of anticipation, especially when the hoped-for Austrian uprising actually occurred. He stated his reaction with disengaging frankness in his memoirs: "Young as I was I could not be insensible to a prospect at once so near and so flattering, nor does it surprize me even now that when the promised land proved to be a *mirage,* some feelings of personal disappointment mingled with those of sorrow for the down-dashed fabric of European delivery and British glorification." [5]

The mirage referred to was the swift and terrible French reaction. Napoleon smashed the Austrians at Wagram and then forced upon them the humiliation of Schönbrunn. Not only did the Hapsburgs have to recognize the hegemony of Bonaparte but, in addition, they had to turn over to him as his empress the Princess Maria Louisa, one of their fairest daughters.

This catastrophic turn of events actually proved to be a blessing in disguise as far as the subsequent career of Stratford Canning is concerned. Had the fortunes of war developed in favor of England at this time they would have undoubtedly led to the earlier downfall of Napoleon, and in the subsequent return to peace Canning could not have looked for anything but relegation to a rank more befitting his age and experience. As it turned out, the new setback cemented the position of Bonaparte ever more firmly, kept Russia in a proper state of fear and subjection, and isolated England that much more completely.

The Austrian defeat also resulted in Adair's continued residence in Constantinople, but the shock and tragedy of it all weakened his health considerably. It was not long before he begged to be relieved of his post.

A further tragedy followed in the wake of the Austrian fiasco, and it was one which affected the personal fortunes of Stratford Canning most intimately. The rivalry in the Cabinet between George Canning and Castlereagh, the Minister for War, exploded in a volcanic eruption of blame and recrimination culminating in a predawn duel between the two in which Canning was wounded. The volatile Foreign Minister submitted his resignation to the Prime Minister, the Duke of Portland, and it was accepted as the only solution to the ministerial impasse.

It must be remembered that the lapse of time between the occurrence of events in England and the advent of the news in Constantinople was considerable, encompassing a period of two months or more. When a similar period is allowed for a return of mail from that remote corner to London, one can see that it often required a third of a year, at least, merely for an exchange of views. As a consequence, attitudes and judgments which had a basis in reality when committed to writing were oftentimes reduced to the level of moot questions by the time they reached their destination. Stratford Canning's acceptance of his ministerial commission, for example, and his mental adjustment to the eventual departure of Adair were founded largely, if not wholly, on the presumption that a friendly and guiding hand would be at the helm of the Foreign Office. Scarcely had he resigned himself to the whole design when, as a matter of fact, George Canning was actually out of office and a radical alteration of circumstances had taken place.

The deposed Foreign Minister, though, was by no means blind to the disastrous consequences which this bewildering upheaval could have for his protégé, and his first thoughts were for the budding diplomatist at the Porte. By personal

letter and by marshaling the assistance of his nephew's friends
at the Foreign Office and elsewhere, he contrived to shower
a veritable rain of appeals upon Constantinople importuning
Canning to be neither rash nor romantic, but to stay where
he was and do the duty England required of him. As much
as the youth was enamored of a parliamentary career, just so
much was the seasoned M.P. aware of its merciless uncertainties; and he sent what he called his "most positive
injunctions" to the other to remain where he was. "I may
or may not," he advised his nephew, "have it in my power
at some future time to take you by the hand again. If not,
you have a profession in which you may be useful to your
country and do credit to your friends and to yourself, and
you must not lightly abandon it." [6]

Stratford Canning's response to these pleas proves that
they had their effect, but they also reveal the reluctance with
which he yielded to them against his own desires and also
in the face of some obvious disadvantages of a more practical
nature. His final letter on the affair bears extensive quoting
for the picture as he saw it. He wrote to George Canning on
the eighth of January, 1810:

> I have at length had the satisfaction of receiving your
> two letters of 9 and 20 October last. They reached me on
> the 23rd ultimo [December], together with a large packet
> from Planta containing a full account of the late eventful
> history in which you have had so large a share. You will

have perceived by my last letter of 14 Novr. that we had
long been in possession of the principal facts, without
knowing that they were correct . . . .
. . . .
    You did me but justice to suppose that the first impulse
of my heart, upon learning the circumstances of your resignation, would be to give up the employment which I
received at your hands. Not that I could so far forget my
duty as to run away from my post without permission; but,
had you left me to myself, I should have lost no time in
writing for leave to return to England: not as an act of
flattery by which I might claim merit in your eyes; but
merely to gratify my own feelings by doing my utmost to
testify the opinion which I entertain of the late events.
. . . In this instance your injunctions have a right to out-
weigh my own feelings. Therefore as you have advised me
in such decided terms to prolong my stay here, I have no
intention but to follow that advice, as far at least as acquiescence in it is consistent with the end for which I understand
you to have given it. That end cannot be any other but my
interest. Now though it is certainly my interest not to
offend your successor by betraying any unwillingness to
serve under his directions, I think you will agree with me
that it is very far from being to my advantage to remain
here after I shall have once secured the rank of minister
plenipotentiary by actual service in that situation. I will not
dwell upon the disadvantage of being for so long a period
thrown out of all society and cut off from my friends of
my own age at the very time of life when alone by habits
of intimacy and continual intercourse the most useful con-
nexions are formed and strengthened; nor upon the peculiar
state of this Court, which presents to a foreign minister no
one compensation for the numberless causes of inconvenience and disgust by which he is hourly overwhelmed.

. . . There is another circumstance which you may not be aware of, that makes it impossible for me to reside here, even should I be permitted to do so. The expenses of this Mission are so great that Mr. Adair finds even the appointments of Ambassador insufficient to the support of them. They are besides of such a nature, so indispensable, so permanent, and so little dependent upon the will of the Minister, that I almost despair of being able to reduce them materially below their present mark. To bring them within the allowance of a minister plenipotentiary is out of the question. I shall in consequence be obliged either to incur private debts to a considerable amount, or to have recourse to the unpleasant expedient of drawing largely upon Government for extraordinary expenses. Will it not therefore be most prudent for me to get away from this place as soon as I can do so, without appearing to withdraw myself abruptly from the service of the Government? With this view I will stay here quietly till Mr. Adair goes; after his departure, which will probably be about the end of February, I will take an early opportunity of writing for permission to return to England simply on the score of health. . . . I venture to persuade myself that you will not disapprove of the conduct I propose to adopt, which though not in exact conformity to the letter of your injunctions as I believe most strictly so to the spirit of them . . . . I shall be very anxious until I am assured by your own words that you are contented with the manner in which I intend to act.[7]

Canning's assessment of this very practical problem indicates that even at this time he was anything but a dreamy-eyed youth. Later on in that same year he alluded briefly, but cleverly, to the same idea; but this time he was writing to Richard Wellesley, whose father had succeeded George Canning at the Foreign Office! With a touch of good-humored envy he first contrasted his own lot with that of his friend who was about to take a seat in Parliament:

> I shall, *for the present,* abstain from reproaching you for not having acknowledged a lengthy epistle which I sent to you *many* months ago . . . . Indeed I can readily excuse you, when I consider how much your thoughts must have been occupied by the immediate prospect of going into Parliament . . . I, too, after four months of anxiety and putting off, am in the act of passing into a state of responsibility, which one can hardly do in times like these without certain feelings of apprehension. Mr. Adair has been detained here since the end of February . . . by several unexpected events. His departure is now fixed for the middle of next week [July 12, 1810], and then my diplomatic labours will begin in earnest. How long they are to last, I know not: that depends upon the noble Marquis your father. But I most sincerely hope not very long, at least in this part of the world. This climate has made several rude assaults upon my health . . . . one of the advantages of this place is that there is not a physician in it above the rank of dog-doctor. Another is that the expenses of the Mission are enough to ruin a much richer man than I am . . . . I thank you for your wish that I could meet you in the House of Commons; perhaps the day may come; I am disposed to hope it.[8]

A few days after writing this letter he escorted Robert Adair to the water's edge and bid him a fond goodbye. So it

was that by a convergence of factors almost entirely beyond
his own control, and in spite of his own desires, Stratford
Canning's diplomatic career was born. He had no inkling of
how long that life would be. On July 12, 1810, he remained
alone in Constantinople. At the age of twenty-three he was
"the voice of England in the East."[9]

1. Lane-Poole, *op. cit.*, I, 41-42.
2. Cf. F. E. Bailey, *British Policy and the Turkish Reform Movement*
(Cambridge, Mass.: Harvard University Press, 1942), pp. 26-29. Selim
III's reform movement, begun in 1793, was mainly a reconstruction of the
army along modern lines (the Nizam-i-Jedid). As this struck at the heart
of Janissary power it provoked strong resistance on the part of the Corps.
This resistance finally broke out in successful rebellion and the eventual
deposition of Selim III in May of 1807. See also A. J. Toynbee, *A Study
of History* (12 vols.; New York and London: Oxford University Press,
1939-54), VIII, 239 ff., for a wider discussion of the same.
3. Lane-Poole, *op. cit.*, I, 51.
4. *Ibid.*, p. 47.
5. *Ibid.*, pp. 53-54.
6. *Ibid.*, p. 79.
7. *Ibid.*, pp. 77-79.
8. *Ibid.*, pp. 87-88.
9. The quotation is from Tennyson's poetic eulogy inscribed on the
tomb of Stratford Canning in Westminister Abbey.

III

THERE are few men who could long have weathered the dismal and tragic atmosphere that enveloped the new British Minister at the Sublime Porte. England was at war, nominally, with every nation within the sweep of a French bayonet. Her king, George III, had lapsed into his final madness; the Prince Regent and his royal brothers were a disgrace to the Crown and to the nation; her finances were nearing their end and her commerce gasping for life. In Portugal Wellington's holding action made him seem more a victor than he was, for he could do nought but maneuver for position and husband what, in his own words, was "the last army England has." This tenuous English grasp on the continent plus a lingering friendship with the Kingdom of the Two Sicilies were scarcely any more of a domain than the infinitesimal area of the British Embassy at the Porte ruled over by

His Excellency, the Minister Plenipotentiary, Mr. Stratford Canning.

As if to dramatize the stark isolation of his country the British Minister had also to face the bleak conditions surrounding him in Constantinople. The Christian suburb of Pera, wherein the "palace" of the British Embassy was located, had shortly before been ravaged and gutted by fire. The Embassy building itself was of stone and had withstood the flames, but its outbuildings were gone, and it stood naked and alone amid a landscape of destruction. Stratford was shunned by all but a handful of the foreign diplomatic society and virtually ignored by the Turks. His secretary and friend, David Morier, a stripling of his own age, was often far removed on necessary business of state in Persia or Mesopotamia or elsewhere in the myriad corners of the Levant, thus depriving him of the companionship and friendly conversation that might have compensated somewhat for all the rest.

If in spite of all this he might have looked forward to at least a regular flow of dispatches and counsel from his superiors at home, he could have accepted the situation as being part of the fortunes of war. Even here an unfortunate chasm had developed between Whitehall and the Embassy at the Porte. Lord Wellesley seldom seemed to think of the plight and need of his subordinate in the East, and the young Minister was singularly devoid of instructions and guidance. While it may be reasoned that London, with all its problems in Europe, the Americas, and India, saw no occasion for high-level diplomacy in the Levant, there were, nevertheless, countless daily problems which obstructed the work of its only major outpost in the East.

" . . . I was thereby empowered for the time being to act with full authority on behalf of my government," Canning inscribed in his memoirs. "The instructions under which I had to act were simply those addressed to the late ambassador, in so far as they remained in vigour. They could not of course be followed without due attention to fresh experience and change of circumstances. No provision had been made in them for my particular guidance when left alone, and it is remarkable that during the whole term of my independent service, I received no further directions on any but the most ordinary matters. This is the more strange as our Minister for Foreign Affairs, Lord Wellesley, enjoyed so high a reputation for talent and activity. To the best of my remembrance the most important despatch addressed to me by him related to some manuscript copies of classical works supposed to have been stored away in the Seraglio. I concluded that the great man overlooked so insignificant a youth as myself . . . . Whatever may have been the cause of this apparent neglect, I thought it the more incumbent on me to shun no responsibility which the exercise of an unshackled judgment might entail if I ventured in urgent cases to steer rather by the stars than by compass. The electric telegraph had no existence in those days. Steam had not been practically applied to navigation . . . . our despatches came as they went, by sea . . . . In one instance no official communication reached me in the space of fifteen weeks."

"A correspondence," he noted with regard to his responsibilities, "more occasional than regular had to be kept up with various points. Our consuls in the Levant were not so numerous as they are now, but their dependence on the Embassy was greater. They had to report on passing occurrences, to transmit intelligence from quarters more remote, and to receive instructions from the ambassador, or his substitute . . . . Communications were to be carried on with our admiral in the Mediterranean, with his delegate in the Archipelago, with the governor of Malta, and with the commander of our troops in the Ionian islands. I had also to feed a correspondence with Vienna and Petersburg through such by-channels as might still be used in secret for mutual information."[1]

Almost all of the news that reached London from the eastern part of Europe and the Levant filtered through the listening post at Constantinople. The failure to maintain better liaison is inexplicable, unless it be laid to stupidity, as it probably deserves to be. In response to one urgent query, for example, the best that London could give in reply was an earnest plea to all its foreign service posts that the personnel use larger and better envelopes to enclose their reports!

Criminal and inexcusable as the desertion was, it nevertheless played a positive role in shaping the future of Stratford

Canning. In the first place, any thoughts he may have had of asking to be relieved were probably discarded by him as being futile. The time that would elapse before the requisite arrangements could be made would, in all probability, be about as long as would be required to produce a transfer or reassignment in accordance with ordinary procedure. At any rate, Canning seems to have left the matter to that. More importantly, the void forced him to develop his own talents at an unusual pace. Left to his own devices by his government, cut off from his diplomatic colleagues by circumstance, slighted by the Turks because of his youth and the precarious position of his country, he was thrown back on the one certainty left to him: his unbroken faith in eventual English triumph.

Building on this conviction, he was obliged to acquire habits of self-reliance and self-confidence in his judgments which, when joined to an alert, native intelligence, became the hallmarks of his career. With an ardor that older heads would quite likely ascribe to the imprudence of youth, he plunged more than once into situations and commitments a more experienced diplomat might have hesitated to engage in. Even in his first trials of diplomacy, he showed an ability to perceive the central problem, and he left nothing to chance in clarifying it or solving it in accordance with his own lights. He could be patient where patience was required, and it was often required to an almost limitless degree, but he could not be diverted.

Such clarity of mind and determination of will were sorely needed by anyone attempting to treat with the Turks of his era. As intimated above, the administration of the Ottoman Empire was an irritating mixture of medieval pride and fanaticism combined with moral no less than material weakness. Its sovereign, the Sultan, reigning with the borrowed prerogatives of the Caliphate, was unlimited by any law save the strictures of the Koran.[2] Yet, for all his authority, he was bound to the cloister-like isolation of the Seraglio by immemorial custom and tradition. The daily administration of the Empire and its relations with the outside world were in the hands of the Divan, or Council of Ministers, headed by the Grand Vezir, the "alter ego" and prime minister of the monarch.[3] As far as internal order was concerned, it was a government in name only, since it had little authority outside the environs of the capital. Local government was in the hands of the provincial rulers—the pashas and beys—while a great number of feudal landlords, the derebeys, were as sacrosanct in their own domains as independent princes.[4]

"The old political system of Turkey had worn itself out," the new British minister observed. "A depreciated currency, a disordered revenue, a mutinous militia, dilapidated fortresses, a decreasing population, a stagnant industry, and general misrule, were the monuments which time had left of Ottoman domination . . . . The tottering empire was beset from without and from within: Russia, France, Austria, and even Persia had by turns contracted the area and drained the resources of the empire. From the corrupt monotony of his seraglio the Sultan had to send forth his firmans, his emissaries, his bands of irregular soldiery, or, it might be, his naval armaments, against an invading enemy, a rebellious chief, or an armed insurrection. Several great families, several unsubdued tribes, and here and there an over-powerful pasha had succeeded in braving and circumscribing the imperial authority. The Mamelukes still prevailed in Egypt. The most important part of Syria was under the sway of a Christian Emir. Ali Pasha of Janina exercised royal power in the provinces bordering on Greece, and Greece itself, excited by Russia, was preparing to burst the fetters . . . . Servia, Montenegro, and the Danubian Principalities were all more or less in league with Russia, and the Porte, at war with that formidable Power, had everything to apprehend from the Russian forces concentrated upon her northern frontier. The Sultan's fleet was manned with Christian Greeks from the island population of the Archipelago; the Barbary powers were scarcely even in nominal dependence on the Porte . . . . "[5]

Small wonder, then, that an empire so constituted was arrogant toward the weak, and obsequious toward the strong, that the young English effendi bore little weight and was accorded little respect in contrast with his French counterpart. Small wonder, too, that his overtures were greeted with patronizing smiles, his representations received with perfunctory nods, and that in one audience with the Reis Effendi (the Foreign Minister) he was told to lower his voice.

Canning had found ample reason to raise his voice. He had come to the Reis Effendi on this particular occasion to demand redress for a clear violation of neutrality which the Porte was indulgently tolerating to the detriment of English commerce. The eastern Mediterranean and the Aegean waters were swarming not only with French-commissioned privateers but with pirates of all creeds and nationalities. Again and again these maritime scavengers sallied forth from the protection of an island or harbor—and there were hundreds of such hiding places available—to pounce upon some helpless and unsuspecting British merchantman. They would seize the ship and bring her back to port, where the cargo, and sometimes the ship itself, would be sold or otherwise disposed of— all without benefit of admiralty court and in complete disregard of the recognized law of nations.

Privateering, of course, as distinct from piracy, was a recognized and legal instrument of war. The disposition of the prizes in a neutral port, however, and the usage of neutral ports as bases of attack and havens of protection against retaliation and recapture of prizes was not legal. It was clearly incumbent on the neutral power to take measures sufficient to insure legal procedure on the part of the belligerents. Hardly a week went by without the report of some violation, some depredation of British property, reaching Stratford Canning's ears.

Almost immediately on his accession to the position of authority at the Embassy he made his first approaches on the question, respectfully calling the attention of the Porte to the existence of such violations and seeking a cessation. The protocol of the Ottoman court, it is well to note, was not devised to facilitate the approach of an envoy to the proper ministers of government. All ordinary business had to be transacted through the agency of an interpreter, or dragoman, who had to be personally acceptable at the Seraglio and at the Porte, as well as to the particular foreign government in whose employ he functioned. These dragomans, or go-betweens, were really a privileged caste in the capital. They were invariably either Greeks or Italians whose forebears had long lived within the confines of the Golden Horn. Originally the institution had served as a most wonderful instrument, a compromise between Moslem hauteur and the demands of international intercourse.

Theoretically, a Moslem could never treat with an infidel—the despised *giaour*—as an equal; yet it was necessary to find some method of dealing with the European monarchies, especially as Ottoman power began to decline relative to the strength of the Western nations. The dragoman was the ideal answer. He could bring the messages of his masters to the court of the Sultan where, as circumstance and Ottoman dignity required, he could be abused—even killed in some cases—or, depending on the favors sought from his employers, he might be treated most handsomely—all this, of course, without detriment to the dignity of either side. The extreme harshness had largely disappeared by Stratford Canning's day, but the theory remained. For all practical purposes the system had become a most admirable means of vacillation and pro-crastination for the hard-pressed Turks. The endless possi-bilities for using up time in sending the dragoman back and forth from embassy to Porte with official exchanges, while a word was changed here or a phrase deleted there, was a method they found most appealing. Add to this the necessity of securing appointments and arranging audiences and one can form some idea of the amount of patience required of an eighteenth- or nineteenth-century diplomat in Constantinople.

This was the sole medium of communication open to Stratford Canning while almost daily British ships were being seized, British wealth was being consumed, and, in some flagrant instances, whole crews were disappearing into ap-parent slavery. The situation was similar to that faced by the Americans in the matter of the Barbary pirates; but British affairs were not simple enough to allow the same kind of direct reaction. Canning was limited to the time-honored mode of Ottoman procedure. Only when the end of negotiations was in sight or when the direst emergency had arisen was it permissible for the foreign envoy, be he ambassador or minister, to seek a personal meeting with the Reis Effendi. Even more difficult were the opportunities of contact with the Grand Vezir, and never was the Sultan himself violated by the presence of so lowly a being except for formal audiences of presentation or leave-taking.

To most outsiders and casual visitors the sytsem was banal, corrupt, and totally suspect. Corruption there certainly was, but the practice had many advantages, not the least of which, as Canning was to discover, was that the delay and evasion occasioned by it could become a two-edged sword, to be employed by its intended victim as well as by its instigators. He was to avail himself of the opportunity often in the years to come. Then, too, the casual observer often lost sight of one other important aspect: the institution had become a matter of family tradition and pride. The individual dragoman had found himself bound by a proud code. He was aware that a reputation for honesty brought longer life and, eventually, greater wealth than chicanery and bribery; Moslem and Christian alike could be fooled—but not often.

Thus began the long and honorable association between Stratford Canning and the Pisani brothers, Frederick and Stephen, sons of an old and respectable family. They served through long years as his chief dragomans, and never once did he suspect them of misrepresenting his position to the Porte. Soften his words they might, or postpone the delivery of an insult to either side, as they saw fit, but never did they alter the real substance of his notes to the Porte nor of the replies sent back to him through them.

It was through Frederick Pisani that the British Minister began the protracted negotiations leading to an amelioration of the distressing conditions afflicting British commerce in the Levant. They were to occupy a period of almost two years. A journal which Canning kept of the proceedings reveals the uninterrupted series of notes, memoranda, protests, etc., he directed to the Reis Effendi, one Buyuklu Oglu Mustapha, whom he describes variously as "ignorant," "obstinate," "negative," among other such terms of esteem.

As early as December, 1810, when it was apparent to him that only a display of real intent on the part of the English could win the necessary respect from the Turks, he presumed to request the commander of the British Mediterranean fleet to send additional patrol vessels into the waters of the Archipelago. Stratford further suggested that these ships should operate under orders to retaliate in kind against the enemy. In making the request the young Minister manifested his own realization that he was not battling against Turkish obstinacy alone but also against French intimidation at the Porte. His opposite number in the French Embassy was being just as insistent that the Turkish government take no action to interfere with the operations of French privateers, under threat of offending the Emperor Napoleon who stood far more prepared to exercise a restraining influence on the Sultan than did the embattled English.

The admiral at Malta courteously side-stepped this first move of Canning's by pleading lack of instructions from the Admiralty and his current inability to spare more ships than those already operating in the theater. Rebuffed but not dismayed, Stratford turned again to diplomacy. He spent more months in discussion but accomplished little besides evoking expressions of regret and promises of redress. Finally he began to seek personal audiences, in which he did raise his voice, and in no uncertain terms. When this, too, met with little response—other than being told to lower his voice and not to allow his face to become so red—he reverted to the more direct diplomacy of a show of force. Instead of approaching Malta on the question, he sent an order directly to the local British commander in the Aegean. Fortunately, that individual was also at the end of his patience, and at the Minister's direction (the order was sent, incidentally, on the eve of Canning's twenty-fifth birthday, November 3, 1811) he entered the harbor of Napoli di Romania and exchanged fire with a French privateer. The English were serving notice that the three-mile limit which was protecting the illegal traffic would not be indefinitely honored, not when it was being unilaterally observed in favor of the French.

Characteristically, this action made the Turkish ministers sit upright on their cushions and regard this impertinent youth with something more than the curiosity they had heretofore granted him. Though it did not end the problem immediately, the beginning of the end was in sight. The first exercise of his own judgment in a delicate issue proved to be a success. The outcome crystallized his self-confidence, more than all the counsel and guidance he ought to have been receiving could ever have done.

The determination he showed here was not the sole reason for the Turkish change of heart. Far more than he realized, they were beginning to count on him in another and far more important matter. They wanted him to continue a course of action which they knew he had initiated, one much more to their liking and in their interest, and so they made moves to satisfy him on the issue of neutrality. At any rate, an appropriate firman was issued outlawing the offending practice. British merchant captains at least had an argument to present to Turkish officials, and British warships could demand the assistance of local authorities in righting illegalities.

1. Lane-Poole, *op. cit.,* I, 91-93.

2. The precise nature of the Ottoman Sultan's title and claim to the Caliphate is a matter of some difficulty, traceable, in the main, to the fact that there is no exact counterpart in Western civilization. In discussing the ideal concept of Islamic society, Wilfred Cantwell Smith points out: "The underlying notion is of a society in motion. In relation to this the individual must not get out of step, must not turn deviationist; while group leadership is responsible for seeing that the whole venture knows and follows the right direction. In order that it know there is the body of *ulama,* the *mufti* (the religious scholars); in order that it follow, there is, ideally, the *khilafah (imamah)* [caliphate]" (*Islam in Modern History* [Princeton, N.J.: Princeton University Press, 1957], pp. 20-21).

Historically this leadership which pointed the way to follow was vested in elected successors of the Prophet. The Caliph was the leader of the *muslim* ("the followers"). In a short time he became the leader of the Islamic state with the initiation of Moslem "empire," first under the Ommayad, and then under the Abbasid Caliphates. The succession of factional disputes in the years following Mohammed's death soon brought about the demise of the elective principle and the gradual substitution, early in the Abbasid dynasty, of the Byzantine principle of hereditary succession. This tendency had begun under the Ommayads, and resistance to it actually paved the way for Abbasid power; but soon the Abbasids themselves turned to the practice. "In an adroit propaganda campaign throughout Islam the Abbasids posed as the champion of each disgruntled group, thereby benefitting from the shifting sands of Arab politics and establishing themselves as the royal family in possession of the Caliphate" (S. N. Fisher, *The Middle East* [New York: Alfred A. Knopf, 1959], p. 83). The original Caliphates, however, had the benefit of being able to claim either a blood tie with the Prophet or a lineal succession from one of his immediate disciples.

By the time the Ottoman Turks established their hegemony over the Middle East the last vestiges of the Abbasid Caliphate existed in a weak claimant to the hereditary title, the Caliph al-Mutawkkil. He was imprisoned by Selim I and later permitted to return to Cairo, where he died, in the middle of the sixteenth century. "It has been claimed," Fisher notes (op. cit., p. 206), "that he transferred his caliphal authority to the Ottoman ruling family before he departed; and in later years the Ottoman sultans based their use of the title of caliph and the exercise of its power on this incident." Historians differ on when the Sultans began to claim or exercise the prerogatives of the Caliphate. The question is not pertinent here for we are concerned not with the theoretical aspect of the title but rather with the *de facto* situation that existed when Stratford Canning began his career at the Porte. Even Bailey, who disputes the connection between the Sultanate and the Caliphate, admits that "Traditionally, then, the Sultans did possess the power of the ancient caliphs in addition to that which they claimed as head of the Ruling Instituiton" (op. cit., p. 21). In the nineteenth century, then, it was commonly accepted in the West that the Sultan was also the Caliph. Hence Stratford Canning could write as late as 1880, "Caliph as well as sovereign, he commands the consciences as well as the persons of his Mahometan subjects" (*The Eastern Question* [London: John Murray, 1881]).

What was the origin of this Western misconception? Toynbee gives a satisfactory explanation within an extended discussion of the Caliphate (op. cit., VII, 11-27). He quotes Sir T. W. Arnold, *The Caliphate* (Oxford: Clarendon Press, 1924) as follows: "This confusion was due to the misinterpretation of both the history and theory of the Caliphate by insufficiently instructed Western observers, who drew a false analogy between an Islamic institution which they failed to understand and a Western institution with which they were familiar. They equated the Caliphate with the Papacy; explained it as a 'spiritual' office in the Western sense (an abstraction which was quite foreign to Islamic thought); assumed that the double title of Sultan-Caliph implied a personal union of the 'spiritual' and 'temporal' powers in the Ottoman Padishah . . . . Their error obtained wide currency in the West (except among scholars without influence in international affairs) *and even among Muslims* who had received a Modern Western in place of a Classical Islamic education."

Faced with continual contraction of their political sovereignty the Ottoman Sultans found their "spiritual" sovereignty a source of additional strength vis-à-vis the Western powers and hence did nothing to upset the idea. So successfully did they exploit this mistaken concept, even among their own people, that the revolutionary government of Mustapha Kemal, when it abolished the political entity of the Sultanate on November 1, 1922, saw fit to declare in the same law that the office of the Caliphate (the spiritual office) still resided in the house of Osmanli and elected a member of that house to the office. When the office of Caliph was finally abolished in 1924, there were severe repercussions throughout the Moslem world. Thus had the original Western mistake come full circle!

3. For a good, concise description of the governmental organization of the Ottoman Empire, cf. Fisher, *op. cit.*, pp. 209-17, and Bailey, *op. cit.*, pp. 10-13. The center of power was the Sultan who reigned in his palace or Seraglio. Of almost equal importance (and at times more, depending on the character of the monarch) was the Sublime Porte, or government building presided over by the Grand Vezir and other ministers. Here met the Council, or Divan, which was variously expanded to include lower officials—both civil and religious—as occasion warranted. When it was so expanded it was called simply the Council.

4. Cf. Bailey, *op. cit.*, pp. 13-16; see also C. W. Crawley, *The Question of Greek Independence* (London: Cambridge University Press, 1930), Appendix VI(d), for a table showing in great detail the administrative organization of the Ottoman Empire both in the capital and in the provinces. Note also that Crawley shows the Sultan-Caliph at the apex (see note 2 of this chapter).

5. Lane-Poole, *op. cit.*, I, 49-50.

IV

ALL during the time in which he had been occupied with the vexations of Aegean piracy, Stratford Canning felt that he was doing no more than his obvious duty. If the representatives of His Majesty's Government could not lift a finger to protect the basic rights of English commerce, there would be little value, in his opinion, to their functioning in any way whatsoever. Consequently, the forthright stand he took on the matter did not appear to him to be either dramatic or remarkable.

He also conceived it to be his duty to align his efforts at the Porte with the general outlines of British foreign policy. He was mindful of the fact that in dispatching the Adair mission in the first place, George Canning's intention had been not only to restore peace between London and the Porte, but to break, or at least weaken, the Franco-Russian entente. Turkey had to be made the stumbling block that would upset the friendship.

That the continued pursuit of their mutual goals would inevitably bring Napoleon and the Czar into conflict in the East was obvious to every European statesman. Bonaparte's dream of becoming a latter-day Alexander the Great was in direct opposition to the Russian goal of restoring a Christian Empire of the East with the Romanov eagle perched above the waters of the Bosporus. England's best interests lay in hastening the collision.

Ambassador Adair, therefore, had been instructed to point out to the Turks the malevolent designs of each of the two great continental powers. As the lesser of two evils, he was to urge peace with Russia, based on the grounds that even if the Sultan were to find himself capable of holding off the Russians for the time being, his forces would be so weakened that they would fall an easy prey to the Corsican, who was a danger either as friend or foe.

Turkey, however, was just as suspicious of Russian "friendship" as England wanted her to be of a French partnership. In order to counter these Turkish fears of her northern neighbor, Adair's first hope had been to construct a tripartite alliance between Austria, England, and Turkey. A restored and strengthened Austria would have been a sufficient guarantee against further Russian incursions along the Danube. The Porte, then, could make peace with Russia under the protection of that coalition. That hope, of course, was wrecked by the Treaty of Schönbrunn, and when both Adair and George Canning were shortly thereafter removed from the active scene, their plans were evidently consigned to the archives of the Foreign Office. The English Cabinet apparently expected to be able to accomplish nothing along those lines, for they would surely have replaced Adair with a seasoned diplomat.

The London ministry, however, was not considering the statesman-to-be who had stepped into Adair's shoes. Stratford Canning assumed, since he had no notice to the contrary, that he was in turn bound by the instructions given to his former superior. The mutual benefits that peace would bring, moreover, to Turk and Russian alike, made the immediate pursuance of that objective appear even more logical.

Indeed, the hoped for falling out seemed to have already begun. Hard upon the heels of Schönbrunn had come the whispers and rumors of French designs upon Russia. The catapulting of the sometime-sergeant Bernadotte to the line of succession to the throne of Sweden had made Czar Alexander take hard notice of his "ally's" intentions. Neither did the preference of an Austrian archduchess over a Romanov candidate for the Empress of the French serve to endear Napoleon to the Czar. Finally, the plans announced by Napoleon for Poland seemed an undue invasion of the Russian sphere of influence. All in all, it was becoming increasingly clear that the Russian troops deployed along the Danube would, in the near future, find far more important employment elsewhere. There appeared to be no better time for the Turks to look for an advantageous peace.

The British Minister to the Porte was soon to find out that
logical analysis was not the same thing as judicious synthesis.
However expedient peace might appear to a third party, the
difficulty of overcoming national pride and prejudice, the
tendency of each of the antagonists to hope that one more
campaign would improve its bargaining position, and the
mutual suspicion engendered by long years of conflict—all
hindered a real exploration of the path to peace. The Turks,
despite the weakness of their position, were obstinate, and
the Divan was prone to magnify the slightest successful
skirmish into a victory of momentous proportion.

Notwithstanding this intransigence, Canning could at least
talk to the Turks, whereas he had no official liaison with the
Russian court. Further complications arose from the fact that
Russian troops had made real progress in the campaign of
1810. They had cemented their positions in the Principalities
and were established in several places on the Turkish side of
the Danube. The Czar and his ministers were understandably loathe to give up the advantages thus obtained. As 1810
drew to a close, an impasse had resulted in the relative positions, with the Russians planted in Bulgaria but showing signs
of being able to go no further and with the Turks unable to
take to the offensive but dreaming of vast new levies appearing
from nowhere in the spring. Mutual stubbornness was playing
directly into Napoleon's hands.

It was at this juncture that the twenty-three-year-old
Canning decided to step into the picture more actively. He

had learned that Russian finances were straining under the double jeopardy of conducting a war against an avowed enemy, the Sultan Mahmud, and preparing at the same time to ward off the pending attack by an ostensible ally, the Emperor of the French. Stratford Canning's source of information lay in the friendship he had established with the unofficial Neapolitan minister at the Porte, Count Ludolf. This diplomat was, naturally, in contact with the Duke of Sierra Capriola, the envoy of the Kingdom of the Two Sicilies at St. Petersburg. Between them these gentlemen had contrived to let the Russian court know of the efforts being made by the British Minister at the Sublime Porte to convince the Turks to bring to an end what was becoming a ruinous drain on their feeble resources. In the same unofficial vein they were able to acquaint Canning, in December of 1810, with the Czar's intention of sending to Bucharest a representative empowered to function as plenipotentiary in any exchanges considered desirable by the Porte. The bid for Canning to try his hand at mediation was clear. It was to be followed by eighteen months of protracted and devious diplomacy.

The privateering question, one must remember, had already been brought into the foreground, and Stratford Canning's seeming insolence had already rankled the Reis Effendi. When, on top of this, the young Englishman ventured to broach the matter of treating with the Russians, even to the point of making some concessions to them, it is no wonder that he was accused of being a czarist agent! The Porte even gave heed to French-inspired rumors that a secret treaty was

being drawn up between England and Russia by which
Britannia would once again woo Muscovy at the expense of
Turkey. The Reis Effendi went so far as to hint that the
Sultan, if he could not expect English help against the
Russians in the form of a naval demonstration in the Black
Sea, might well turn to France and Austria for such help.

Canning's reply to this form of pressure was as daring as
it was masterful. He reminded Buyuklu Oglu Mustapha that
British aid had been offered when Mr. Adair was on the
scene but had been turned down by the Porte for fear of
French reaction. He cautioned the Turks that they could not
hope to treat with a victorious Bonaparte nearly so well as
they could with a victorious Russia, a Russia held in restraint
by the benevolent influence of England. In effect he disposed
of the challenge by accepting it.

This unlooked-for reaction had its desired effect, for although the Reis Effendi remained cool toward Canning for
some time, he nevertheless allowed the dragoman to report
to the English envoy that the Sultan was sending a plenipotentiary to the Turkish camp in the area about the mouth of
the Danube. So by March 15, 1811, Monsieur Italinski, on
behalf of Czar Alexander I, and Ghalib Effendi, representing
Sultan Mahmud II, were physically near enough to each other
that a meeting could be arranged as soon as one side could be
induced to make the necessary approach.

The battle was by no means over; it had just begun, and
there would be many obstacles thrown in the path of the
British Minister. In addition to the piracy issue, there were

incidents such as the disposition of the Spanish Embassy building. It had been seized by the French envoy, Maubourg, on behalf of a representative newly sent to the Porte in the name of King Joseph, the Bonaparte puppet in Spain. Canning protested violently to the Porte that this was an unjust usurpation of the property of the Spanish people and an affront to their English allies. His objections were so strongly worded and so vigorously entered that, once again, he was reminded to keep his voice lowered and his visage free of a ruddy wrath. The Turks were coming to know his temper but were not prepared to accept it at this early date. Quite to the contrary, the Reis Effendi threatened to ignore him and go over his head to London. Canning thereupon let this matter drop, and the action attests to his good sense and ability to distinguish essential from nonessential. The obvious prudence he demonstrated also gives the lie to allegations made against him later on that he let his temper rule his reason. He was content to make his point against the illegality of the procedure and let the matter rest.

This was not the only attempt that Maubourg made to frustrate Canning, for the Frenchman clearly foresaw the consequences that British mediation could have. Unlike Canning, however, Maubourg had constant guidance from his government. He could, and did, moreover, enlist the additional services of the Austrian internuncio at the Porte to thwart every move the young Englishman made. All through the negotiations Maubourg attempted to throw suspi-

cion on the motives of England, and, more positively, he
showered an endless series of alternating threats and promises
upon the Porte and the Seraglio.

Again and again Canning appealed, in vain, for some
direction, some expression of confidence in its Minister by
the London government in order to sustain his efforts. He
kept Lord Wellesley completely informed as to his actions,
but never received either commendation or disapproval. In
desperation, at one point, he begged the Foreign Secretary to
reprove him if he had gone too far.[1] To all his pleas there
came only silence or, at best, routine and irrelevant messages.
Lane-Poole puts the total dispatches from London to Constantinople at sixteen during the period from the summer of 1810
to the spring of 1812.[2] None of them was pertinent. To
counter personal letters of cajolery to the Porte from Napoleon
himself, Canning had nought to offer but the warnings his
own reason drew from the sad experiences of other governments who had been similarly trapped. Against the threats
emanating from the proven might of France, he could place
only the promise inherent in the minuscule successes of
Wellington.

In St. Petersburg, too, French diplomacy worked against
him. Up to almost the very eve of the 1812 campaign there
was always the real possibility of Franco-Russian rapprochement as Napoleon sought to gain by trickery the ends for
which he was preparing to wage war. The Russians did
not know, however, the incessant pressure that a combined

Franco-Austrian approach was bringing to bear upon the Porte. An alliance between these powers and the Sultan against Russia looked very tempting to the harrassed Mahmud.

While Canning continued to warn the Porte against accepting the destructive help of Napoleon, he turned his attention directly to the Russians. He communicated to Italinski, at Bucharest, and to St. Petersburg through the Duke of Sierra Capriola, advising them of the headway that Paris and Vienna were making in Constantinople. The danger of postponing peace was as serious for Russia as it was for the Porte, he pointed out, for in the event that Russian terms were too harsh the Turk would surely turn to the French. The British Minister sketched the terrifying picture of an unbroken front against Russia running from the Baltic to the Black Sea. By way of contrast he held out to the Russians the proposition that a peace with Turkey would speedily result in a peace and alliance with England. The letter to the Duke of Capriola fell under the eyes of Czar Alexander,[3] and Italinski soon received instructions to cultivate and continue his correspondence with the English representative at the Porte.[4]

This happy development coincided with an outbreak of rebellion within the ranks of the Turkish army along the Danube (February-March, 1812). Ill-fed and unpaid, lacking spirit and patriotic fervor, the troops refused to go on the planned spring offensive. The Divan was in a state of near panic, and on the seventeenth of March the Grand Vezir was instructed to work for the conclusion of peace on the best terms possible.

The French and Austrian embassies made frantic, last-minute attempts to divert the course of events. Napoleon hurried an ambassador extraordinary to the scene, and the Austrian internuncio proposed that an Austrian military mission be assigned to assist the Sultan's generals. Canning struggled to maintain his advantage in the face of each new thrust, desperately aware of the lack of help he had a right to expect. "I am very much in want of instructions," he pleaded in a message to Wellesley on the twenty-first of April. "Even the smallest communication direct from H.M. Government, if greater means cannot be employed would be of great service. The French are making every possible exertion. Courier upon courier arrives from Paris." [5]

If his isolation had not been bad enough in itself, there was a new cloud on the horizon. He had heard months before that a new ambassador had been appointed to the Porte, but he had received no notification to that effect from the Foreign Office. Much as he desired to return home, he was now so deeply involved that he wished to carry the negotiations through to the end. Yet he did not know from day to day whether he was still empowered to act, nor in whose name he was empowered.

Unofficially he had been commissioned by the Turks to act for them in the approaches to the Russians. But he did not have their full confidence and trust because of the precipitate naval action he had ordered at Napoli di Romania the preceding November. They demanded that he submit every communication to them for prior approval. This he could not do if he were to accomplish anything, for, as he put it in his memoirs, "I had to persuade the adverse parties."[6] Matters of substance had to be phrased in different language to meet conflicting viewpoints, not to mislead but simply to clothe the same item in garments that would make it more presentable. In order to meet this difficult demand of the Turks, his work was doubled, for he now began to compose two sets of dispatches, one for submission to the Turkish ministers and one to send to the Russians at Bucharest. He had, too, to contrive to get this second set to the Russians by secret couriers, with all the attendant danger of that course of action.

To complicate the whole business, before his last desperate appeal to Lord Wellesley had cleared Aegean waters, he received a notice from Viscount Castlereagh on May 1 which announced the latter's succession to Lord Wellesley as Foreign Secretary. To Castlereagh's great honor it must be stated the hostility he felt for George Canning was never transferred to Stratford, but certainly the initial shock of the announcement must have been unnerving at the very least.

In spite of everything Canning pushed doggedly ahead. Ignoring the rebuffs and taunts of the Reis Effendi, he worked more and more through Ghalib Effendi, the plenipotentiary. The Grand Army of Napoleon mobilized beyond the Vistula and drew near the Niemen. The fruits of Tilsit were in poisonous bloom. The Russians had been holding out to the last for annexation of the Danubian Principalities, but they finally withdrew their claims in exchange for some minor concessions along the Asian boundaries of the two empires.

In Europe they accepted the river Pruth as the boundary, along with the right to guarantee autonomous administration of the Principalities, but the semi-independent provinces still remained under the suzerainty of the Sultan.

The treaty, known as the Treaty of Bucharest, was signed in that city on the twenty-eighth of May, 1812. Historically, it was not definitive; the dispositions and arrangements it made have been modified many times since. Yet, when it was signed, and then ratified less than a month later, it freed the Russian armies under Chicagov from their Danubian stations. These were the forces which moved northward, hit the Grand Army on its flanks during the catastrophic retreat from Moscow, and finally broke it at the Beresina. Years afterward, the Duke of Wellington, mistakenly thinking he was paying tribute to his brother the Marquis of Wellesley, had this to say of the treaty he thought the latter had concluded: "If the great statesman . . . had never rendered to his own country or the world any other service . . . his name would have gone down to posterity as the man who had foreseen and had afterwards seized the opportunity of rendering to the world the most important service that ever fell to the lot of any individual to perform." [7] From the Czar of Russia the following message was sent to Lord Castlereagh: "The Emperor of Russia congratulates M. de Stratford Canning for his share in making peace with Turkey, cet événement si important par les conséquences qu'il devait avoir." [8]

While it is undoubtedly true that other factors entered into the total scheme which led to the Peace of Bucharest, Stratford Canning role was a principal one.[9] The success he had achieved was remarkable for a twenty-five-year-old neophyte. In addition to the message cited above, the Czar sent his personal commendations to Canning in the form of a snuff box with the Czar's portrait set in diamonds. The Prince Regent also sent his personal approbation. The Turks, curiously enough, were complained that he had not procured enough for them. They dubbed Stratford Canning a "Russophile."

Most happily Canning surrendered the keys and archives of the Embassy to the new ambassador, Robert Liston, who arrived on the twenty-eighth of June. In the following month, on July 12, almost four years to the day since he had departed from England, Stratford Canning shook the filth and dust of the Golden Horn from his heels and began the journey home.

1. Lane-Poole, *op. cit.*, I, 129.
2. *Ibid.*, p. 128.
3. *Ibid.*, p. 162.
4. *Ibid.*, p. 170.
5. *Ibid.*, p. 167.
6. *Ibid.*, p. 168.
7. Cited in *ibid.*, p. 176.
8. Harold Temperley, *England and the Near East: The Crimea* (London, New York, and Toronto: Longmans, Green and Co., 1936), p. 49.
9. *Ibid.*, p. 51. Temperley cautions that the other factors are not known as yet. He feels that the decision was Mahmud's own but may have been influenced by his mother, a French Creole, who was anti-Napoleonist.

V

THERE are numerous letters dating from Canning's first residence in Constantinople which testify to his never-ending desire to be free of the place. Its streets and alleys were dirty and foul-smelling; its people ignorant, disease-ridden, and crawling with vermin. Moslem officialdom was corrupt, and the justice it administered hardly deserved the name, for it was arbitrary and cruel. The Ottoman Empire was a land in which murder was dignified under the guise of legal or religious execution whenever it suited the convenience of authority, be that authority the Sultan himself or any of the myriad of lesser officials. On one occasion, for example, Canning was present when the head of the rebellious Pasha of Baghdad was ceremoniously presented to Mahmud. The lives of the Sultan's subjects, especially the Christians, too often depended on the whims of pashas and beys, any one of whom could take a life on the slightest pretext, and without the least fear of being held accountable.

One most not suppose that the youthful diplomat spent the entire four years within the walls of his residence, or journeying back and forth to the Porte. He did get away for occasional excursions and periods of relaxation, but never very far from the capital—Smyrna was as far as he got—and such holidays seldom lasted longer than a few days. There was, also, a fairly steady stream of visitors, some of them friends of his, but many complete strangers bearing appropriate introductions from London. Some of these expected more service than the Minister could give them and complained about his hospitality to the Foreign Office, but these instances bothered him little and apparently did not upset his superiors.

Besides these diversions there were idyllic spots on both sides of the Bosporus and elsewhere in the environs of the capital where he enjoyed riding or walking in solitude. Such pleasures, of course, and many more, he could find in the English countryside, and he longed constantly for the day when they would once more be within reach.

His exile he still saw as a preparation for service at home; and not long after his return, he was at George Canning's side, electioneering in Liverpool and enjoying it to the utmost. What he enjoyed, incidentally, was his cousin's popularity and his proficiency in the rough-and-tumble of partisan politics. Actually, he was along merely as an observer; his own yearnings for a Parliamentary career had to be set aside for the time being. For one thing, the Tory party had a sufficiency of able candidates, and, of greater practical weight, his means did not allow him the luxury of a seat in the House of Commons. Lacking the independence of personal financial resources, he was forced to accept a statutory pension or allowance granted by the Foreign Office. It amounted to about 1200 pounds a year, and he could not do without it. The emolument was granted, however, only on the condition that the recipient accept the next assignment offered him and on the further stipulation that he not take a seat in Parliament.

Consequently he found it expedient to allow himself to be considered a member of the Foreign Service. But he was in a paradoxical position. By virtue of his rank and experience he could not be relegated to an inferior position such as a clerkship or secretaryship, nor, because of his age and lack of seniority, could he expect an assignment equal to or above his rank. Napoleon had not yet gone down to defeat, but the end was in sight. With the coming return to peace there would be a whole college of senior diplomats awaiting the various posts that had long been vacant. Furthermore, although George Canning was successful in his own bid for election, he was still out of favor with the dominant faction of the Tories and was not included in the Cabinet when it was organized. The portfolio of the Foreign Office was given to Castlereagh, and Stratford Canning was forced to bide his time.

There followed a two-year hiatus in his career, and we do not have much in the way of detailed information as to how he spent his time. In his memoirs, he unwittingly revealed how little these years meant to him by passing over them without much attention. In the fashion of the times, of course, there were clubs and literary circles, and he did meet with one group composed of former school associates which was known as the Grillion Club, taking its name from the coffeehouse which its members frequented. He was a welcome guest at Madame de Staël's circle in its early days, but he did not seem to be overly taken with the lady herself. His willingness to visit there was due, no doubt, to the variety of charming people to be found in attendance. Otherwise he seems not to have adjusted to the prosaic pace of this kind of life after having been so intimately involved in the fate of men and nations.

Canning was still publicly and privately disavowing the choice of a career in diplomacy when an appointment as Minister Plenipotentiary and Envoy Extraordinary to Switzerland came as a welcome relief to boredom and inactivity. The opportunity came in a most unusual way, too, since it was tendered to him by Lord Castlereagh in Paris. Canning had gone there in the spring of 1814 to witness the formalities of the Allied triumph and the restoration of the Bourbons. At one of the many soirees and receptions he attended, he had a brief meeting with the Foreign Secretary during which the offer was casually made. Stratford accepted it immediately.

This change of scene cheered him as nothing else had been able to. We find him writing some of the most enthusiastic and lighthearted letters of his life, "Put on your spurs," he wrote to one of his small circle of close friends, "mount your yacht, and come the shortest possible way to this delicious country. When once here, you will acknowledge that you have spent twenty years of your life most unprofitably. . . . The finest mountains—the greenest hills—the richest plains— the neatest houses—the best inns—the most limpid streams, and for aught I know the most delightful fair ones, ever yet beheld in this transitory sphere!"[1] And he sent this message to his sister the next day: "Good-bye, my dear Bess. Unless you bring your spouse and children here, I much doubt that you will ever see me again. How the deuce will it be possible to tear oneself away from this delicious country . . . ?"[2]

The challenge of the new post probably served to revivify Canning even more than did the idyllic scenery. The downfall of Napoleon had left the Swiss in a turmoil peculiarly their own, for here, contrary to the mood prevailing in the rest of Europe, there was little desire for a return to the status quo ante. Up to the time of Napoleon, Switzerland had been a federation of thirteen independent cantons with five subject provinces, but all of it under the domination of the towns. Bonaparte had erased this urban preponderance by setting up, within the "Greater Empire," a Swiss Confederation of nineteen equal and sovereign cantons. This arrangement was far more attractive to the rural districts, and, although they welcomed their deliverance from French hegemony, they wanted no part of the previous urban control.

When, following Napoleon's defeat, the towns moved to reclaim their leadership, the country people made plain their resolution to defend their new "freedom" by force of arms.

Besides this conflict of urban and rural interests, the country faced further barriers to political stability. Its unique geography, for one thing, made communication between its different areas a matter of great difficulty, requiring long and circuitous routes of travel for all but experienced mountaineers. Superimposed on this natural disadvantage was the crisscross of religious antagonism dating from the bitter years of the Reformation and the religious wars. Linguistically, too, it was a Tower of Babel: though basically trilingual, it was zigzagged by as many dialects and sub-dialects as there were valleys and meadows in the shadows of its peaks. Stemming from these divisions of religion, race, language, and geography were a dozen or more parties and factions, each determined to impose its particular viewpoint on the whole.

The victorious allied powers, though they cared little about the mechanics of a solution, wanted the problem solved, since they were agreed on the need for an independent Alpine state to serve as a buffer between France and Austria.

The simple task given to Canning was to bring order out of the chaos. His first few months were spent patiently listening to delegations, deputations, and even individuals by the score. These visitations, incidentally, had begun in Paris as soon as his appointment was announced.

On one item, at least, there was universal agreement among the Swiss. The great powers were assembling in Vienna to redraw the map of Europe following the upheavals of the previous decade. If the Swiss hoped to gain anything from the Congress of Vienna, they realized that they must put on the face of unity even if they did not yet have the spirit of unity. So well, apparently, did Stratford Canning listen to one and all, and so impartial were his stated views, that he was a nearly unanimous choice to express their desires to the Congress of Vienna. A draft of constitutional machinery was put together, and he took it with him to Vienna.

Although the disposition of Switzerland was but a tiny item on the agenda, Canning was officially accredited as a member of the Committee for Swiss Questions and, as such, a recognized member of the diplomatic corps then swarming about the Austrian capital. He spent the winter of 1814-15 going to balls, banquets, soirees, and receptions and rubbing elbows with the great and near great. His descriptions of Metternich, Talleyrand, and other powerful men in attendance are lengthy and perceptive. His relations with Castlereagh became even more cordially cemented, though not at the expense of loyalty to George Canning. When Castlereagh departed for London after the first of the year and was succeeded at the Congress by Wellington, the young diplomat had many an occasion to see the great duke at close quarters. Wellington spoke to him warmly of his brother, Lt. Col. Charles Canning, who had been one of the hero's aides on the Peninsula. (Later Charles was killed at Waterloo as he carried an order from the Duke to one of the field commanders.)

The Committee on Swiss Questions did not meet more than once or twice a week in formal session, but there was much behind-the-scenes work. Here Canning was in continuous contact with his Russian colleague, Count John Capodistrias. Canning had previously known the Count as one of the Russian plenipotentiaries at Bucharest. He was a native of Greece, with a Venetian title (Capo d'Istria), who had done yeoman service in diplomacy for Czar Alexander I. Later on Capodistrias was to become President of the provisional government of Greece and a leader in the struggle of his people against the Turks. The mutual respect and friendship that arose between Stratford Canning and Capodistrias at this time was to serve them in good stead during the difficult years of the Greek Revolution.

The Congress of Vienna proceeded at a leisurely pace all through the winter until it was galvanized into activity by the news of Napoleon's escape from Elba. Canning was present at a major conference when the report was brought in, and he described, in his memoirs, how faces turned white and voices became stilled. One after another, the major participants departed from the table to look to their own affairs. His most vivid description is of a scene composed of the stately figure of Wellington descending a spiral staircase with his own officers in train. Trooping along with them were officers of the principal allies listening to the calm reassurances that were being spoken by the Duke as he gave orders and made suggestions for marshaling troops and armies.

Before it dispersed, the Congress of Vienna ratified the proposed constitution for a Swiss Federation without any major changes. This put the burden of securing its acceptance on the shoulders of Stratford Canning, and no small burden it was. Each of the Swiss factions had been confident of being able to turn the provisions of the proposed constitution to its own good at the Congress. Each, therefore, had given its assent to the draft, but conditionally. Canning had the task of visiting the various cantonal legislatures to plead for affirmation of something none of them found quite agreeable. The uncertainty of the Swiss regarding a resurgent Napoleonic empire did not serve to ease his path, and at times he doubted that the Swiss Federation would survive. Its viability, however, was insured by the field of Waterloo, and gradually the various cantons fell into line behind it.

The Swiss Federation, under the terms of the constitution, was to be a loose one of some nineteen cantons. A central directorate was established that would rotate its sittings between Berne, Zurich, and Lucerne, with the chief officer of the respective city occupying the presidency in turn. The constitutional machinery has been modified since, and the power of the central government has been stabilized more effectively, but the political entity we know today as Switzerland dates from that time. Of even greater import for the world at large was an act of the Congress of Vienna when it reconvened in the fall of 1815. This was a solemn guarantee on the part of all the powers of the perpetual neutrality of Switzerland. Never, even in the darkest days of the two world wars, has that neutrality been seriously threatened. That agreement has allowed the name Geneva to become the symbol of peace.

With the coming of peace Canning journeyed about "selling" the new Swiss Federation. And he had the time to enjoy the country to the utmost. The winter of 1815-16 was one of the calmest he ever spent, and a modern travel bureau could profitably search his memoirs and letters for the passages wherein he extolls the beauty of the mountains, valleys, lakes, and hamlets of the Alpine paradise.

He was to have one glorious year more. The deprivation of the normal intimacies of youth which he complained about in Constantinople was finally mitigated by the joys of human love. While on leave in the summer of 1816, he went back to England; and to the surprise of all his friends in London and in Switzerland, he married a Miss Harriet Raikes, a daughter of one of the governors of the Bank of England, The marriage was idyllic, but tragically short. Less than a year later she died along with their stillborn child and was buried at Lausanne.

The charm that Switzerland held for him disappeared with her death. The routine duties of his work rapidly began to bore him. The following year saw an exchange of letters with George Canning, Joseph Planta, and others—all discussing his desire for office at home, or for reassignment to some other post. He could not afford retirement, for his mother was becoming more and more dependent on him. An older brother, Henry, had all but lost the family business, and with Charles's death Canning had become her main support.

On the sixteenth of August, 1819, he obtained permission to resign his commission on the understanding that he would receive either a post in the government at home or be promoted to a higher-ranking mission. In the ratings of the Foreign Service Switzerland was then a fifth-class mission, the lowest ministerial level. On September 24, Lord Castlereagh nominated Stratford Canning as the Envoy Extraordinary and Minister Plenipotentiary to the United States of America, a new fourth-class assignment. Canning's former Secretary at the Swiss mission, Henry Addington, wrote to him: "If you can succeed in keeping those schoolboy Yankees quiet and saving us another hundred millions of debt, you will . . . come home . . . a G.C.B. with a handle to your name."[3]

The American mission was commonly agreed to be among the most difficult in the Foreign Service. The Americans, in their resentment of the mother country, were extremely sensitive to any hint that England might be patronizing them or, even worse, dictating to them. That Canning was selected was testimony of Castlereagh's opinion of him. For once George Canning had the warmest applause for a Castlereagh decision. It did not escape Stratford Canning's notice, either, since he seemed destined for diplomacy for the time being, that his immediate predecessor, Sir Charles Bagot, had gone to St. Petersburg as a reward for his American service. That embassy, along with Paris, Vienna, Madrid, and the Hague, constituted the cream of the diplomatic world. Even if he did not aspire to that, a tenure of office among people of his own race and language could, he reasoned, help ready him for a career at home.

1. Lane-Poole, *op. cit.*, I, 222.
2. *Ibid.*, p. 223.
3. *Ibid.*, p. 285.

VI

BECAUSE he did not want to make the long and arduous Atlantic crossing in the winter, Canning did not depart for America until the early summer of 1820. The delay gave him time to frequent his usual haunts in London and to sit in on as many sessions of Parliament as he could. The economic dislocation of the Napoleonic Wars, the clamor for electoral reform, and, more than anything else, the tempestuous relationship between George IV and his estranged queen made that winter sitting of Commons one long series of bitter debates. Charges and countercharges which involved careers and reputations flew across the floor irrespective of party lines. Scandal and recrimination were personally distasteful to Stratford Canning, and, though he still looked upon the benches of Commons as his ultimate goal, the lustre of domestic politics became somewhat dulled as he observed its workings from the galleries.

The preparations for his trip to the United States went on apace, and they were more than were usually necessary for a departing envoy. Furniture, servants, cooks, secretaries, and sundry items—including a cabriolet—all had to be transported with him to the primitive new capital growing on the banks of the Potomac. Since he had pledged himself to a stay of three years, he had to plan carefully lest he be unduly dependent on the meager comforts available in muddy, fever-ridden Washington.

The chances for normal intercourse between the mother country and her former colonies were as uncertain as the physical appointments of the new assignment. Canning came to Washington at a time of transition in the relations between England and the United States. Memories of bitter conflict were still too fresh, especially in the new nation, to allow for for compromise where it was needed, or for any real search toward mutually satisfying agreement. The best that could be hoped for was an easing of the tension, so that time might heal old wounds without new ones developing. The United States was just beginning to feel its way among the powers. She was gradually becoming aware that her own security was no longer threatened by European military might, and her statesmen were finding that they could engage in the normal give-and-take of foreign relations. In the forming of foreign policy, although it was long to be dominated by the stricture of George Washington against "foreign entanglements," American leadership had begun to recognize the necessity of treating with the rest of the world.

Specifically, there were problems to be discussed with England. The Treaty of Ghent, which ended the War of 1812, had not really solved the issues that led to the conflict; actually, those conditions most obnoxious to the Americans had ceased to exist once a general peace had come into effect in Europe. England had no longer to resort to every means possible to enforce a blockade of the Continent, nor was she driven any longer to the impressment of seamen to man her far-flung navy. American commerce was now unmolested on the high seas, but there was still one sore point: the question of the slave trade. The Congress of Vienna had outlawed trafficking in human life, and the English government felt it had the right to stop and search any ship thought to be carrying slaves in contravention of international agreement. The United States, although it had forbidden its merchantmen to engage in slaving, insisted, nevertheless, that only its own naval forces had jurisdiction over vessels flying the American flag. This was the thorniest issue remaining between the two nations. There were other issues, of course, less provocative for the time being but, potentially, major irritants. For one thing, the demarcation of the boundary between the United States and Canada remained unsettled, and, for another, the future of vast tracts and territories belonging to the crumbling empire of Spain had to be established.

These and a half-dozen or more minor questions were items included in Canning's instructions. Pre-eminent in those instructions, however, was Castlereagh's insistent admonition for caution and prudence. Painfully aware of England's need for uninterrupted peace, and sensible of the American proclivity to look askance at any English claim or overture, no matter how trivial it might be, he urged upon the Minister to the United States a special forbearance. In dealing with American statesmen, the Foreign Secretary warned Canning, he would be treating with many men who, besides harboring hatred of England and anything English themselves, often felt called upon by their easily aroused countrymen to stand up to the British. In such circumstances there were frequent occasions for insult and affront.

Typical of the prejudice Canning had to face were the anti-British sentiments of John Quincy Adams, the Secretary of State in the administration of President Monroe. Strik ingly alike in the intensity of their convictions, Adams and Canning were almost foredoomed to come into serious conflict. That they did not reach an open rupture can probably be laid to the inherent good sense of each man, and also to the fact that Stratford Canning did not have the antipathy to Americans that John Quincy Adams did to the English. Mindful of his written instructions, Canning never pushed as far as he might have been tempted. Their relations are best summed up by their own evaluations of each other. Adams, in his diary, candidly described the British Minister as "a proud, high-tempered Englishman . . . with a disposition to be overbearing, which I have often been compelled to check in its own way. He is, of all the foreign Ministers with whom I have had occasion to treat, the man who has most severely tried my temper . . . He has, however, a great respect for his word, and there is nothing false about him . . . Mr. Canning is a man of forms, studious of courtesy, and tenacious of private morals. As a diplomatic man, his great want is suppleness, and his great virtue is sincerity."[1] And Canning found the American Secretary of State "much above par in general ability, but having the air of a scholar rather than a statesman, a very uneven temper, a disposition at times well-meaning, a manner somewhat too often domineering, and an ambition causing unsteadiness in his political career. My private intercourse with him was not wanting in kindness on either side. The rougher road was that of discussion on matters of business."[2]

In one of their early conferences Canning gleaned from Adams what was to become the first major foreign policy position of the United States. They were discussing the Spanish colonies in Central and South America when Adams broached the concept of spheres of influence which was later to culminate in the Monroe Doctrine. Fortunately, the idea involved here met with sincere approval in London, especially when George Canning was renamed Foreign Secretary (Castlereagh ended his life by suicide in 1822). The elder Canning had always cast a wary eye at the Holy Alliance, which had come under the domination of Metternich;[3] and when he heard rumors of a scheme by the Continental monarchs to restore Spain's American colonies to her by concerted force, he was deeply disturbed. Therefore, he reacted favorably to the American proposal and subsequently suggested a joint Anglo-American action to forestall such an eventuality.

Monroe was inclined to accept the British offer, as were his predecessors, Jefferson and Madison, whom he consulted, but Adams could neither wholly trust British motives nor suffer it to appear that the American cockboat was trailing in the wake of a British man-of-war, as he phrased it. The idea of a joint project came to naught, therefore, but the later promulgation of the Monroe Doctrine was due in no small measure to American awareness of its favorable reception in London. It had been Stratford Canning's good fortune to be able to relay the initial American thinking on the matter to the British government.

The cordiality engendered in early exchanges such as the matter just described eased, somewhat, the vexing problem posed by the slave trade. The issue was not definitely settled, but the American government agreed to co-operate to the extent of ordering its naval vessels to pursue and search any American ship reported by British navy patrols to be suspect. The United States, however, refused to countenance search by foreign warships, nor would she engage in it herself when ships of foreign registry were involved.

The other weighty issue, that of the Canadian-American boundary in the area of the Columbia River, both Castlereagh and George Canning after him chose to leave in abeyance for a more propitious moment. Stratford Canning made it clear that the British government did not abdicate its claims in this area but that it chose to abstain from attempting a definitive demarcation until such time as a capable boundary commission could effectively penetrate the wilderness and make a reasonable determination of rights and interests.

Thus, there were no momentous decisions made in the course of Canning's Washington stay, but he made definite gains for his country. England was cast in a much more agreeable and friendly light because of his presence, and when he left Washington in the summer of 1823, he left with the accolade of more than one journalist, and without any bitterness on his own part. Ruffled feelings had been smoothed over, and tensions were markedly reduced.

Canning's success in America can be traced in no small way to a change of attitude within himself. For once, he had committed himself to a definite tenure and was not looking for early relief. His correspondence does not continually refer, as it used to, to the proximity of his homecoming. He had given his word, and there was no further discussion. This mental composure enabled him to take the physical discomfort of Washington with ease, and for two years he never left the environs of the capital. When one considers that the temperature ranged from six degrees below zero to 105 above—according to his own records—one can assume that he had achieved a rare equanimity of disposition. He even became a very agreeable host, and, indeed, during one session of the Congress he took it upon himself to entertain all of its members, either individually or in groups. The American Congress interested him as an institution, too, and he was frequently seen in the galleries of the Senate and of the House.

Of course, the language and customs of the country were familiar, and this no doubt made it easier for him to adapt himself to the American scene.

The British Minister was entertained, in turn, by several of the leading American figures. The aging Charles Carroll of Carrollton, at whose Maryland estate he was a frequent visitor, was one to whom he was most attracted. Chief Justice Marshall was another object of his admiration, as was the young Henry Clay. He also dined at Mount Vernon with a nephew of George Washington and privately wondered when the Americans would erect a suitable monument to the memory of the man who had done the most to win their freedom.

He took one extended trip through the northern states and Canada. The letters, notes, and diaries he kept of this and other, shorter, trips reveal him to have been an acute observer of the American scene. It is unfortunate, perhaps, that he never compiled them into a single account. Such a collection would have made for an interesting comparison with the more famous reports of Trollope and Dickens. One curious entry is a detailed comparison of the costs of living in Hagerstown, Maryland for the years 1816 and 1822. Similar memoranda appear for Niagara and other places along his route, but he left no explanation as to why he made the compilation.

With these exceptions he spent his time in and about the city of Washington. During the days of summer heat, when Congress was adjourned and the life of the city came to a complete halt, he occupied himself with reading and writing.

He developed a fascination for the Waverly novels of Scott and devoured them as fast as they came over to him, or whenever he could purchase a new one in the city.

His last year was brightened considerably by the appearance of Henry Addington, who had come over to fill his old post as Secretary to the Minister. The two had gotten along famously in Switzerland and the collaboration was renewed. It was Addington, too, who succeeded him in Washington when Canning relinquished the American mission in June of 1823. The ex-Minister arrived back in England in the following September, no longer a fledgling diplomat but a Foreign Service officer of rank and distinction.

1. *The Diary of John Quincy Adams, 1794-1845,* ed. Allan Nevins (New York, London, and Toronto: Longmans, Green and Co., 1928), pp. 296-97.

2. Lane-Poole, *op. cit.,* I, 308-9.

3. The original purpose of the Holy Alliance as conceived by its principal architect, Czar Alexander I, was to unify the policy of the Christian European states. It was brought into being at the time of the Congress of Vienna, with adherence to its principles by the monarchs of Austria, Prussia, and Russia. Alexander of Russia, though farseeing and liberal for his day, was too weak to overcome the domination of Metternich, and under the leadership of the Austrian Chancellor the Holy Alliance "gradually became an alliance of kings for the suppression of the liberal movements in various countries. Alexander made one concession after another to Metternich. The opinion was expressed that Alexander had completely lost any independence of view. This seemed to be confirmed by the events of the Greek revolution against Turkish rule" (George Vernadsky, *A History of Russia* [New Haven: Yale University Press, 3rd rev. ed., 1951], p. 146). Cf. Winston Churchill, *op. cit.,* IV, 7: "Its [the Holy Alliance] main purpose was to intervene in any part of Europe where revolution appeared and in the name of legitimacy instantly to crush it."

VII

BY the time his thirty-seventh birthday had occurred (November 4, 1823) Stratford Canning had seen service in Denmark, in Constantinople, at the Congress of Vienna, in Switzerland, and in the United States of America. He had been a party to conferences, negotiations, and conventions involving men, nations, and dynasties, yet still regarded all of this as a prelude to eventual service in Parliament. His return home from America, however, coincided with a turn of events in Europe, and George Canning felt that his cousin's services were sorely needed, and at the highest level of diplomacy. In order to put this next phase of Stratford Canning's career in its proper light, a brief recapitulation of the European situation is necessary.

The reverberations of the Napoleonic explosions had nearly toppled several of the major thrones and dynastic lines on the continent. In the wake of the near catastrophe those who had come so near to disaster trembled in fright at the apparition of rising nationalism and republicanism. The Congress of Vienna had been convened not only to dispose of the problems arising from the aftermath of war but to solidify the established regimes and political institutions. One of its offspring was the Holy Alliance of Russia, Austria, and Prussia. Its purpose soon became an undisguised effort to preserve the status quo.[1] The deity of the Alliance was absolute autocracy and its demon was democracy or any form of popular rule. Not only were its participants determined to preserve their own positions but they took it upon themselves to act as sort of a police force for legitimacy. Thus their presumption to act on behalf of Spain when her American colonies began to sever the ties which bound them to Madrid.

In England this was seen as a retrograde movement, and there was little sympathy for it. The island kingdom had a long and hallowed tradition of parliamentary democracy (though the dream of universal suffrage was as yet far from a reality). The current thinking of English theorists and political leaders was in the direction of broadening still further the basis of government. The clamor for electoral reform was growing louder each year. In political thinking, therefore, England was moving in the opposite direction from the nations for whom she had bled at the beginning of the century. The result was a growing tendency to withdraw from Continental embroilments except in those cases which involved the legitimate interests of England. Of course, there was a rub in such a position: almost any continental settlement affected England's trade and commerce, and therefore she was involved whether she liked it or not. In order to have a free hand to deal with such questions as they arose, George Canning had adopted a policy of non-commitment with regard to continental disputes. No one country was England's definite ally; she was free to agree or remonstrate with any one whom she chose. But no sooner were these theoretical positions taken than certain political dilemmas arose which threatened their soundness.

In 1821, a loose confederacy of Greek nationalists and revolutionary factions had joined forces in open revolt against the misrule of Constantinople. The Porte reacted vengefully, and the ensuing reports of massacre and atrocity visited upon innocent victims soon became items of marketplace talk throughout Europe. For the champions of the Holy Alliance, Alexander and Metternich, the problem was a cruel one. Without a doubt the Greeks were in revolt against their legitimate and absolute sovereign. At the same time, the picture of Christian blood flowing at the hands of Moslems was enough to cause the greatest embarrassment, to say nothing of the anguished pleas for help coming from the Greeks. The Czar, in particular, was beside himself. All previous Russian intervention in the Balkans and in the Danubian Principalities had been based on Russia's right to alleviate the sad lot of her coreligionists. Alexander could not, at this juncture, backtrack on that position without serious consequences at home and without relinquishing future pretexts

for action against the Turks.[2]   He had to cast about for some
means of action outside the Alliance.

Metternich and the Austrian emperor, though not as seriously concerned on the religious score, could not afford to
ignore it completely.   They were more disturbed by the
probable consequences of a separate Russian move than they
were with the fortunes of the Greek people.   To Metternich
the Greeks were rebels against authority pure and simple.
Were he to abandon them on those grounds, however, he
would face the danger of leaving to Russia a clear field for
unilateral operation.   This could lead to eventual Russian
pre-eminence in the Balkans as well as along the course of the
lower Danube.   In order to thwart any such eventuality Austria had to pretend to be concerned for the Greeks.

Despite George Canning's aim to be free of Continental ties,
England could not hope to remain unconcerned.   The English government had to cope with a vocal and powerful public
opinion.   The romance of the Greek revolt had already led
to public subscriptions for financial aid, and there had been a
substantial number of philhellenic volunteers sallying forth to
do battle alongside the revolutionaries.   The deep attachment
for Greece in the classics-steeped upper classes threw the
weight of British popular sympathy to the side of the revolution immediately.   The death of Lord Byron at Missolonghi
further intensified these sentiments.

Both the Cannings secretly wished for Greek success as
avidly as did their more romantic countrymen.   Stratford had

written from America in 1821 expressing the hope that the Sultan would be driven bag and baggage into the heart of Asia. There were wider and more consequential issues at stake, however, than a sentimental attachment to a romantic ideal. Whatever the ultimate outcome of the struggle was to be, George Canning was determined that it not include the precipitate downfall of the Ottoman Empire. Such a calamity could only lead to grave results for England in that her lines of communication to India would be seriously jeopardized and her Levantine commerce put at the mercy of the power or coalition of powers succeeding to the hegemony of the Sultan. Above all else, he was determined that Russia not use the Greek question as a means of establishing herself astride the Bosporus and casting her shadow to the Persian Gulf. Stratford Canning agreed with his cousin's reasoning, and furthermore he felt that the scramble for spoils which would inevitably follow the collapse of the Turk would plunge Europe into a bloodbath alongside which the Napoleonic Wars would pale into insignificance.

The Foreign Secretary had to move very carefully. A highly vocal faction was all for instant action, but George Canning fended them off temporarily by prevailing on the Cabinet to recognize the belligerent status of the Greek Provisional Government, in March of 1823. In doing so England put herself in the position of being able to claim early support of the Greek nation should the revolution be successful. Like Metternich, George Canning feared the consequences of unilateral

Russian action. Unlike Metternich he had no disposition to throttle the revolt if it could make headway without destroying the integrity of the Ottoman Empire. In spite of all the romance attached to it, the chaotic amalgam of sincere nationalists, professional revolutionaries, and self-seeking factions composing the revolutionary movement had little appeal for George Canning, and he could not bring himself to look upon them as the ideal heir to Ottoman rule. He believed that the Greeks were not yet ready for complete independence, but also he felt that there should be no return to the *status quo ante*. Some middle way had to be found. As far as public opinion was concerned, the difficulty of his job was eased somewhat by the reports of the early volunteers, who began to find to their sorrow that all was not well with the revolt and that many of the factions were as desperate and as inhuman as their oppressors. Many Englishmen were beginning to think that complete independence was not the answer.

When, therefore, in January of 1824, the Russian government circulated a memorandum among the major powers which called a conference in St. Petersburg to adjudicate the dispute, George Canning reluctantly agreed to send a plenipotentiary to represent England. His agreement was based on the necessity of making England's position known relative to the solution proposed in the Russian memorandum. By its terms Greece was to be divided into three autonomous provinces, each of which was to remain under the sovereignty of the Sultan. On the surface this arrangement seemed to meet

George Canning's requirements for a way out of the crisis, but
the Foreign Secretary was suspicious of Russian motives. He
feared that their game would be to play one faction against
another and then to step in as the dominating element. He
himself preferred a unified state, preferably one small enough
not to be able to make aggressive moves which would disturb
the peace. Sir Charles Bagot, British Ambassador to the Russian Court, was instructed to sit in at the conference but not
to commit England to any decisions of the kind envisioned
by Russia.

The conference began slowly and dragged, chiefly because
no prior agreements had been made and little groundwork
had been done to effect a unanimity of view. Then, in May,
the secret terms of the memorandum were published in a Paris
journal, and there were explosive repercussions in Greece.
The Provisional Government, seeing anything less than complete independence as a negation of all they were fighting
for, defiantly rejected the proposed mediation. They appealed
to England to protect them from the dubious benevolence of
those who would save them in this manner from the hated
Turk.

Now George Canning had long believed that any attempt
at mediation must have the support of at least one of the conflicting parties. In such a case the concerted pressure of
the mediating nations could be brought to bear on the recalcitrant party with some reasonable hope of success. But
where both parties were resolutely opposed to a suggested

solution, as they were in this instance, the mediation was doomed to failure. The only alternative was for the professed peacemakers to impose their remedy by force of arms, a policy which he felt contradicted itself and carried with it the seeds of general war. Bagot was accordingly called home and the conference ground to a halt.[3]

By this time a wholly new ingredient had been added to the stew and changed its flavor radically. The Greeks had been buoyed considerably by British recognition of their belligerent status in the previous year. With the aid of volunteer officers and other outside assistance they had managed to win some impressive victories over the Sultan's forces and were holding several key positions. Mahmud, disgusted with his Janissary generals and bitter over the performance of his army, turned to his Egyptian vassal Mehemet Ali Pasha for help. In return for crushing the Greek revolt Mahmud promised to cede at least the Morea and Crete to Egyptian rule. Mehemet assigned the task to his son Ibrahim, who set sail from Alexandria with a large fleet and thousands of well-trained troops. It looked like the beginning of the end for the Greek Revolution.[4]

George Canning was afraid that Alexander would intervene. The uncertainty as to what the aggressive and ambitious Egyptian viceroy would do after that disturbed all the European powers, and the Russian conference was reconvened. Canning still refused to participate but wanted an observer on hand.

Accordingly, he prevailed on Stratford to accept the assignment as the Ambassador to the Porte until the Greek question should be resolved. Prior to going to Constantinople, however, he was to go to St. Petersburg, ostensibly to settle a Russo-British boundary matter in the northwest Pacific, but really to keep an eye on the proceedings of the conference and to present Britain's views should they be sought.

Stratford Canning, in the meantime, had been meeting with the American Minister Richard Rush in an attempt to iron out the difficulties still remaining with the United States. He had also found time to engage in another courtship, and the prospect of an ambassador's pay and subsequent pension were too attractive to decline.

Before Canning departed, the Foreign Secretary supplied him with a clear statement of English policy to guide him:

> To preserve the peace of the world is the leading object of the policy of England. For this purpose it is necessary in the first place to prevent to the utmost of our power the breaking out of new quarrels; in the second place, to compose, where it can be done by friendly mediation, existing differences; and thirdly, where that is hopeless, to narrow as much as possible their range; and fourthly, to maintain for ourselves an imperturbable neutrality in all cases where nothing occurs to affect injuriously our interests or our honour.[5]

Armed with these general principles, Stratford Canning set out in the fall of 1824 for St. Petersburg by way of Vienna, where he was to discuss the situation with Metternich.   On one important point the instructions from the Foreign Office were deficient, and that was on the matter of just how England would settle the dispute, or even narrow its range. George Canning had not found a practicable middle way between the repugnant extremes, between putting down the revolt in the name of legitimacy and using force to compel the Sultan to acknowledge Greek independence. The Russian compromise had already been repudiated by the Greeks and was known to be equally unacceptable to the Turks.

If Stratford Canning, therefore, were to be challenged to come forward with a means of mollifying both parties, he would be forced either to improvise on the spot or to confess his inability to offer a better plan than the one to which his country objected. It is quite probable that his ability to improvise is what the Foreign Secretary counted on, and for this reason he wanted his cousin in the role. Stratford Canning's personal task would be to arrive at a solution consonant, as far as possible, with intrinsic merits of justice and based on the worthy aspirations of all parties concerned. In a sense, then, his mission was exploratory: to ascertain just what would be suitable to the European powers as well as to the belligerents.

At Vienna he found Prince Metternich, as expected, adamant in his absolutism. The Greeks, according to that architect of restoration, were nothing more than a backwash of the worst elements of Jacobinism. While he proclaimed sympathy with the plight of the Sultan's loyal Christian subjects in Greece and declared his intention of doing what he could for them, Metternich made it clear that he in no way considered the rebels to be representative of the Greek people as a whole. That they were able to continue their resistance to lawful authority at all was a sin he laid at the feet of George Canning, whom he suspected of secret republicanism. There was no doubt in the Austrian's mind but that English money and English sentimentalism alone sustained the Greeks. Metternich agreed with the English Foreign Office in one respect only, namely, that Russia would seek to use the situation to her own advantage. That was the sole reason for Austria's participation in the conference: to discourage and destroy the hopes of the impertinent Greek rebels and to tie Russia's hands by removing the pretext for intervention. He implied that in order to do this Austria might have to support a move for some kind of semi-independence. (The Austrian Chancellor had high hopes that by the time the conference convened Ibrahim would already have settled the matter and the Greek revolt would be a thing of the past, although he did not indicate this to Canning.[6])

There is an interesting sidelight to this meeting between Canning and Metternich. Although the Englishman had been a minor member of the Congress of Vienna, he had never had any real exchanges with the *doyen* of European statecraft. Undoubtedly Metternich knew of Stratford Canning and his work, and there is every reason to suspect that he looked upon the latter as a formidable diplomat in the making. Hoping to unnerve him at the outset, the Prince received him correctly but coldly, and his first words were uttered with

great disdain: "You have a bug on your sleeve." And as
Canning noted, "the remark was not pleasing."[7]

With little gained in Vienna other than the conviction that
the cause of Greek independence would find little more than
grudging support from the Hapsburg camp, Stratford Canning departed for St. Petersburg in January, 1825. The
journey occupied some twenty days (including some all-night
stages), and in the course of it he drew up precise notes and
memoranda to serve as agenda and check lists for himself in
his bouts with Alexander and his Foreign Minister, Count
Nesselrode. In one instance, for example, he drew up a
parallel tabulation of policy positions for England on the one
side and the members of the Holy Alliance on the other, so
that every point of agreement and divergence would be crystal
clear in his mind.[8] He also drew up a lengthy explanation of
the change of position England had assumed on the conference, emphasizing that opposition to the conference arose not
from intransigence or equivocation but from the inherent
impossibility of successful mediation at the moment. Should
further exploration of the subject with the Porte and with the
Greeks lead to a substantial alteration of these chances, then,
he felt, and then only, should the proposed conference be
attempted. For the powers to take substantive positions beforehand would leave them with little recourse but to abandon
the Greeks to their fate or to take up arms against the Sultan.

To point up England's position that further groundwork
was needed, he had something definite to suggest to the Russians, and that was the return of their ambassador to the Porte

as an evidence of good will to the Sultan. The ambassador had been withdrawn some time before when Russian representations in behalf of the Greeks had met with severe rebuff (the Sultan hanged the Greek Patriarch of Constantinople in public),[9] and the two powers had almost come to blows. To return the ambassador as a prelude to the conference would be proof of pacific intent, and might lead to the spirit of compromise required. Refusal to do so would make every Russian move suspect in Turkish eyes and, he might well have added, in English eyes as well.

The reception he met with in St. Petersburg was almost as cold as the Russian winter, at least as far as the subject of Greece was concerned. He was given to understand that since England had seen fit to withhold her influence from the conference there was no point in discussing the matter. For several weeks he was kept completely in the dark; as he put it, "one might imagine there was no such land as Greece in the world." He spent his first few weeks exclusively on the question of the North American matters he had come to negotiate. Although he was sure the Russians were burning with curiosity to know more of England's attitude and intent, he maintained a studied and consistent silence with respect to Greece. When the North American business was disposed of, he suggested to Count Nesselrode that if there was nothing additional to be discussed he should like to arrange his audience of leave-taking.

The conference was now in full session and Stratford knew that it was not going well. Rather than being a peace conference, it had developed into a meeting in which the several participants found it hard to avoid a serious falling out as they maneuvered for positions considered most advantageous to themselves. All of them knew that without England's co-operation a resort to force against the Sultan was really impossible, and for Stratford Canning to depart without divulging a hint of English intentions was more than Nesselrode could stand. A series of meetings ensued between the two with serious attempts on each side to come to an understanding, but they always ran into the stone wall of whether or not Russia intended to resort to force. Canning, seeking to narrow the range of the dispute, demanded a declared disavowal before England would partake in the deliberations, while Nesselrode, though pleading nothing but good intent, would not go that far.

What did come out of it, however, was a clearer picture for Stratford, who had yet to go to the Porte and attempt to persuade the Sultan to accept a friendly mediation. For one thing, he was satisfied that as long as England maintained her firm stance against an imposed settlement, there was little danger that Russia would precipitate a conflict. Secondly, he was in a stronger position to warn the Greeks that they must give in on some of their more unrealistic aims or face the probability that they might end up with nothing but an exchange of foreign rule. There was even the more ominous danger that, if Russia and Austria should fall out completely and nullify each other, the Greeks might be abandoned entirely to the mercies of a vengeful Sultan.

Over and against these warnings, Canning felt he could suggest to the Greeks that if they accepted England's sincere desire to mediate unselfishly in their behalf, they might achieve a measure of independence. Finally, he had been able to persuade the Russians that the English Cabinet, far from sponsoring revolution as such, was actually in agreement with the Alliance that complete independence for Greece was impracticable at the present time. The conviction that he thus left with them was to be important in George Canning's eventual decision to act in concert with Russia rather than to allow her to go it alone.

Canning came back to England in May to begin his preparations for another residence in Constantinople, the despised "dust hole" he had quit thirteen years previously. He had also to attend to a personal matter of some moment. At the end of his American mission he had met one Eliza Charlotte Alexander, a pretty young girl close to half his age. Miss Alexander was not the dutiful Victorian type of young lady, and in spite of her parents' approval of Stratford Canning had turned him down when he originally proposed marriage. She had actually gone to Holland in the summer of 1824 to avoid his attentions, but Stratford, just as insistent in love as he was in diplomacy, pursued her there before he went to Russia. Apparently he improved his chances by his persistence, for when he renewed the courtship and the chase after the Russian interlude, she finally accepted him.

Stratford Canning and Eliza Alexander were married on
the twenty-fifth of September, 1825. It was to be a long,
happy union, one that was marked by mutual respect and
confidence. Despite his strong personality Canning was not
the domineering male usually associated with the Victorian
age.

1. See above, chap. VI, n. 3.

2. Cf. Vernadsky, *op. cit.*, p. 146: "Public opinion in Russia demanded
support of the movement. Metternich, on the other hand, saw in it only
a rebellion of the subjects of the Sultan, their legal ruler, and on this
basis the Alliance expressed itself against support of the revolution.

"Alexander did not want to quarrel with the Alliance, which had come
into existence at his own initiative, but his diplomacy during this period
sought for independent means of expression outside the Alliance. He
sought separate agreements with its members."

3. Cf. Crawley, *op. cit.*, p. 36.

4. Cf. Temperley, *op. cit.*, p. 53.

5. Lane-Poole, *op. cit.*, I, 343.

6. Cf. Crawley, *op. cit.*, pp. 39-42. Crawley says, in this connection,
that Metternich's seeming reversal on the matter of Greek independence
was not seriously advanced but was merely a means of forestalling Russian
action.

7. Lane-Poole, *op. cit.*, I, 349.

8. *Ibid.*, pp. 359-62.

9. This had occurred in 1821 at the beginning of the revolt. Mahmud
held the Patriarch personally responsible, under the millet system, for the
behavior of the entire Greek Christian community. After the execution
by public hanging in front of the patriarchal palace, the body was ill-used
by the mob. The Russian ambassador protested vigorously and shortly
thereafter quit Constantinople. See Crawley, *op. cit.*, pp. 17-18.

VIII

SCARCELY had Eliza Alexander become the new Mrs. Canning than her husband whisked her off to the Aegean on a most unlikely honeymoon. Canning had arranged preliminary conferences with several members of the Greek Provisional Government and with some of the factional leaders involved in the struggle. To Count Capodistrias, his old colleague of Swiss days who had fallen from the Czar's favor by reason of his part in the insurrection,[1] he emphasized the dire possibilities inherent in too resolute a stand for complete independence. The Count was sufficiently aware of general Russian policy to see the force of the argument and began to throw his weight behind some form of peaceful approach to the Porte. Prince Alexander Mavrocordatos was another one of the leaders to whom Canning's candor and sincerity became immediately apparent. His calm words of warning coupled with promises of real support on a middle ground were beginning to have their effect.[2]

There were other developments which tended to turn the Greeks toward a position more in keeping with English policy. The Petersburg Conference had come to an agreement on the part of Russia, Austria, France, and Prussia whereby they warned the Sultan to come to terms on the pain of severe penalties should he fail to do so. It was no secret, however, that Prince Metternich had let it be known at the Porte that Austria had no intention of following through with any sanctions whatsoever, and thus the strength of the demands was immediately vitiated. The Porte remained as intransigent as ever.

This meaningless arm-waving was further weakened by the death of Czar Alexander I at the close of the year, which removed from the scene one of the founders and props of the Holy Alliance. After some uncertainty about the succession, his younger brother Nicholas ascended to the throne. Nicholas' ambitions were unknown. His first utterances seemed to negate the sometimes warlike threats of his predecessor and to imply that Russia no longer thought of armed intervention.

All in all the Greeks felt they were being abandoned to their fate; the possibility of English mediation was the sole remaining hope. At a meeting on shipboard off the island of Hydra their representatives intimated to Canning that they would accept a settlement granting independence to the Morea, that is, the lower portion of Greece excluding Epirus, Macedonia, and Thessaly. They were willing to tolerate the presence of Turkish garrisons on the border and promised indemnities to satisfy legitimate Turkish claims.

A year earlier it would have been a major and perhaps efficacious concession, but now it came at a time when Greek fortunes were at a very low ebb. Not only was their foreign support dwindling and their cherished dreams of Russian aid vanishing in the mist, but a series of Egyptian military triumphs over their crumbling armies had reduced them to despair. The already stubborn Turkish attitude had stiffened correspondingly. Consequently, when the English Ambassador reached the Dardanelles in the spring of 1826 after a long and tiresome trip, delayed by meetings, by sickness in his party (Mrs. Canning had been laid low with fever), and by weather, he faced a rather defiant Porte. They were not thirsting for the opportunity to make any concessions.

It was quite a change from his earlier experience: the basic structure had not changed so much, but the authority of the government had been appreciably strengthened. The Sultan Mahmud had solidified his power. He had effectively curbed the feudal autonomy of the derebeys, the great land-holders, and had replaced them with appointed officials. He had brought all his vassals under control save one, Mehemet Ali, and the Egyptian was being bought off by the prospects of rich rewards in Greece. Bushels of human ears were reaching the Seraglio daily and no attempt was made to hide them or the glee with which they were received. The depredations of the Egyptian troops had already been a matter of personal experience for Stratford Canning and his party. At one tiny port where they had put in for food and water they had found a ghost town, devoid of all life but birds of prey, and these were busily picking the bones of the slaughtered inhabitants.

Stratford Canning had come back to Turkey as an Elchi, the term reserved for the full ambassadors of the major powers. Neither he nor the Turks knew yet that in the years to come the title would be his almost exclusively. He was to be the great ambassador, the Elchi par excellence. A hint of things to come can be seen in his behavior at his audience with the Sultan, when he presumed to wear a ceremonial sword in the presence of the great Caliph himself. Mahmud spoke not a word throughout the audience but neither was any attempt made to induce the English Elchi to forgo the side arm. It was the beginning of the revolution he was to effect in the relationship between the Seraglio and foreign envoys.

Before he was able to press any of his views upon the Porte, Canning had first to defend the right of England to meddle at all in the internal affairs of the Empire. With perfectly good logic the Turks asked him what the reaction of the English Cabinet would be should they enter a protest in London on behalf of the Peterloo rioters and other political malcontents then disturbing the peace in his homeland. Canning countered, with little effect, that there was a great difference between legal prosecution of rioters and the barbarities being inflicted in the Sultan's name on the women and children of Greece.

At the beginning he could make no progress in Constantinople, but other developments were working to help him.
The reports of the conference at Hydra and the accession of
Nicholas I in Russia had prompted George Canning to send
the Duke of Wellington to St. Petersburg to take up the
negotiations that the Elchi had begun the previous year.
Nicholas, in an evident pose of desiring to appear as peacefully inclined as possible, entered enthusiastically into the
proceedings, and the Wellington Protocol which resulted
from the meeting (April 4, 1826) adopted almost in detail
the lines of settlement advanced at Hydra. By its terms
England and Russia agreed that Greece was to have full
autonomy, with a payment of annual tribute to the Sultan
who was also to have a voice in the nomination of its officials.
The news of the agreement was joyfully received in England,
but Stratford Canning, who doubted the sincerity of the
Russians, had some misgivings, especially about their guarded
disavowal of the use of force as a method of mediation. Nor
was his doubt unjustified, for hard on the heels of the
Wellington Protocol came a severe ultimatum to the Porte
from Russia (April 5, 1826). While it is true that it made
no mention of Greece and concerned Turkish laxity with
respect to several items of the Treaty of Bucharest, the intent
was clear. It was the same relentless pressure brought to bear
to keep the Turks off balance in hopes that the walls would
finally crumble without the need for high explosives.[3]

Canning viewed the ultimatum as a double blessing,[4] since
it not only disspelled any rash hopes that might have been

arising in England for a quick and easy way out of the problem but also removed for him a dilemma that would face him if the Turks were to be convinced that no force would be used against them. By now he was sufficiently grounded in his understanding of Ottoman mentality to realize that no matter how much they appeared to resent the sword-rattling of the European powers, it was the only language they understood. Once it ceased they would return to their old ways. If the Wellington Protocol were to be taken in Constantinople for what its terms implied,[5] the Turks would turn a deaf ear to the thought of Grecian independence and he, as Ambassador, would be at a loss as to what pressure he could bring to bear upon them. As things turned out, the necessary pressure remained along their Danubian border because of the Russian move. Before too long, consequently, there was a surprising reversal of Turkish recalcitrance. The Porte suddenly agreed to send representatives to meet the Russians at Akkerman. It was not only the Russian pressure that motivated the Sultan, however, for the embattled Mahmud had a surprise in store for everyone.

If the Greek War had taught Mahmud anything it was the lesson that his army was hopelessly inefficient and incapable of meeting the trained modern armies of Europe. In his relations with foreign powers, therefore, he would perpetually be treating from a position of weakness. The root of this inefficiency, moreover, lay in the control wielded by the Corps of Janissaries, and in their unwillingness to pursue anything but their own ends.

It has been noted that Mahmud had made several strides toward improving the administration of the empire since the time of Canning's earlier term at the British Embassy. These improvements, let it be emphasized, were not made in the name of progress as commonly understood in the West: not in the interests of enlightened justice and humanitarianism, but solely to reconcentrate power in the hands of the Sultan and the Divan. If anything, they were to make it easier for the Sultan to be the autocratic Oriental monarch of old. The Janissaries, with their bureaucratic network in the capital and in the provinces, were the single greatest barrier remaining.

Apparently Mahmud had decided to move against them some time before. He had freed himself from dependence on the Corps by employing the ruthless machine of Mehemet Ali in Greece. When the Russian pressure was renewed, Mahmud evidently concluded that he would lose less by treating with the Czar than by remaining a moment longer under the shadow of the praetorian guard the Janissaries had become.

He himself had come to power and his two immediate predecessors had met their death as a direct result of an attempt to crush the Janissaries.[6] There had been many Turkish leaders then, civil, religious, and military, who had applauded the attempted reforms of Selim III, but the hold of the Janissaries had been too strong and opposition to them too unorganized. In the intervening years, however, Mahmud had seen Mehemet Ali rise to a level of real power through his destruction of the Mamelukes in Egypt and the adoption of army reforms.[7] The Ottoman Sultan was not to be outdone, and he planned carefully. Over the years he had gradually removed the members of the Corps from one key position after another. Then, in June of 1826, he resurrected the Nizam Jedid. The Janissaries were given the opportunity of enrolling in the new army if they wished, but the Corps itself was disbanded. The Janissary units in the capital began a revolt by murdering the Sultan's emissaries, but Mahmud was ready. On the night of June 15, a ruthless campaign was begun against them. They were seized and slaughtered by the thousands in the capital and provincial cities.[8] Their barracks were put to the torch, and artillery was turned on those who tried to make their escape. For months afterward, the city was a scene of horror. The bowstring and scimitar were steadily plied, and the very name Janissary meant an automatic death sentence. As is common in such explosions of revenge, the damning indictment of being listed on the rolls of the Corps was used against personal and political enemies. There was no investigation and no defense.

Predictably, the violence brought with it xenophobic outbursts, and often the only safety for the Embassy staff was to be found within the confines of the Embassy itself. Poor Mrs. Canning watched in fear and dread late one night as her husband hurried down to the Embassy courtyard in his dressing gown to save the lives of the Embassy guards, who happened to be listed among the Janissaries.

While all this was going on, Canning was on guard against an inside danger as well. Treachery had been uncovered in the Embassy staff, involving one of the lesser dragomans who was known to be revealing secrets to Baron Ottenfels, the Austrian Internuncio. The delicacy of the affair was complicated by the fact that the individual in question was a favorite at the Seraglio, and the Ambassador did not want to dismiss him summarily. It was better, he thought, to keep him in sight and to remove the danger by not entrusting him with information of any importance. In this quiet and unobstrusive way, Canning removed what might have been magnified into a major incident at a time when there was enough to worry about. After all, the machinations of the Internuncio and Prince Metternich did not depend on the services of a single corrupt dragoman. Metternich's devotion to the principles of absolutism had made him insensible to all considerations of humanity and justice. To try to thwart him directly in each and every instance would have been, in Canning's opinion, a waste of time and perhaps the very diversion the Austrian Chancellor was contriving to effect.

Obviously, in this period of upheaval, there was little to be accomplished in the way of solving the Greek crisis. Mahmud's violence showed no signs of abating all through the summer, and the Ottoman Court seemed to be in a state of hypnotic trance. One eye was feasting on the continuing bloodbath and the other was fastened hopefully on the masses of recruits drilling European-style in every empty space and campground for miles about. Gradually the comic-opera aspect of this new army dwindled for European observers, as Mahmud gave evidence of imposing his will, and what had initially been assumed to be the last gasp of a tottering dynasty imperceptibly transformed itself into the prospect of a new birth of power.

It is difficult to judge just how unnerving this unexpected possibility was to the European courts and chancelleries, but it would be foolish to assume that it had no effect. The Porte also was showing some new astuteness in her foreign relations. For concomitant with an increasing stubbornness about Greece, where the Egyptians were all but smothering the rebels, the Turks displayed a marked willingness to appease the new czar of Russia. Turkish plenipotentiaries acceded to Russian demands relative to the border disputes along the Danube and signed a treaty with the Russians at Akkerman. It was a strategic retreat that cost Turkey little in the way of actual surrender while it removed any immediate pretext for Russian incursions southward. This affair was concluded in October of 1826, and the customary winter lag in negotiations and communications left all participants in a state of confused indecision.

Even George Canning was at a loss as to how to proceed. He admitted that the barbarities in the Morea had put a distinctly different coloration on the grounds for mediation than had heretofore existed. There was also a recurrence of piracy in the Aegean which was proving detrimental to

British commerce. The rising clamor on this score plus a new wave of sympathy on behalf of Greek independence seem to have influenced him to countenance the use of force after all.

When Stratford Canning protested the piracy to the Reis Effendi, he was met with indifference. The piracy, according to the Turks, was simply a result of the rebellion, and the rebellion would long ago have foundered but for support from England and the other powers. Let the Sultan deal with the Greeks as they deserved and there would be no further difficulty. The conviction grew in the Elchi's mind that, once again, only a display of force would sway the Turks. They ignored all evidence of cruelty presented to them, or denied the facts as they chose, and he saw no hope of persuading them to a different mode of action by words alone. His reports to London bear this conclusion out and undoubtedly they had their effect on his cousin's outlook.

By the spring of 1827, George Canning had finally become the Prime Minister of England. He was faced with the choice of allowing Greece to be subjugated anew, of standing by while Russia took unilateral action, or of moving in concert with the other powers to bring effective pressure on the Porte. He welcomed a move by France to associate herself with the aims of the Wellington Protocol, and in July, the Treaty of London was signed by France, England, and Russia. It restated the provisions of the Protocol, whereby the powers bound themselves to mediate in behalf of Greek independence, save for Turkish rights to indemnification and interest

in the foreign affairs of the new state. It also contained a
secret article binding the three powers to interpose themselves
between the belligerents should an armistice be refused.[9] A
time limit was annexed to the treaty when it was presented to
the Porte, but as Stratford Canning reported, the Reis Effendi
refused to look at the treaty and did not even bother to have it
translated.

Exactly how the interposition was to be made and how the
armistice was to be enforced is not known. Three allied
squadrons set sail for the Aegean under the loose over-all command of Sir Edward Codrington with orders to prevent the
Sultan's armies in Greece from receiving either reinforcements
or supplies. On his arrival in the waters of the Archipelago,
the Admiral sought the advice of the British Ambassador as
to the lengths he was to go to thus "prevent," and in reply
Stratford Canning wrote that he presumed the Cabinet intended Codrington to use "cannon shot" if necessary.

The measure of prevention intended by the Prime Minister
is a secret that died with him on August 6, after he had been
Prime Minister for little more than one hundred days. His
death came at the very time that Codrington was seeking
clarification of his orders, and it was tragic for the cause of
peace. There is little doubt that the Prime Minister would
have restricted the Admiral to the use of warning shots unless
he were attacked. As matters stood the orders were indefinite,
but warning shots were all that Stratford Canning intended.
He never failed to accept a share of the responsibility for what
transpired a few weeks later, however, and freely admitted

that he should have been more judicious in his choice of words to a man of Codrington's fighting instincts.

Early in October the allied fleet sought shelter from a severe storm in the harbor of Navarino. Unfortunately, the bulk of the Turco-Egyptian fleet was also at anchor in the same port. An incident ensued and a fierce battle followed, in the course of which the entire Moslem fleet was destroyed with the loss of countless seamen. The disaster could not have been more complete.

Only the slightest chance warned Canning and his diplomatic confreres in Constantinople of the danger they were in before the news reached the Porte. Well aware of the frayed condition of Turkish nerves, they had all feared just such an eventuality and had made some moves to send away the women and children of the embassies but had not yet done so. Only fifty years earlier the lot of a foreign ambassador in a like situation would have been certain death, and the various envoys were not yet sure that the idea of diplomatic immunity had taken root in the minds of the Turks, especially after the violence of the preceding year in the Ottoman capital.

Some time previous to this the ambassadors of France, England, and Russia had begun the practice of meeting daily to discuss the developing crisis, and on a Sunday afternoon following the coup at Navarino, the English Ambassador was on his way to the French Embassy when a passerby thrust a crumpled note into his hands. It was a message from an English merchant captain informing the Ambassador of large-scale naval action he had heard while sailing in the vicinity of

Navarino. Correctly interpreting the sounds of cannonade and intermittent explosions as harbingers of danger, the seaman had skirted the area and made a dash for Smyrna, from where he dispatched an overland messenger to Pera. Being thus warned, the diplomats had the opportunity of seeing to it, at least, that all their people were safely gathered in the respective embassies to await the outcome. Escape was impossible; to move staffs and families would have required fair-sized vessels, and none were available. Even had they been, a dash through the Sea of Marmara and the Dardanelles was inconceivable.

Fortunately, no attempt was made upon their persons, but the embassies were surrounded by troops and the envoys accused of violating the law of nations. The fact that further intelligence indicated the first shot had been fired by the Turks themselves did not assuage the anger of the Porte in the least, and for a time the foreigners felt they were living in constant peril of their lives. However, as the weeks passed without further retaliation, Canning thought that the Turks might have been brought to their senses by the shock of their losses. He ventured to send a dragoman to ask for a conference with the Reis Effendi. He reasoned that it was possible the Divan might be awaiting an approach on the subject of peace rather than wishing to appear fearful of the allies by making the first move.

He was able to get his conference—several of them, in fact— but his hopes for Ottoman surrender to the inevitability of Greek independence were soon crushed. Actually a struggle of vast proportions had been raging in the Divan ever since Navarino, with the Sultan himself urging a war to the death, and being restrained only by a majority who were in favor of coming to terms. The Sultan, accordingly, had withheld a declaration of war but he was resolute on Greece. Let the Greeks submit to his authority and he would listen to and repair their grievances. He would give them kind and friendly government but never independence.

When it was apparent that negotiations would be fruitless, the allied envoys asked for their passports. They were refused permission to leave, however, on the grounds that they were asking of their own accord and not under instruction from their respective home governments. Notwithstanding this refusal the ambassadors resolved to leave with their missions and repair to Corfu to await the decisions of their superiors. Canning described the departure in his memoirs:

> The position, it must be allowed, was sufficiently delicate and hazardous. It was also attended with much inconvenience and embarrassment. We were acting under a heavy responsibility towards our respective Governments. We had to provide for the protection of the merchants, for the conveyance of the official correspondence, and for the safety of the crown property which must be left behind. We could not foresee into what fanatical agitation the Musulman populace might be thrown by our departure. . . .
> On 8 December I embarked on board a small merchant vessel. . . . My wife went with me. Our companions were numerous. . . . We had to walk a considerable way through the town. It was already dark when we started. It blew

hard from the north, and rained plentifully. We had the
streets in consequence to ourselves; there was no hindrance
to our exodus. . . . The French ambassador had weighed
anchor an hour or two before us, but we passed him in the
night and were the first to reach the Dardanelles. . . . We
had to encounter the officers of the Custom House, and here,
if mischief was intended, we should have to undergo an
awkward detention. . . . I got into a boat and waited on
the Pasha, who treated me as a mere English traveller with
becoming hospitality. The windows of his Excellency's
apartment looked out upon the water, and when I saw
that our vessel had cleared the line of his guns, I told him
who I was, and explained the circumstances under which I
had left Constantinople. He took my communication with
Turkish gravity and personal good humour. It looked as if
he had received orders to let us pass. . . . We had scarcely
cleared the Dardanelles when we were told to be on our
guard as pirates were supposed to be in the neighborhood.
The warning was thrown away upon us, for our vessel
was not armed, and I doubt whether there was a single gun,
pistol, or cutlass on board. Our business evidently was to
push on, and we were fortunate enough to reach the Gulf
of Smyrna without accident or alarm. A royal frigate was
waiting for us there.[10]

Canning and his wife returned to England in 1828, just
after the turn of the year. He looked upon his mission as a
dismal failure, and he had suffered a grievous loss in the death
of his cousin. He was somewhat heartened by a warm welcome from the Duke of Wellington, now the Prime Minister,
and the personal approbation of the King at Windsor, but
otherwise the outlook was very dismal.

1. Cf. Crawley, *op. cit.*, p. 16: "When the revolt broke out sooner than the cautious friends of Greece had hoped or expected Capo d'Istria soon lost his position at the Emperor's side."

2. *Ibid.*, pp. 45 ff. A sizable number of important leaders had already submitted an "Act of Submission" to England whereby they sought an English Protectorate over Greece. This measure followed the Greek rejection of the terms outlined in the Russian memorandum. Although the idea of a Protectorate was immediately dismissed by the Foreign Office, nevertheless George Canning did take it, together with other overtures being made to various European royal houses looking for a candidate for a Greek "throne," as a sign that the Greeks were ready to accept a semi-independent autonomy along the lines he had been urging. He thus felt free to attempt mediation along with Russia. Accordingly, Stratford Canning was instructed to press the Turks to accept similar mediation.

3. *Ibid.*, p. 2: "The Russian Cabinet liked always to have some unsettled claims which could be pushed forward at favourable moments as an excuse for further encroachment."

4. *Ibid.*, p. 54: "The awkward paradox was this: Stratford's lever of negotiation with the Turks was admitted to be the prospect of a war with Russia: yet Wellington, so far from admitting the right of the Tsar to make war, was to obtain if possible an undertaking from him not to do so."

5. *Ibid.*, p. 61: "The protocol made it quite clear that meditation was to be *offered to*, not *forced upon*, the Turks . . . ." (my italics).

6. See above, chap. II, pp. 22, 33 n.2.

7. See Toynbee, *op. cit.*, VIII, 232-49, for a full treatment of Moslem reaction to and adoption of Western military organization in the nineteenth century.

8. Some historians think that Mahmud intended the slaughter as an act of revenge. Others feel that the violence of the Janissary reaction drove him to it. It seems safe to say that he expected the reaction and was prepared to meet it in any way necessary. Cf. Fisher. *op. cit.*, pp. 273-74, who notes that 14,000 artillerymen were gathered in the capital.

9. Cf. Crawley, *op. cit.*, p. 76.

10. Lane-Poole, *op cit.*, I, 455-57.

IX

THE death of George Canning signalled the end of an era of great Tory leadership in England. Incompetence and indecision became the order of the day in Westminster and Whitehall. The months immediately following the Prime Minister's death had seen a caretaker Cabinet under Lord Goderich function until a new government was organized under what should have been the able leadership of the Duke of Wellington, but it was an administration which proved to be highly ineffective. Before 1830 was out, it was to go down to defeat opposing the Reform Bill being supported by the Whigs and young Tories.

For Stratford Canning the untimely death of George Canning was a great personal blow. Not only did it sever the deep ties which bound him to his cousin and mentor, but it shattered his hopes for home office as well. Stratford had now to face the realization that there was to be no place for him in the Cabinet in the foreseeable future. He had, however, resolved to finish the task entrusted to him by his cousin: the liberation of Greece as an independent country, free from both Turkish and Russian domination.

The leadership which George Canning had maintained in European affairs, particularly with reference to Greece, was on the point of being abandoned to Russian ascendancy. Indeed the new Czar's intentions had been quickly manifested by a declaration of the war which the late Prime Minister had feared. Stratford Canning had barely reached England when Nicholas I declared war on the Porte.[1]

In view of this turn of events Canning did not go through the usual formalities of submitting his resignation to the new Cabinet but decided instead to press them to pursue the goals delineated by the Treaty of London before time had erased the meaning of the agreement. He had assumed that as a matter of honor if not of policy the Wellington Cabinet would feel constrained by the terms of that treaty to implement the intentions of the previous government. If it were to do so, it was imperative that steps be taken to return the Ambassador to the scene and to re-establish contact with both the Greeks and the Turks. Canning urged that there was every reason, now that England had used force, to follow it up to its logical conclusion by pressing upon the Porte the determination of England to see the independence of Greece realized before the Sultan should undo himself by miscalculation. The danger was, of course, that should Britain suddenly abstain from the imbroglio the Sultan might well try his new army against the might of Russia. He would inevitably be crushed,

to the detriment not only of Turkey but of England as well.
To dispatch the English fleet to the Dardanelles, on the other
hand, was a measure Mahmud would understand, and it
would likely bring him to senses before a catastrophe occurred.

However, the logic of this reasoning found little support
at the Foreign Office, where a new face had appeared.[2] The
Earl of Aberdeen who soon succeeded Lord Dudley as Wellington's Foreign Secretary was a conviced pacifist. Despite
his early philhellenism he could not countenance force even
to help the Greeks. Aberdeen refused to believe that the
very horror he detested was actually going on, that savagery
was continuing in Greece because no one had taken effective
means to put an end to it. The apparition of possible violence
to come blinded him to the bloodshed at hand. Nor did he
know the Turks as Stratford Canning did, or he would have
recognized that firmness might bring not the conflict he feared
but the peace he desired. Under the domination of Wellington, furthermore, Aberdeen had become something of a legitimist, and the Greeks were not doing much to convince him
that they were worth fighting a war for. Factional strife and
assassination had become rampant; there were two; and sometimes three groups, each of which claimed to be the legitimate
provisional government. Their greatest leader, Count (President) Capodistrias, was soon to fall under an assassin's knife.

Understandably under the circumstances, it was exceed-
ingly difficult for the Elchi to press his views home with the
Cabinet. It is worth noting, however, that the very policy

he was advocating was the same the Czar had lately offered to London. The invitation was embodied in a memorandum that was rejected by the Wellington Cabinet in January, before Nicholas had decided to act alone. In desperation Canning resorted to every stratagem he could think of to spur the Duke to action. Once he appealed to Wellington to imagine what would happen if by some chance the Turks did succeed in beating off the Russians. Was Christendom to bow before a new wave of Moslem terror in Greece? On another tack, he proposed a joint Anglo-French occupation of the Morea. When this drew no response, he suggested that France alone proceed on such an expedition, with England giving its blessings.

This last suggestion apparently did not conflict too harshly with Aberdeen's principles or with Wellington's parsimoniousness.[3] The Cabinet sanctioned the move and by July a force of 18,000 French troops landed in the Morea. The non-intervention principle of George Canning was thus effectively buried along with the legitimist pretensions of the Holy Alliance.

The Wellington Cabinet sanctioned the French move on the grounds that it was in line with that article of the Treaty of London which required that the signatories interpose themselves between the belligerents should an armistice be refused. Here was an interesting paradox: the government of France was considered to be acting in behalf of the three signatories of that document, and Russia, now at war with the Sultan, was one of the three! But that technicality was easily disposed of. Russia was neatly fitted into the scheme of things by being judged to be at war in the Balkans and the Black Sea but neutral in Greece.

Mediation, at any rate, was resurrected, and a meeting of plenipotentiaries representing the signatories of the Treaty was called to convene at Poros, an island near the northeastern coast of the Peloponnesus. There they were to draw up an instrument of peace in accord with the terms of the same Treaty. Stratford Canning was the English plenipotentiary, and was, as Crawley notes, the wrong man for the Wellington Cabinet to send in view of the limitations they wished to put upon the new state.[4] Of course, these limitations were not yet known or Stratford would never have gone out.

The joint instructions given the ministers were correctly broad on all three points they were to consider: the territorial limits of the new state; its form of government; and financial indemnification to the Porte and to Turkish subjects likely to be effected by the change of sovereignty. The settlement of these points was to be determined by local conditions. On the matter of territorial extent, for example, they were to judge on the basis of two criteria: first, to include within the boundaries of the new state any area whose populace had been involved in open insurrection, so that that area was not to be abandoned to certain revenge; and second, to select a naturally defensive boundary with a mind to "mountain ridges and deep ravines." Anyone who is familiar with the terrain of Greece will know how indefinite the last admonition was. On the matter of the form of government the plenipotentiaries were to keep in mind the factional strife among the Greeks, and they were to consult the Greeks themselves. It was a fore-gone conclusion that the respective European governments favored a monarchy, but until a suitable prince could be un-covered it was possible that the conferees would have to go along with the provisional president, Capodistrias. Such was the extent of their orders.

Mrs. Canning's health was not good in the summer of 1828 so she remained home in England. Canning joined his French and Russian counterparts at Poros, and they plunged into the morass of detail awaiting them. They were joined for long periods of time by Capodistrias whose objections and truculence at this juncture became a constant thorn. As Can-ning put it, England and the civilized world wanted to see an independent Greece, but not a Greece powerful enough to keep the eastern Mediterranean in a state of perpetual fer-ment. Turkish agreement was going to be hard enough to obtain without dismembering her still more to suit the dreams of a "greater Greece."[5] With Capodistrias, Stratford could be patient and understanding, and in spite of extreme provoca-tion he kept the Greek president from leaving, and thereby upsetting, the meeting.

Day-in and day-out shipboard existence was not easy for Canning, who never prided himself on being a mariner. Seasickness and summer heat bothered him constantly, but his powers of endurance were such that he kept himself and his colleagues at their tasks until, item by item, they forged a vehicle that seemed able to traverse the rest of the distance to the "promised land." Subject to ratification by all concerned, the Poros Conference set the continental boundaries of Greece along a mountain range bordering Thessaly, somewhat to the north of the one Stratford Canning preferred (he had urged a line running from Arta to Volos just above the thirty-ninth parallel). Here he acceded to the judgment of the French ambassador who was an expert in geography. The insular boundaries included most of the islands in the far-flung Aegean Archipelago, including Crete. Where populations were so mixed as to ensure continued violence, there was to be a transfer of population depending on individual choice. A further recommendation was that a kingdom be set up, with a Crown to be offered to a foreign prince as the means best calculated to stifle factional disputes. Finally, the outlines of a constitution were drawn, centering much authority in the Crown to allow for stabilization at first, but containing machinery for a later broadening of the base of government. The solution was agreed to by the plenipotentiaries and the Greeks. There remained the tasks of obtaining Turkish acquiescence and finding a king—a king who would not need an expensive court and one strong enough to be what he was supposed to be.

For the winter the diplomats decided to withdraw to Naples, then the favorite retreat of European society. There Mrs.

Canning joined her husband. But it was not entirely a period of relaxation. In the midst of the social whirl Canning had several discussions with Prince Leopold of Saxe-Coburg, who seemed to be a nearly unanimous choice for the throne of Greece. Whether or not Canning influenced Leopold adversely is an open question. The Ambassador clearly hoped, along with the others, that the Crown would go to Leopold, but told him quite frankly that it was a throne which might drive its occupant to despair.[6] At any rate, Leopold declined the homage of Greece to become, a short while later, the King of the Belgians. Had he accepted the throne of Greece it is interesting to speculate on what the subsequent history of that land might have been.

Stratford Canning's plans suffered a rude jolt when he heard of Lord Aberdeen's reactions to the decisions of Poros. He unequivocally rejected the northern boundary and accused Canning of openly flaunting his instructions with regard to Crete.[7] That island, it is true, had not been included in the agenda but, in the opinion of the ambassadors, would have been if the home governments had been aware of local conditions. Hard fighting had been going on there for years, and it would have been unfair to abandon the rebels to the vengeance of the Turks. The plenipotentiaries had included it in accord with their general instructions to pay heed to the needs of the local populace.

Unfortunately, strong and severe expressions were used on both sides, and the rupture resulted in the inevitable. Stratford Canning offered to resign as Ambassador rather than to try to undo what he had done. The resignation was accepted in April of 1829, and Aberdeen's brother, Sir Robert Gordon, replaced Canning for the coming negotiations in Constantinople. For the time being the Elchi was removed from the scene of action.[8]

By an ironic twist of fate his retirement from diplomacy ushered him, at last, into the benches of Commons, but at the very time he would have wished otherwise. While he had been engaged in the discussions at Poros, he had been elected to represent the constituency of Old Sarum. It was one of the most rotten of the "rotten boroughs," to be sure. However, he was a Member of Parliament and had some consolation from the fact that his seat was once held by no lesser a light than Chatham, the elder Pitt.

In December of that same year, Wellington, by way of compensation and appreciation for Canning's services, recommended to the King that the new M. P. be awarded the Grand Cross of the Bath. He was henceforward known as Sir Stratford Canning.

1. See Temperley, *op. cit.,* pp. 54 ff. Nicholas was not entirely unprovoked. Smoldering with rage over the blow delt him at Navarino, Mahmud issued a blistering proclamation at the close of 1827 repudiating the Convention of Akkerman and virtually calling for a holy war in defense of Islam. It was more than the war party in Russia could tolerate, and war began in April of 1828.

2. *Ibid.,* pp. 53-54: "The policy of acting with Russia, in order to restrain her from attacking Turkey, was one which none but a great

statesman could conceive or execute. Wellington and Aberdeen, who succeeded [George] Canning, made no attempt to do so. They could not conceive that support of Russia might really be a benefit to Turkey." (See also Stratford Canning's memoirs in Lane-Poole, *op. cit.,* I, 458-61.)

3. Wellington did not want to spend a single shilling on a Greek war: ". . . Thank God, it has never cost us a shilling, and never shall." See Crawley, *op. cit.,* p. 121.

4. *Ibid.,* pp. 109-12.

5. See Stratford Canning, *The Eastern Question,* pp. 188-99, for a full account of the Poros meeting.

6. Leopold did talk to others about the matter, of course, including Capodistrias.

7. Cf. Crawley, *op. cit.,* p. 147. Aberdeen feared that the new Greek state would be nothing but a tool of Russia and that a Russian foothold in Crete would give the Czars a strnglehold on the Levant.

8. *Ibid.,* p. 154: "Stratford was deeply disappointed at the result, but he was perfectly right to resign; he wrote to Dawkins [the English Resident in Greece]: 'As matters now stand the fate of Greece will turn almost exclusively on the fortunes of the Russian campaign.'"

X

THE tentative arrangements of the Poros Conference were
approved without change through a separate group of French
and Russian representatives sitting in a superior conference
with the English in London. This ratification took the form
of a protocol which became known as the Protocol of March
(1829). To the protocol the English Cabinet added an
Annex of its own whereby Lord Aberdeen specified that the
new state was to end at the Isthmus of Corinth. This was
the new departure from the Poros agreement that the Foreign
Secretary wanted Canning to follow, and it was more than
the Elchi could stomach. He considered it a glaring injustice
to the Greeks. It was also Canning's opinion that if Aberdeen
wanted, as he had professed he did, a trouble-free Greece and
a Greece that would not cause trouble, he should be willing
to grant her a defensible boundary with the Turks. To choke
her off at Corinth was to leave her hopelessly weak and subject to later attack. It was because of this difference of opinion
that Canning was superseded by Sir Robert Gordon.

Upon his arrival home from Naples, Canning found that there was an evident lack of liaison between the Duke and the Foreign Secretary, for, according to Wellington, the Annex was to be brought forward only if the Sultan refused the more northerly boundary. Furthermore, it had been Wellington's intention that the Annex be used as a device to force the Porte to accept either a semi-independent larger state (that is, up to the northerly line) or a completely independent smaller state.[1] Whatever Wellington intended, the opportunity to remedy the situation had passed, as Gordon was already engaged in pursuing Aberdeen's private policy in Constantinople.

It is not clear just what Aberdeen hoped to accomplish by this open and major break with his allies, but the whole enterprise came to nought when thus presented. Mahmud would countenance neither the Protocol nor the Annex, and Gordon was reduced to useless thumb-twiddling while the Czar worked with the tool the Turks understood best: an advancing army.

The whole substance of the Poros Convention and the March Protocol became practically academic in September when the Russians captured Adrianople. Constantinople was but a short march further, and the Sultan had no better defences there than he previously had at Adrianople. The populace became panicky and mourned the absence of the Janissaries. Mahmud and the Divan were frightened as much by the thought of revolt as by the threatening Russians. When, therefore, the Russian commander, General Diebitsch, halted and offered an armistice, the Porte hastily agreed.[2] The famous Treaty of Adrianople was signed on September 14, 1829. It included some territorial arrangements in Circassia and recognition of Russian right to hold the mouth of the Danube, plus further rights respecting the Christian populace in the Principalities of Moldavia and Wallachia, but its most important feature was the enforced acceptance by the Turks of the terms of the Treaty of London and the March Protocol. The independence of Greece was finally recognized by the Porte.

Many questions remained to be settled: the definitive demarcation of a boundary, the amount and method of indemnification, the selection of a monarch for the new state. The still primitive communications of the time allowed for an incredible lapse of time between the initialling of a diplomatic document and its practical implementation. This factor, combined with Turkish skill in vacillation, was still delaying a final settlement in Greece when the Wellington Cabinet fell in 1830.

When the Ministry of Lord Grey assumed office in 1831, Turco-Egyptian troops were still on Greek soil, although there was no more fighting. On the contrary, the former masters stood on the sidelines while the erstwhile Provisional Government fell apart and the cruelties of civil war superseded the horrors of subjugation. There was every chance that the Greeks would yet be their own worst enemy. President Capodistrias had been murdered and had been succeeded by a much less capable brother, Count Agostino Capodistrias, who seemed unable to bring even a semblance of unity to the country.

However, the new Foreign Secretary, Lord Palmerston, was a person not unlike Stratford Canning in his ability to perceive the right course of diplomatic action. Though they were often to differ substantially in the coming years, Palmerston and Canning understood each other and were to work well together. Without any hesitation Palmerston asked Canning if he would go to the East and help bring order out of the chaos. Canning could not respond with the same assurance, however, for he was doubtful that anything could be salvaged out of the miserable mess. He was in Parliament, moreover, and his misgivings were strengthened by the continued poor health of his wife. There was some embarrassment, too, in that Sir Robert Gordon still held the ambassadorship to the Porte and the Grey Cabinet seemed to be ignoring Gordon very pointedly. On that score Palmerston persuaded Canning that his special mission would in no way detract from Gordon's position or prestige inasmuch as the peace effort might better be handled by a plenipotentiary accredited to none of the conflicting parties. Because of his deep devotion to the goal of final peace and independence for Greece, Canning was finally persuaded to leave his wife. He accepted the assignment.

Prior to his leaving England his previous recommendations had been justified and his hand appreciably strengthened by a new agreement among the three powers, the Protocol of September, 1831. It overturned Aberdeen's restrictions and re-established the more northerly Arta-Volo line as the boundary. Further, a loan was arranged to enable Greece to indemnify the Sultan and the dispossessed Turkish landowners.

Once again Canning set out for the Levant. He was approaching his forty-fifth birthday, and nearly a quarter-century had gone by since he first set sail from Portsmouth with the Adair mission. He had suffered much in the way of privation and personal loss in the intervening years, and the knighthood which had been bestowed upon him was small consolation. His first wife was long buried, and with her was entombed the body of their stillborn son. The second Mrs. Canning continued in poor health as the result of another stillbirth amid the scenes of carnage that surrounded their first years in Constantinople. One brother had died at Waterloo and another, Henry, had passed away with the last year. George Canning was gone and his name was fast becoming a memory. The dreams of youth had evaporated.

His mood of depression did not lighten as his ship approached the shores of Greece. "It grieves me to the heart to say that I hear nothing good of the Greeks," he wrote to his wife from on board. "No fresh crimes . . . . But disunion, and party hatred, and political intrigue carried to the worst extremes. The Scripture expression—'to the Greeks foolishness'—is forever running through my head . . . ," and again, as if trying to determine his own role in all of this, "my only hope is that Providence may possibly choose to glorify itself by employing the weakest of its instruments in effecting the general good."[3]

Perhaps the bitter reflection that almost three years had been wasted by Aberdeen's misconception of reality caused the picture to appear darker than it actually was; for notwithstanding his sense of despair, Canning plunged into the shambles as though there were nothing so beyond repair that it could not be made to yield to the craftman's skill. Undoubtedly he was able to communicate his feelings of extreme danger to those with whom he came in contact, for he proved to be able to inspire a new surge of national unity in the quarreling National Assembly of the provisional government of Greece.[4] Although his success was not immediately apparent to him, the progress he made is attested by a letter from Palmerston which reached Constantinople some weeks afterward: "The Conference are delighted with what you did in the Morea," the Foreign Secretary wrote on the seventh of March, 1832, "and all agree how lucky it was that you should have dropped down there at the moment you did. You seem at all events to have re-established union . . . ."[5]

At the end of January he approached the Golden Horn of Constantinople for the third time in his life. This time he arrived in a steamship. Modernity was coming to Turkey at a snail's pace, but inevitably and inexorably. It is possible that it was at this moment that Canning began to feel a sympathy for the Turks. Perhaps he began to wonder then

what conditions would have to be established before this un-
happy empire could take its place in the community of nations.
At any rate, we find him beginning to allude to such feelings
at this time.[6] They were to be intensified by what he saw
in Turkey, for the country was developing in a way he had
not thought possible. Almost singlehandedly, the Sultan
Mahmud seemed to be making a heroic effort to lift his country from the morass of outworn tradition and to shake off the
torpor of centuries.

The first thing that struck Canning was the remarkable
change in court etiquette. At the audience of reception the
Elchi was received with dignity. Not only did the guards
present arms to him but the Sultan himself spoke warmly and
entered into real conversation with the whole staff of the
mission. It was evident that Mahmud wished the representative of the British court to consider the Sultan of Turkey as
being approachable. Sir Stratford was struck, too, by the relative freedom with which a foreigner could walk about the
streets of the ancient capital and wander through a slave market without being stopped and questioned.[7] (The existence of
the slave market indicates that only a subtle observer would
have perceived that Turkey was undergoing a complete reversal of its way of life, for though there were signs of change,
there was no revolution taking place.)

Canning's task was to obtain the Sultan's final acquiescence
to the surrender of sovereignty over the land and people of
Greece. He was aware that there was more at stake than mere

sentiment. That territory had been conquered in the name of the Prophet and at the cost of Moslem blood. Its surrender to the infidel meant sacrilege and cowardice of a degree to which no follower of Mohammed could be indifferent. He knew, too, that even by agreeing to negotiate the final transaction Mahmud might be exposing himself to a dire fate at the hands of fanatics. The Elchi could not expect the Sultan, therefore, to take the public lead in the amputation. A stratagem had to be found that would allow the Sultan to submit to the inevitable.

The opportunity to open discussions readily presented itself in the form of a new cloud on Mahmud's horizon. Mehemet Ali Pasha, enraged at the reversal of his fortunes in Greece, and blaming the weakness and cowardice of the Porte for all of it, had invaded Syria, and he now demanded that it be turned over to him. He had besieged and captured Acre and had sent word that Ibrahim would come to Constantinople with a powerful army to demand the heads of the Sultan's ministers. Mahmud was virtually helpless, but even so he could not proceed carelessly on the Greek matter, or appear indifferent to the sensibilities of the Moslem populace. There was no telling which of his ministers might seek the favor of Mehemet Ali by arousing the people of the capital against the Sultan.

Canning's stratagem was simple: " . . . to awaken the Sultan's hopes of eventual assistance from England [against Mehemet], without committing my Government or compromising my own character."[8] But he could not go through the

regular ministerial channels. He had to have an instrument
of direct and secret approach to Mahmud himself. That instrument was found in the person of a professional under-
cover agent, a Phanariot Greek[9] by the name of Stefanaki
Vogorides, whom Canning knew to have uncanny access to
the Seraglio. Secrecy was of the utmost importance for all
concerned, and the dignified Elchi now began to engage in
cloak-and-dagger operations of the best fictional type. A
nocturnal meeting between himself and Vogorides was arranged:

> His house, at some considerable distance up the Golden
> Horn, was to be the scene of our interview. I promised to
> go at night, and he undertook to send his own boat for
> my conveyance. The night appointed for my visit chanced
> to be most boisterous. A strong north gale with driving
> rain blew down the harbour. I had to walk no small distance
> to the water, and then to embark alone on its troubled
> waves. On board I crouched in utter darkness under my
> umbrella, and shivered to the blasts that rushed over it. The
> return was so far better that the wind no longer beat against
> our teeth.
> My conversation with the agent in question led to a
> satisfactory understanding between us. He engaged to work
> in my favour with the Sultan; I displayed a readiness to
> consult his Majesty's wishes to the full length of my tether.
> A confidential intercourse under his auspices would be
> maintained simultaneously with the official negotiation.[10]

In the nest of intrigue that was Constantinople it would have
been impossible to conceal a succession of such meetings, and
after that Canning employed the embassy physician, Dr. Mac-

Guffog, as the go-between with Vogorides, thus bypassing even the embassy dragoman. The secrecy was not melodramatic, however, and was utilized to relieve Vogorides' fear as much as for anything else.

Once the contact was effected the Elchi lost no opportunity in impressing upon the Sultan the ultimate good that would come to his realm by co-operation with the European powers, not only in Greece, but over the whole range of international intercourse. In many of his messages there are indications of the reformer-to-be:

> I want to see her [the Porte] in a situation to receive the full tide of European civilization, to enlist the whole force of the country in support of its independence, to take her proper place in the general councils of Europe, and to base her military and financial systems on the only true foundations of security for persons and property. Beg of him [Vogorides] to reverse this picture and to imagine the Sultan wasting the remains of his strength in civil war with Egypt, alienating himself from his natural and most tried friends by rejecting their proposals, making himself unpopular at home by half-measures of innovation, without carrying them far enough to acquire confidence and sympathy abroad, and left to struggle as he best may . . . . I say that it would be better for him to revive the Janissaries, to resume the turbans and pelisses of ancient times, and to demand the restoration of Greece. The choice lies between *fanaticism* and *discipline*; there is no middle line.[11]

The Sultan could procrastinate as well as his ministers, and the contest was long and tiresome. But Canning was persistent and Mehemet Ali was as threatening as ever. The pressure of Mehemet and the thought of British help eventually broke the back of Mahmud's resistance, and the agreement on Greece was ready for signature.

While these secret negotiations between the Sultan and himself were in progress, Canning, in company with the French and Russian envoys, was forced to carry on wearisome discussions with the Divan. The agreement of the Sultan's ministers to all territorial particulars as well as to the details of financial indemnification had to be won before Mahmud could publicly assent to a settlement. Verbally the Turks would agree to this detail and that, but again and again they refused to sign written agreements. At one stage of the dealings the Grand Vezir absented himself on official business in the provinces for weeks on end. Not to be outdone Canning sent a subaltern to his camp in Albania to get the needed assent.

Perseverance finally wore down procrastination. At one of the final meetings Canning arranged through Vogorides for a messenger to arrive from the Sultan (he referred to the incident as a *"coup de théâtre"*) expressing his Majesty's desire that the conferees agree to the Arta-Volo line as the most satisfactory to all. At long last the agreement was handed to the clerks to be put into final form, and the twenty-first of July was appointed as the day for formal signing.

The plenipotentiaries met in an imperial kiosk some miles up the Bosporus. They started what should have been perfunctory proceedings at ten o'clock in the morning, only to have their Turkish member begin all over again with the usual delaying tactics. Canning held them all to their tasks and at length accused the Ottoman dignitary, Suleiman Nejib Effendi, of attempting to thwart the will of the Sultan. The Turk remonstrated and declared he would sooner cut off his right hand than sign the document. Whereupon Canning retorted that he would then have to sign with his other hand as they had met for that purpose alone and not for new debate. When the Elchi insisted that they would remain around the clock until they were finished, Suleiman realized the end had come. At three o'clock the following morning Suleiman signed the hated document in the name of the Sultan.[12] The ten-year Greek War was over! It was a war that could have destroyed Mahmud and his realm and embroiled all of Europe. Sir Stratford Canning had played a significant role in it and could be proud of his service. He had seen leaders die—George Canning and Czar Alexander and Capodistrias, among others. He had seen nations change and reverse policies of long standing. The echoes were not soon to die, but the struggle was over.

That his patience had worn thin in the end is best shown by the tone of the message he sent Palmerston later that same day: "You can hardly refuse to join with me in swearing at the Turks. No man in Christendom can have an idea of what we have gone through. I defy even a Dutch negotiation to be worse. . . . if you are satisfied I shall soon forget my vexation . . . . to make up matters with the Turks, we have just been dining with one of the plenipotentiaries, who, in spite of his beard and his Koran, drinks champagne like a Christian."[13]

By way of postscript to the story of Greece, Prince Otho of the royal house of Bavaria landed in Greece in January of 1833 as the first king of independent Greece. He was the choice of the powers when other desirable candidates were eliminated or eliminated themselves for one reason or another.[14]

Sir Stratford Canning received plaudits from the King, from the Sultan, from Palmerston, and even from the aged Talleyrand. But the best of all his rewards was the infant son he found in Lady Canning's arms when he arrived home in September.

1. Cf. Crawley, *op. cit.*, p. 153.

2. *Ibid.*, p. 162. Actually, Diebitsch's army was in a precarious position. It was greatly reduced by illness and there was a Turkish army advancing on it from the rear. But this weakness was not realized in Constantinople, and Mahmud feared to order his remaining troops to advance to what must have seemed certain defeat.

A further explanation of Diebitsch's sudden halt lies in a policy change adopted by Nicholas I. Realizing that his vaunted military power was not what it was represented to be, the Czar had lately changed Russian policy vis-à-vis the Porte. His advisers pointed out that Russia would not be able to hold the Straits against the rest of Europe. Better, then, to have a weak Turkey as a neighbor to be saved for future action than to expose Russia in an awkward, indefensible position. (Cf. Temperley, *op. cit.*, p. 57.)

3. Lane-Poole, *op. cit.*, I, 496.

4. Cf. Crawley, *op. cit.*, p. 199.

5. Lane-Poole, *op. cit.*, I, 498.

6. Cf. The "Memorandum on the Turco-Egyptian Question" of Stratford Canning to Palmerston, Paris, December 19, 1832, and discussed in chap. XII below. The memorandum is reprinted in full, as Appendix V, in Crawley *op. cit.*, pp. 237-45.

7. See the letter to Lady Canning, February 24, 1832, Lane-Poole, *op. cit.*, I, 503.

8. Lane-Poole, *op. cit.*, I, 507.

9. That is, a Greek of the Phanar section of Constantinople where the headquarters of the Greek Patriarch was located. Generally these were members of old families in the city and were in high esteem at the Porte. They were not nationalist in the sense of the revolutionaries, and, indeed, there was often great animosity between the Phanariots as a group and the leaders of the sevolt.

10. Lane-Poole, *op. cit.*, I, 506-7.

11. *Ibid.*, 508.

12. See *Ibid.*, pp. 501-11, for the account.

13. *Ibid.*, p. 511.

14. Cf. Crawley, *op. cit.*, pp. 205-8.

XI

PASSING reference has already been made to the fact that Stratford Canning had been elected to Parliament in 1828 while he was still at Poros and the official Ambassador to the Sublime Porte. The term "election" is used loosely, for his first constituency, Old Sarum, had a grand total of eleven voters, all of them tenants of the Alexander family. Upon request, they had dutifully sent their landlord's son-in-law to sit in the House of Commons. Reflecting on this event in later life, Canning revealed his feelings about the effects of his career in Parliament: "They voted in obedience to their landlord. Not one of them did I ever see. Their votes, however, served to gratify a long-cherished wish of my heart. But did they enable me to attain the object of that wish? No: I cannot say that they did."[1]

When he made that assessment in the winter of his life, he was testifying to the fact that from his very first days in

Commons he was out of his element. One can only wonder why he did not recognize it at the time. Several opportunities for him to take his leave gracefully soon arose, but he persevered for the better part of a decade. His failure to withdraw from Parliament most probably arose from a natural reluctance to admit, even to himself, that his most cherished ambition had been illusory. How else can one explain the paradox of a man returning again and again to an arena in which he feared even to walk to his seat and trembled when he felt called upon to speak? From afar, of course, we can readily measure the disparity between the image of his dreams and the reality he encountered in Commons, however we might puzzle over his inability or refusal to see it. For long years Canning had been involved in matters of world-wide significance; the destiny of men and nations was something he had lived with day in and day out. Suddenly he was face to face with the petty haggling of everyday politics. He was unable to feign a passionate interest in ephemeral issues, and, when weightier questions were before the House, he shrank from the snap judgments required in the give-and-take of floor debate. He had become habituated to a careful analysis of any problem to come before him and refused to adopt positions merely at the behest of party leadership. These were qualities that quickly marked him as unsuited for advancement to ministerial rank where, above all, party loyalty was considered an indispensable prerequisite. He was immediately identified as an independent and remained so throughout his Parliamentary career.

This does not mean that he was indifferent to the domestic issues of the day. Quite the contrary, for when he ceased to represent Old Sarum on the accession of William IV in 1830 (a member of the Alexander family decided to take the seat), so intense was his interest in the Reform Bill that he paid one thousand pounds, in April of 1831, for the right to sit for Stockbridge. He had canvassed earnestly about for a constituency in which he might stand in a real election but had found none. Stockbridge was his for the taking simply because it was high on the list of boroughs to be dissolved under the Reform Bill introduced in Commons in March, 1831, and in consideration of this impending doom, the price, as he ruefully noted, was "somewhat high." The per diem expense of this seat was greatly increased, moreover, when Palmerston sent him to Constantinople a few months later. While he was absent on that mission, the Reform Bill was passed, and Stockbridge was abolished as a constituency of Parliament.

This might we have meant the last of domestic politics for him but for a strange combination of circumstances. Upon his return from Constantinople in the fall of 1832, he was without a post of any kind. The Embassy at St. Petersburg was vacant at the time, and he was named by Palmerston as the British Ambassador to the Court of Czar Nicholas I. But Canning's appointment to the Embassy was rejected by the Russian court, an action almost unheard of in diplomacy save for instances in which relations between governments were already strained.

There are several theories which have been advanced in explanation of the Czar's rejection.[2] Most historians agree that the Czar and Count Nesselrode did not consider Canning pliable enough for them to work with, but whether that was because of their prior experience or because of plans they had concerning the future of the Turkish Empire is an open question. It became the conviction of Canning and his friends that the latter was the case.[3] However, it is a mystery why Palmerston made the appointment a matter of public record in the official *Gazette* without first having ascertained its suitability to the Russian court. This has led some observers to conclude that the Foreign Secretary was acting in a predetermined manner to effect the recall of the Russian Ambassador, Prince Lieven, whose wife had made herself particularly obnoxious to Palmerston. The supporters of this theory hold that Palmerston was well aware of Canning's *non grata* status in St. Petersburg and gazetted him precisely because he knew of the coming rejection. He could, therefore, refuse to send an ambassador at all and leave it to protocol to force the Czar to withdraw his.

At any rate, the immediate result was, of course, that Canning did not go to Russia, although he remained for some time the officially designated "Ambassador to the Emperor of all the Russias" and was sent, so titled, on a special mission to Madrid that lasted from December of 1832 through April of 1833. The purpose of the mission was to offer the friendly mediation of England in the dispute over the succession to the throne of Portugal. Dom Pedro, the Emperor of Brazil and eldest son of the late King John VI of Portugal, had relinquished his claim to the throne of Portugal in favor of his seven-year-old daughter. The Regent, Pedro's brother Dom Miguel, had seized the crown for himself in 1827, but at this time Dom Pedro, having been turned out of Brazil, was leading his partisans in a civil war against his brother. A similar situation was building up in Spain where the long recognized heir to the throne, Don Carlos, had suddenly and unexpectedly been supplanted by a daughter who issued from the king's (Ferdinand VII) fourth marriage. The peace of the whole Peninsula was threatened, and Palmerston was anxious to remedy the situation. The Grey Cabinet wished to enlist the aid of the Spanish court in favor of Dom Pedro and his daughter, but the Spanish king and his ministry politely and firmly refused. Inasmuch as the bulk of European absolutists favored Dom Miguel, the English overture came to nought and the mission was withdrawn at the end of April.

Shortly before the conclusion of the Spanish mission, Palmerston offered Canning the permanent post at Madrid. It was an admission that he would not be able to force the Russian appointment through. But Canning declined it, first of all because he would have to displace his former secretary, Addington, the current envoy, and secondly because he found nothing attractive about Spain other than the marvelous collection of art in the royal museums. In July he graciously allowed Palmerston to withdraw his nomination to St. Petersburg, and this chapter was closed. Palmerston, in great embarrassment apparently, tried to secure a peerage for him, but even here circumstances militated against the unfortunate diplomat. Lord Grey had to reject Palmerston's request simply because the claims and pressures for peerages were so heavy at the time. A widespread unemployment of deserving politicians had resulted from the Reform Bills![4]

The Grey Cabinet toppled in 1834 and was followed by the first Peel Government. Peel offered the Governor-Generalship of Canada to Canning, but as the latter had again entered Parliament, he declined the honor (which was subsequently given to Lord Amherst).

Canning had re-entered the lists in the course of the party realignments which saw the appearance of the Stanleyites and Peelites prior to the emergence of the new Conservative party. He was elected as one of the two members for King's Lynn in Norfolk with the understanding that he would support Stanley (the future Earl of Derby) in divisions of the House, with the further understanding that Stanley, in turn, would give Peel a chance to prove himself and his newly emerging party group. As things turned out Canning found that he was usually closer to Peel on most issues than was Stanley. Once more his inability to be a party man caused him to lose favor with all. He was personally satisfied, however, when his constituents returned him to office in two successive elections, those of 1837 and 1841. He felt that the endorsements were a tribute to his fidelity in attending sessions regularly if to nothing else.

It would be tempting to engage in a lengthy discussion of the intracacies of party politics in this transition period, but it is outside the scope of this study since Canning did not make a material contribution to any of the developments. In 1839, when the days of the Melbourne administration seemed to be numbered, Canning had a discussion with Sir Robert Peel, the obvious successor, relative to his future employment. Peel told him quite frankly that there would be no place in a Cabinet of the future government for him and urged him to return to the field of diplomacy. He promised a suitable appointment, and Stratford Canning prepared himself for re-entry into the Foreign Service.

1. Lane-Poole, *op. cit.*, II, 2.
2. See E. F. Malcolm-Smith, *The Life of Stratford Canning* (London: Ernest Benn, Ltd., 1933), pp. 147-53.
3. See letter from Planta, July 23, 1833, Lane-Poole, *op. cit.*, II, 21-22.
4. See letter from Grey to Palmerston, August 31, 1833, *ibid.*, pp. 22-23.

XII

THE dependence of the young queen, Victoria, on Lord Melbourne enabled his administration to hang on into 1841. Melbourne, however, was loath to face the mounting domestic quarrels centering about the Corn Laws, which imposed a high tariff on wheat imports in order to protect the price of the domestic product. He finally induced the Queen to accept his resignation and a general election followed. The resulting Parliament clearly showed Sir Robert Peel as the obvious leader and the second Peel Cabinet was formed in September. Within a fortnight Sir Stratford Canning had once more been designated Ambassador to the Sublime Porte and had accepted the post.

Canning's decision to go back to Constantinople was carefully considered. He had the option of other assignments, for, prior to his choice of Constantinople, Peel had again offered him the chance to go to Canada as Governor-General.

When he declined that honor, he could have become Treas-
urer of the Queen's Household, but neither was the thought
of being a courtier particularly appealing, so he refused that
honor as well. When the new Foreign Secretary, Lord Aberdeen, proposed that he return to Constantinople, Canning
assented with unexpected enthusiasm. On the eve of his
fifty-fifth birthday, Sir Stratford Canning had finally found
himself, and he set out with a determination to effect a
foreseeable good: the revivification of the Ottoman Empire
as an integral unit in the community of nations. That end
he saw now as being not only desirable for the internal
welfare of the Empire, but as a necessary condition of world
peace. Further, he saw now the possibility of its realization,
for his ten-year withdrawal to the periphery of diplomacy had
given him time to think calmly about the necessary means to
that end. Broadly stated, he had concluded that there were
two overriding objectives: first, a general reform of the
internal structure of the Ottoman Empire to assure it a
contented and loyal citizenry; second, a freedom from foreign
pressures that would allow concentration on the first objective. These were germinal concepts dating from his previous
tenure. Much had happened in the intervening decade to
corroborate them. A review of those events will reveal why
Canning believed the stage was now set for the final drama.
    When Canning had returned home in 1832 from the
relative triumph of the Greek negotiations, he had come, it
will be remembered, under the obligation of serious personal

commitments to the Sultan Mahmud to do all in his power to secure British help in resisting the ominous advances of Mehemet Ali in Syria. His immediate recommendations, in line with these commitments, were ignored by the Grey government, however, as Palmerston, the Foreign Secretary, had chosen to adopt a "wait-and-see" attitude. Even a personal plea from Mahmud was in vain because Palmerston could see little difference in whether the House of Osman or the House of Mehemet Ali held sway over the Bosporus.[1]

Shortly after this initial rebuff Canning had been sent to Madrid. Lord Grey, in the meantime, had asked Sir Stratford to give the government the benefit of his considered views on Eastern affairs. In compliance with this request Canning put his thoughts on paper and sent them to Palmerston from Paris in December of 1832.[2] This memorandum was a penetrating analysis of the alternatives facing Britain and the Porte.

Canning's thesis was that to leave Mahmud to his fate at the hands of Mehemet Ali was to endanger Britain's whole position in the East. The result would be a weakened Turkish Empire, and Russia would be the beneficiary. By way of an alternative Canning recommended a moderate intervention by which Mehemet Ali and his heirs would become hereditary rulers of Egypt under Ottoman sovereignty. Mehemet's son, and general-in-chief, Ibrahim Pasha, would also remain the lifetime ruler of Syria. Such friendly intervention by England would not only save Mahmud but would give England the opportunity to assist him in his reforms. Inevitably, England would benefit from such co-operation.

To this plea, also, Palmerston turned a deaf ear. He questioned Sir Stratford's arguments[3] and remained convinced that the outcome of the struggle was a matter of indifference to England's place in the East. Palmerston's position was very quickly shown to be an error which resulted in near disaster.

At Konya the Egyptians smashed a Turkish army and captured the Sultan's Grand Vezir; Ibrahim Pasha marched unopposed into Anatolia. Rebuffed by England, and hostile to France because of her actions in North Africa,[4] with Ibrahim advancing rapidly, Mahmud was soon forced to take his one remaining avenue of escape: the intervention of Russian arms. Mahmud, understandably, sought the aid of Nicholas I, and the Czar was perfectly amenable to the idea of giving it inasmuch as Mehemet Ali seemed far too aggressive a potential successor to Ottoman rule, totally out of line with Nicholas' Turkish policy.[5] "The end of February [1833] witnessed a remarkable event in history, for Russian troops arrived on the Bosphorus and camped on the shores of Asia in order to defend the Sultan against his Egyptian rebel."[6] Palmerston and the French reacted as quickly as possible, but the Foreign Secretary's "delay had been fatal."[7] Russia had the situation well in hand. Mahmud was saved from Mehemet Ali and the Egyptian viceroy was forced to recall Ibrahim to Syria, where he was allowed to stay on payment of an annual tribute to the Sultan. In return, Turkey agreed, in June, to the terms of the Treaty of Hunkiar Skelessi.[8]

The Treaty of Hunkiar Skelessi was a treaty of defensive alliance binding Russia and Turkey to come to each other's aid if the need should arise, and confirming all previous agreements between the two empires. More importantly, it contained a separate article by which the Czar could dispense the Sultan of the obligation of assistance and, as a substitute, demand that the Porte "confine its action in favour of the Imperial Court of Russia to closing the strait of the Dardanelles, that is to say, to not allowing any foreign vessels of war to enter therein under any pretext whatsoever."

Palmerston protested the treaty as a key with which Russia might continually open the door to interfere in Turkish affairs, and he showed his contempt for the article on the Straits by sending a naval squadron to demonstrate at the mouth of the Dardanelles. The result of his error, however, was patent, and the Treaty of Hunkiar Skelessi "bred in Palmerston a fatal hostility to Russia, and converted even Whigs to the Tory policy of bolstering up Turkey."[9]

Palmerston's introduction to Eastern diplomacy had been educational, even if somewhat jolting.[10] From then on he took a keen interest in Turkish affairs, if only in order to find a way to thwart Russia.[11] When, therefore, Mehemet Ali renewed the conflict in 1839 Palmerston did not stand idly by as he had in 1832 and early 1833.[12] His readiness to act was fortunate, for Mehemet's early victories were as devastating in their effect as they were startling in their rapidity. Mahmud, thinking to strike first, had ordered his army to invade northern Syria, but it was met and destroyed by Ibrahim at Nezib. Within the same week, the Turkish fleet, ordered to attack the Egyptians at Alexandria, was surrendered intact to Mehemet. Worst of all, Mahmud II died on June 30, ill and broken in spirit. He left behind him, as Sultan, his sixteen-year-old son, Abdul Medjid.

As news of the successive disasters flowed into London, Palmerston leaped into action. Even before that he had notified the Austrian government of Britain's intent to maintain the Porte by forceful suppression of Mehemet Ali if need be.[13] Now the pace quickened as he feared unilateral action by Russia under the terms of the Treaty of Hunkiar Skelessi, and by the French in behalf of Mehemet Ali. He immediately proposed concerted European action to preserve the integrity of the Ottoman Empire. Diplomatic channels hummed with activity, and the rapidity with which the British Foreign Office moved forestalled any attempt by either France or Russia to play its own game. In December Palmerston even prevailed upon Russia to renounce its preferential position in the Straits (a position Russia had repeatedly denied) in favor of an agreement for concerted European action, thus voiding one of the major articles of Hunkiar Skelessi. By the following July, England, Russia, Austria, and Prussia had hammered out an agreement known as the Treaty of London.[14] Relative to the Turco-Egyptian conflict, it assured Mehemet Ali lifetime rule in Egypt if he agreed to cease hostilities in twenty days, and, as an added inducement, he was guaranteed lifetime rule in southern Syria if he should accept these terms in ten days. His alternative was to face a combined attack by the European powers.

Mehemet refused to budge, and an Anglo-Austrian fleet bombarded Acre, landed troops in Syria, and eventually smothered the Egyptians. Mehemet Ali was forced to yield to British terms and was retired to Egypt for the remainder of his life. He became senile in 1847 and died two years later. Ibrahim ruled Egypt for one year after the incompetency of his father but preceded him in death. Their descendants ruled Egypt for more than a century after them, outlasting the House of Osman by some thirty years.

It was a tragedy for the Moslem world that Mahmud, the Sultan, and Mehemet, the modernizer, had not been able to work together. Despite their political differences they had much in common, and their talents were such as should have produced complementary effects. They might well have achieved the reform of Moslem society neither could effect by himself.

It was ironic that the final settlement achieved by force of European arms bore such striking resemblance to the solution proposed by Sir Stratford Canning in 1832.

Following the settlement of the crisis, France added her signature to the Treaty of London of 1840, and on the thirteenth of July, 1841, the five European powers and the Porte initialled a new Straits Convention which restated the ancient rule of the Straits, "in virtue of which it has at all times been prohibited for the Ships of War of Foreign Powers to enter the Straits of the Dardanelles and of the Bosphorus; and that, so long as the Porte is at peace, His Highness will admit no foreign Ship of War into the said Straits."[15] Article Two of the Convention excepted light vessels employed in the service of the several diplomatic missions in Constantinople.

By the autumn of 1841, then, when Sir Stratford Canning reappeared on the scene, a relative quiet had settled over the Levant, and the Ottoman Empire was at peace with all of its neighbors. This was the freedom from external pressure that he saw as the indispensible prerequisite for the prosecution of an internal reform.

As early as his first residence in Constantinople, Stratford Canning had sensed the real weakness of the Turkish Empire.[16] It was not foreign pressure nearly so much as it was internal malaise. By 1832 he had come to more definitive conclusions respecting the nature and cause of the illness: "I think the time is near," he had written to Palmerston, " . . . when it is necessary that a decided line of policy should be adopted and steadily pursued with respect to this country. The Turkish Empire is evidently hastening to its dissolution, and an approach to the civilization of Christendom affords the only chance of keeping it together . . . . "[17]

In this letter he had discussed the financial and military maladministration of the Empire, but only as they reflected a more basic disease: the injustice inherent in the whole fabric of its life. The root of this injustice was a religious intolerance based on strict interpretations of Koranic law.[18] According to these strict interpretations, the infidel, the non-Moslem (*rayah*), had no legal standing in relation to his Moslem fellow subjects. Hence, millions of the Sultan's subjects could not look to the monarch for protection and security, nor could they, as a further consequence, generate any sense of loyalty to the Sultan or patriotism for their country. Indeed, it was the helplessness of these people which often generated pressure from the outside, for it was their pleas that brought Russia, England, Austria, or France, as the case might be, to the Porte demanding correction of one thing or another, but always in seeking justice for non-protected subjects of the Sultan.

The cure, it should be carefully noted, lay in "an approach to the civilization of Christendom." Stratford Canning was not dreaming of a holy war, of an imposition of Christianity on the Moslem. What was needed was an adaptation to the Western concept that rights were inherent in the person and did not depend on a man's beliefs. Canning was under no illusion that the task was an easy one. On the contrary, in the same letter, he refers to the chance of securing such an accommodation as "a very precarious one at best," but nonetheless necessary.

The Ambassador's hopes were considerably brighter on this score when he resumed his old post, for there had been a welcome series of internal developments, too, which bolstered the prospects afforded by the general peace. Mahmud II, from the time he obliterated the Janissaries, had tried valiantly to maintain a course directed toward modernity. While cir-

cumstances had forced him to concentrate on the military
aspect of this reform to the detriment of social improvement,
he had not been unmindful of the need for the latter. Shortly
before his death Mahmud had again turned his attention to
the concept of general reform—Tanzimat. With the aid
of his principal adviser, the reform-minded Reshid Pasha,
he had prepared a decree of reform that was sweeping in its
innovations. Reshid Pasha remained at the side of the young
Abdul Medjid and prevailed upon him to issue the decree,
the famous Hatti-Sherif of Gulhane (November 3, 1839).
This *hatti-sherif* ("noble rescript"), or *hatti-humayun* ("imperial rescript"), as some historians prefer,[19] decreed security
of life and property for all subjects regardless of creed, abolished the odious practice of execution without public trial and
judicial sentence, and assured to the condemned the right to
bequeath his property, thus barring its seizure by the con-
demning magistrate and thereby removing one of the major
motives for "legal" murder. The decree also fixed a system
of tax quotas and regulated the terms of military service.
These were all revolutionary concepts.

There had been one serious setback of late, and, once again,
it was casued by external events. The near disaster of Mehemet Ali's final threat had set off violent recriminations
within the Divan and the Seraglio. Reactionary elements
blamed the reform movement for the collapse of Ottoman
defenses, and their invectives had proven too fierce for the
terrified boy who now occupied the throne. They had forced
Abdul Medjid to dismiss the liberal ministers of his father,

and by 1841 reaction seemed to be firmly in the saddle. So, although the Gulhane (Rose Chamber) Decree had been duly promulgated, the outlook for reform was not completely roseate.

But Canning viewed this development as merely a temporary deviation from the path the Turks themselves knew they had to travel. He was full of confidence when he presented his credentials to Abdul Medjid early in 1842, and he was able to testify that his heart went out to the young Sultan; "the graciousness of his manner," he wrote to Lord Aberdeen, "and the intelligent, though gentle and even melancholy, expression of his countenance, warrant a hope, perhaps a sanguine one, that with riper years and a more experienced judgment he may prove a real blessing and source of strength to his country."[20]

For the time being the Elchi decided to leave Abdul Medjid to the normal processes of maturing that would come with time and circumstances. In the meantime he had to gauge the temper of the men who were actually running the Empire and those who might conceivably replace them in the course of the year ahead. Reshid Pasha, the only possible rallying point for the discredited innovators, had been packed off to the Turkish Embassy in Paris, safely removed from the Sultan's ear. Sir Stratford and Reshid had first met in the early 1830's when Reshid had been a member of the Turkish Boundary Commission in the Greek negotiations. One of the few Turks willing to face the stark realities of that era, Reshid knew that the Englishman, Canning, had actually obtained the best possible terms for Turkey. Most Turkish statemen considered Canning, still under the cloud of Navarino, to be under the Russian thumb, but Reshid told Mahmud quite frankly that had it not been for Canning the Turks might have come out far worse. His honesty, in a day when few dared to be honest, had appealed to the embattled Mahmud, and Reshid became a trusted lieutenant. Additional experience in London and Paris afforded Reshid Pasha added opportunities to assess the value of Western political systems, and the facility with which he imparted his evaluations to Mahmud had helped him to emerge as the latter's chief adviser. Together they charted the reforms which Canning had now made his own, and it was Reshid who had authored the salient points of the Gulhane Decree. Reshid had now been shunted aside, but Canning knew that he would have to come back.

The ministry surrounding the Sultan in 1842 was composed, for the most part, of old men who dreamed of a return to the days before Mahmud's meddling had so rudely interfered with their traditions. Their reaction had reached such an extreme that they had even excluded from public service any Turk who could speak the Christian languages. Fanaticism was in full swing. Christians were again being abused in the courts and in the course of their daily pursuits; local pashas were again indulging in instances of legal murder; the Divan was again turning a deaf ear to all reports of injustice and illegality.

In face of this situation the British Ambassador had to exercise the utmost self-restraint. He was well aware that he was not regarded as a welcome friend by this element of Ottoman leadership. "It would be a great mistake," Canning wrote to Aberdeen on March 27, 1842, "to suppose that the Porte is the best judge of her own interests. . . . Her ministers . . . have neither the capacity nor the knowledge to grapple with the difficulty of the times. They have not even the sagacity to recognize their real friends."[21] His first task would be to cultivate the friendship of the Sultan. His second would be to effect a change in the tenor of the ministry.

The man at the top of the Divan was the Grand Vezir, Mohammed Izzet Pasha, a gallant old soldier but a Moslem fanatic. Sarim Effendi, just as reactionary but a shrewder man, was Minister for Foreign Affairs. Most dangerous, in Canning's estimate, was the High Chamberlain, Riza Pasha—dangerous because he was unprincipled. He had been a confidant of Mahmud but had quickly thrown in his lot with the reactionaries. Gossip reported by the dragomans indicated that, in collusion with the Finance Minister, Safti Pasha, Riza was steadily enriching himself at public expense. If Canning were to accomplish anything it was clear that these four ministers would have to go.

Canning waited until June before he brought up the subject of reform. He mentioned it to the Sultan at a private audience where Riza was present in his capacity as High Chamberlain. Abdul Medjid responded freely, and declared that he had ordered the implementation of those humane laws promulgated at Gulhane; that reform was dear to him. The difficulty, unfortunately, was finding even ten pashas to co-operate with him; he would be sure of success with even that little help. Something about his bearing convinced Canning that the Sultan spoke sincerely. The Ambassador became convinced that Abdul Medjid would sanction and promote reforms with the proper urging and assistance. This audience was the beginning of a close relationship between them.

Beyond that one incident Canning studiously avoided giving offense to reaction. There were many items that had piled up in the Embassy archives to concern him—the backwash of years of war and turmoil. There were many cases of indemnity due British subjects whose property had been damaged during the conflict in Syria. Matters involving trading rights and commercial agreements throughout the far-flung Empire had magnified a thousand times, far beyond the capabilities of the limited Embassy staff. He had to plead with the Foreign Office to empower the consular establishments to assume the responsibility in such cases. He had to delineate duties and responsibilities within the Embassy, where he had found laxity and shoddiness of method. The British Embassy in Constantinople was to be a working embassy, and the Ambassador saw to it that it was.

Within a year he saw the rewards of his patience. Mohammed Izzet Pasha retired as Grand Vezir to be succeeded by Rauf Pasha, who was much milder in outlook and correspondingly more tractable. Sarim Effendi was replaced by a new Foreign Minister, Rifat Pasha, a typical Turkish functionary but a man whom Sir Stratford felt to be sincerely interested in what was best for Turkey—one who could be prevailed upon in the long run. Best of all, Reshid Pasha was recalled from Paris and installed as governor of Adrianople—not an honor, to be sure, but desirably near at hand from Canning's point of view. Riza Pasha, on the other hand, became the Seraskier (commander-in-chief of the army), so the current was flowing in both directions.

Slowly the stage was being set in accordance with Canning's plans when an unlooked-for occurrence pushed him precipitately into the director's box. One summer day in 1843, a group of Armenians threw themselves in front of his carriage as it was proceeding from the palace at Pera to the vicinity of Buyukdere. Their plea was simple—that the Buyuk Elchi intervene at the Porte in behalf of one of their loved ones who had been condemned to death. His crime was that of apostasy from Islam; the young man had originally forsaken the Christian heritage of his forefathers to become a Moslem, then repented his act and returned to Christianity. Under Koranic law, the punishment was death by beheading.

The family of the doomed man knew of the Elchi's many exertions in behalf of abused Christians, and they turned to him in desperation. It brought Canning face to face with the inflexibility of tradition. Intervention in behalf of a Christian was one thing; a reversal of the criminal law of Islam quite another. Yet it was the issue that he knew must eventually be faced, for it was not an isolated case. It had happened before and could be repeated indefinitely. He decided the time had come for a test of strength, and he thereupon made appropriate overtures at the Seraglio asking that the Armenian's life be spared. Needless to say, the advances were brusquely thrust aside, and, as if to emphasize the absolute character of the law, a public execution followed. The decapitated body was left exposed for three days in a busy spot of the city and then thrown into the waters of the Bosporus.

Canning's entire staff must have shaken their heads in despair as he girded for battle—Alison, the Oriental secretary, who knew well the traditions and laws of the country; Pisani, the dragoman, on whom would fall the dubious privilege of carrying the protest to the Porte—all of them anticipated the tension of the coming days and weeks and months. Sir Stratford Canning had fixed his eye on a goal, and those who knew him realized there would be no turning back. This time, however, what he wanted appeared to be an absolute reversal of Islamic law, a virtual recantation of doctrine. Even the most hopeful of his associates could not see how he would accomplish it.

The Ambassador's first move was to send a report of the incident to London. He also saw to it that his European colleagues sent similar reports. From the Earl of Aberdeen came instructions to require of the Porte that no further

executions of such nature take place. Baron Bourqueney, the
French Ambassador at the Porte, was ordered by Paris to act
in concert with Canning. Characteristically, there were no
clear orders on what to do upon rejection of any protest, but
they were at least authorized to begin proceedings. Canning
was prepared to counter the certain refusal of what he considered to be the necessary guarantee of correction. The
Turks, he knew, would be quite ready to promise an accommodation to the expressed wishes of the powers, but he was
not interested in a mere *modus vivendi* between opposing
principles of justice. He had seen too many arrangements
wither and die through apathy. He wanted a final and ir-
revocable rejection in principle of the religious law, a legal
foundation for personal religious freedom which, inevitably,
would have a bearing upon wider areas of civil freedom.
If, at the time, this seemed impossible of fulfilment, he could
point back to the history of the Western powers themselves.
They were but a few centuries removed from the days of the
religious wars when devout and sincere men on both sides felt
they were carrying out the will of God if they took the life of a
heretic or non-believer. The growth of religious toleration
had brought in its wake the adoption of legal principles en-
suring civil freedoms. Such freedom had seemed just as
impossible in the West of the sixteenth and seventeenth
centuries as it did in the Moslem world of the nineteenth.

The reaction Canning foresaw came as predicted. When
the joint notes of protest were duly presented at the Porte,

the members of the Divan, one and all, were full of expressions of sorrow and remorse over the execution. Rauf Pasha, the Grand Vezir, affirmed that, personally, he did not have it in his heart to kill even a fowl, but the law of the Koran was inflexible and immutable; it was not within the power of the Caliph himself to gainsay it. Rifat Pasha pointed out that for the Divan to take even an official note of the protest would be to stir the most violent reaction among members of the ulema and among the traditionalists. The Reis Effendi, however, had a plan which, he said, had the Grand Mufti's approval: the Porte would issue instructions that the magistrates turn a deaf ear to reports of apostasies in the future. This was the only way, he asserted, that the Porte could contrive to effect a cessation of the admittedly barbarous practice.

Even as Rifat was urging this arrangement on the foreign envoys, a report of another religious execution, at Brusa, reached the capital. This time five powers protested: Austria, Russia, Prussia, France, and England. Rifat stuck to his position and reaffirmed his previous offer: if the powers would indicate satisfaction with a "gentlemen's agreement" of the kind suggested, the Porte would guarantee the incidents would not be repeated. The offer was tempting and attractive to the others, but Canning held out for a declaration of principle as the only sure guarantee. The Reis Effendi came back with the flat statement that "a law prescribed by God himself was not to be set aside by any human power." Then came the veiled threat that, in pushing too far, the Christian powers might undo everything, that were the Sultan to agree to so revolutionary a demand he might lose his throne. It was a back-to-the-wall threat of a kind Canning had faced as a young man when the Porte threatened to turn to Napoleon in preference to England. Here again he met the threat head-on by reminding Rifat that the sword of revolt had already been raised against the Porte; that Mehemet and Ibrahim were buried in the sands of Egypt only by the force of the Christian powers. If another revolution were to come, the Egptians would most likely be the inheritors of Ottoman prerogatives. What could all the Turkish pashas and functionaries expect at their tender hands?

The impasse was absolute: reform had finally come face to face with the only real barrier, the Koran. The other powers began to waver and draw back, but the Elchi had come too far to flinch at this juncture. He turned to an exploration of the Koran itself. Although he was a convinced Christian, Sir Stratford Canning had a deep and sincere respect for the Moslem moral code. He had begun to wonder how a religion that was capable of its moral heights could, at the same time, endorse the cruelties wrought in its name. The lamps burned for long hours at the Embassy during these weeks, and Alison and the others were kept to the same grindstone he turned for himself. Canning went deeply into Moslem theology and law and found himself agreeably enlightened.

Koranic law, like its Christian counterpart, stemmed from two great sources. There was the basic Scripture, the Koran, and there was the body of traditional commentary, comprising a host of *obiter dicta* attributed to the Prophet himself and to his immediate followers, joined together with exegetic interpretations of the great teachers. These commentaries were grouped together under the name of Sunna, or what might be loosely translated as the Body of Tradition. Indisputably, the Sunna had to have a Koranic basis for validity; it was to the Koran itself, therefore, that final appeal had to be made in disputed cases.

A search of tradition revealed that, beyond the shadow of a doubt, the Sunna decreed death to an apostate. Undaunted, Canning began to scan the words of the Koran with the compulsion of an Augustine reaching for the light. The Koran is divided into 114 chapters (sura), and he plunged into them with the ardor of a True Believer. The further he delved the stronger grew the conviction that the invocation of the death penalty was an unwarranted extension of scriptural admonitions.

All the pertinent verses of the Koran were noted, discussed, and interpreted. Of them all, only one was considered to be open to the traditional interpretation cited as authority for executing the apostates. It was found in the forty-seventh Sura and read as follows:

> Verily, they who turn their backs after the Guidance hath been manifested to them, Satan hath deceived them and emboldened them. How will it be when the angels shall cause them to die, smiting their faces and their backs!

There was general agreement, however, that the context from which this passage was taken was referring to the early warrior disciples of the Prophet who had begun to lose heart and were showing reluctance to rush into battle with the disregard considered necessary by Mohammed. The penalty threatened for such shirkers, far from being a command for human execution, was actually a warning of the revenge to be exacted by the angels of an evil conscience when the souls of miscreants came to pass over the bridge to Paradise. Such was the scriptural basis on which the objectionable practice was founded.[22]

Early in 1844, then, the ministers of the Divan were shocked by the unheard of attempt of a Christian embassy to lecture to them on the fine points of Islamic law. A kind of panic swept through the Seraglio. Hurried consultations were held with individual imams and with the ulema as a whole, but neither the individual theologians nor the ulema could gainsay the points being pressed by the Buyuk Elchi. Alternately he was roundly cursed and privately blessed as he gave no quarter in the following weeks, using every stratagem and tactic which long experience had stocked in his private armory.

By adopting this aggressive stance, Canning removed himself from association with his diplomatic conferers and again stood alone, as one after another the other powers shrank from an internal theological dispute. Privately the several ambassadors cheered him on, but they could do nothing in an official way to help. He had even gone too far for Aberdeen and, had they been closer, the Foreign Secretary might have stayed the hand of his ambassador.[23]

The closing days of February saw him demanding a forthright declaration of principle while Rifat held out just as stubbornly for acceptance of his original compromise. Aberdeen wished to accept this promise, but Canning insisted that "there is . . . no lasting security against the recurrence of the barbarous practice except in a real surrender of the principle. Together with that principle, the main barrier between Turkey and Christendom would be removed."[24] He reminded the Foreign Secretary that there was every possibility that a case of apostasy might occur which would involve a British subject. Now was the time to have a clarification of principles, not later on when relations might be gravely jeopardized.

Meanwhile, he had held several secret meetings with Reshid Pasha in the course of which Canning learned that he had gradually acquired support in the Divan sufficient to sustain his position if he should succeed in winning the Sultan to his side. Armed with this information he peremptorily demanded an audience with the Sultan himself. Now it is true that, in the altered protocol of the Seraglio, an audience was more easily secured than had previously been the case, but it was still bound by rigid formal procedures. The recalcitrant members of the Divan feared that the Elchi's magnetism would easily sway the young monarch. Obviously, they could not indefinitely refuse to set a date for such a meeting as that would have left the Englishman no course but to break off diplomatic relations with the Porte.

There were possibilities open to them, though, of blocking the Elchi in his mad scheme. The Grand Vezir and his advisers had the right to inquire into the nature of the desired audience and then to confine the discussion of the subject to certain points. Once agreed upon, it would be a serious breach of etiquette for an ambassador to go beyond the predetermined points. In this way the Divan could control the nature and extent of agreements entered into by the Sultan, and the monarch did nothing substantially beyond reading a prepared document given him by those whose position demanded contact with the despised giaours.

Seeing their salvation in the involved intricacy of courtly procedure, the Grand Vezir and the Reis Effendi thereupon requested the Ambassador to submit a record of the items he wished to be treated. Canning willingly sent them a memorandum which he requested be embodied in a formal note to be read to him by the Sultan. This was the procedure of the Court. Once his own words were read back to him by the Sultan, they became a formal promise of the Sultan to the Queen of England and, when properly worded, stood as the law of the Empire. Canning's memorandum, naturally, contained a precise abrogation of the law and practice of executing apostates.

One further detail of protocol must be noted for proper understanding of what followed. Once the Reis Effendi accepted such a memorandum on behalf of the Sultan, the

Porte's agreement was understood. Canning, accordingly, was not surprised when Frederick Pisani brought back word that the audience had been granted for the twenty-second of March but that the Porte rejected the memorandum submitted. (This rejection was on the fourteenth of March.) The dragoman later recorded that he trembled in fear as he handed the Elchi the text of a note given him by the Reis Effendi which the Porte considered more suitable. The expected outburst failed to materialize for some reason as the Elchi's eyes rested on the salient clause: ". . . the Sublime Porte will take efficacious measures, the measures which are possible, in order that the executions of Christians who, having become Musulmans, return to Christianity, shall not take place." It was nothing more than Rifat's compromise position, but Pisani reported that the Sultan was to give the English Ambassador verbal assurances that the desires of the Queen of England would be fully and sincerely meet.

Within a few days Pisani was summoned back to the Ambassador's office. He was handed another note and told that it was the only note the Ambassador of the Queen of England would receive. The text of the note was precise and clear:

The official declaration communicated by his Excellency the Minister for Foreign Affairs shall be transmitted to the British Government, who will understand with satisfaction prevent henceforward the execution and putting to death that the Sublime Porte, in taking effectual measures to of any Christian, an apostate from Islamism, relinquishes for ever a principle inconsistent with its friendly professions;

and the further assurances to be given at the ambassador's
audience of the Sultan . . . will fully satisfy the British
Government that Christianity is not to be insulted in his
Highness' empire, nor anyone professing it to be treated as a
criminal, or persecuted on that account.[25]

This was likewise refused by the Reis Effendi and Canning
sent no further communication before the day of the audience.
Eyewitness accounts of that day testify to Canning's determination.   He came to the antechamber of the audience room
bearing a document.   The Grand Vezir and Rifat both knew
what it was.   Canning advanced to the Reis Effendi, who
moved backward, out of reach, only to have the terrible Englishman follow him.   In desperation Rifat clasped his hands
behind him as if to signify that the crime to come was not of
his doing.   Canning thrust the document in his arms, and
they proceeded into the throne room.   The deed was done and
the revolution accomplished without bloodshed.   Abdul Medjid gladly read the document and shook the Ambassador's
hand, whereupon Canning asked if he might be the first
Christian ambassador to kiss the Sultan's hand.   This was
denied as being just a little too much to ask.   It was a quaint
attempt to hold on to the past, and of little moment.   Millions
of the Sultan's subjects now had religious freedom in principle
though the fact might take many more years to realize.

1. See Temperley, *op. cit.*, pp. 63 ff, for an analysis of Palmerston's
policy at this juncture.

2. See above, Chap. X, n. 6.

3. His pencilled comments are included in Crawley, *op. cit.*, Appendix V. Briefly, Palmerston questioned, first, whether anything could help save the Ottoman Empire, which he thought too large to be properly administered under any conditions; second, whether there was much difference between an empire run by a Mahmud or by a Mehemet Ali; and third, whether British help, if given, would actually earn a decent gratitude from the Ottomans.

4. France had lately seized Algiers and was thought by many to be toying with the idea of sharing the rest of North Africa with Mehemet Ali.

5. See above, chap. X, n. 2.

6. Temperley, *op. cit.*, p. 65.

7. *Ibid.*, p. 66.

8. See the complete text in J. C. Hurewitz, *Diplomacy in the Near and Middle East* (Princeton, N. J.: Van Nostrand, 1956), I, 105-6.

9. Temperley, *op. cit.*, p. 74.

10. As Bailey (*op. cit.*, pp. 42-43) notes, Palmerston's previous experience had been in the war department. His first diplomatic interests, beginning in 1830, had been centered in Belgium and the Iberian peninsula.

11. *Ibid.*, chaps. iii and iv. There was added reason, too, because British trade to the Levant was increasing rapidly, and the threat to British commerce was obvious, as Stratford Canning had pointed out in 1832.

12. Cf. *ibid.*, p. 169: "Palmerston was no idle spectator in 1839 as he was in 1833." Metternich suggested an informal conference, but while Austria vacillated, Palmerston took the lead. He forced all the powers, his own government included, to sign the Treaty of London (July 15, 1840). Temperley (*op. cit.*, p. 143) states: "Within less than a year after the signature of the Treaty of July 15 Palmerston had broken the power of Mehemet Ali and forced him to sign the witness of his own defeat."

13. Cf. Hurewitz, *op. cit.*, I, 111: Foreign Minister Palmerston to Her Majesty's Ambassador at Vienna.

14. See *ibid.*, pp. 119-20, for the text of the Treaty.

15. *Ibid.*, p. 123. In his preface to the text of the Convention, Hurewitz notes that this rule of the Straits survived without major change until the outbreak of World War I.

16. See above, chap. II, p. 16.

17. Lane-Poole, *op. cit.*, II, 78.

18. This proposition, a basic view of Stratford Canning's, is felt by some to be an oversimplification. I am inclined to feel, however, that Canning was perfectly correct. Besides my respect for Canning's own wealth of knowledge concerning the Turkey of his day, I base my judgment on the following points: (1) The preamble to the Hatti-Sherif of Gulhane, the great reform decree issued by Abdul Medjid in 1839, states: "All the world knows that in the first days of the Ottoman monarchy, the glorious precepts of the Koran and the laws of the empire were always honored. The empire in consequence increased in strength and greatness. . . . In the last one-hundred and fifty years a succession of accidents and divers causes which have brought about a disregard for the sacred code of laws and the regulations flowing therefrom, and the former strength and prosperity have changed into weakness and poverty; an empire in fact loses all its stability so soon as it ceases to observe its laws" (for the complete text of the decree see Hurewitz, *op. cit.*, I, 113-16). The rescript said, in effect, that a misinterpretation of Koranic law is at the root of Turkey's malaise. This was Canning's thesis precisely, and it was the lever he used in the subsequent apostasy controversy. (2) Toynbee, *op. cit.*, VIII, 252, summarizes well what seems to have been the common aim of the reformers in Canning's time: "The common aim of the liberal Westernizing Ottoman Turkish Muslim statesmen of the post-Malmudian Age was to carry out Mahmud's still unaccomplished work by converting the Ottoman Empire into a *Rechtsstaat* whose subjects of all religions and nationalities would be secured so full a measure of equality before the law, according to standards attained in the enlightened Western states of the day, that the *ra-iyeh* would lose their desire to secede for the purpose of founding or joining separate national states of their own." The reformers were not going to become non-Moslem; they wished to put an end to the penalties suffered by non-Moslem subjects precisely because these people were non-Moslem. (3) Even more weighty, in my opinion, is the analysis given by W. C. Smith (*op. cit.*, pp. 161-205) of modern Turkish Islamic intellectualism in respect to Islam and the civil society. If I interpret him correctly, he develops these propositions: (*a*) Although Turkish nationalism is today Moslem, Turkey is also explicitly a laicized state which the revolution has erected. Because of this the Turks are suspected by non-Turkish Moslems of heresy (i.e., of attempting to create a society that is

both Islamic and lay). (b) The Turkish Islamic intellectual denies this charge and replies that the Turkish sense of history is one of a continuing process, that Islam is developing still, and the "the others [Arabs, Indo-Pakistani, etc.], in their attitude to Islamic society on earth, are thinking of an ancient glory they wish to recapture; the Turks of a recent mis-development they wish to rectify" (ibid., p. 170). (c) The misdevelop-ment which the Turks saw was the confusion of Islam and civil society. The accomplishment of the revolution was the liberation of one from the other. Through the revolution, Turkey "rediscovered true Islam" (ibid., p. 176). This is the liberation that Stratford Canning sought.

By way of contrary opinion, some historians (e.g., Bailey, op. cit., pp. 8-91) point out that in many practical instances the Ottoman Empire was more tolerant of dissident belief than were some contemporary Western states. This is indeed true as far as it goes, but it does not relate to the principles upon which the Ottoman Empire or these states were function-ing. And in the instances where tolerance was practiced in the Ottoman Empire, it will be found that it existed only so long as its beneficiaries minded their own business and did not attempt to exercise any civil right. Bailey himself goes on to declare: "Convinced that any change would ruin their religious hold over the people the ulema tended to oppose all reform. . . . The ulema had become, in fact, a kind of Supreme Court, responsible for all matters relating to justice, and herein lay their danger. Since they were more interested in their religious duties, they neglected their civil functions, allowed disorder to reign in the courts below them, and thus contributed to arbitrary, tyrannical, chaotic government" (ibid., p. 22).

19. Cf. Hurewitz, op. cit., I, 113, in his commentary on the rescript.

20. Lane-Poole, op. cit., II, 81.

21. Ibid., p. 84.

22. An instance of the invalid extension of Koranic law. See n. 18, this chapter.

23. See Lane-Poole, op. cit., II, 95.

24. Ibid., pp. 94-95.

25. Ibid., p. 96 n. 1

XIII

THE successful outcome of the apostasy controversy presented Sir Stratford Canning with an opportunity that was at once golden and full of danger. A revolutionary principle had been established which cleared the way for major reforms, but no one realized better than he that the gap betwen principle and practice was enormous.[1] If the victory were to mean anything, it had to be followed up by practical implementation or it would remain an empty monument to good intentions. On the other hand, if he alone were to push too hard in this direction, he could easily undo in a moment all that had been accomplished. He was under no illusion that fanaticism and reaction were buried. He was never in doubt that there would be retrogression from the established principle of religious freedom. That there would be sidestepping, backsliding, open defiance and contravention, he freely predicted.[2] Reform could not be permanent until the Turks themselves

wanted it; the great design of Mahmud and Reshid had to
be put into practice by Turks for the whole Turkish people
and all subject peoples of the Empire. The best a friend
could do, be he the British Ambassador or anyone else, was
to help those few Turks who saw the light to overcome the
obstacles by whatever means wisdom and prudence offered.[3]
This was the attitude he adopted.

Since permanent and effective change depended, ultimately,
on the character of the ministry in the Porte and the general
tenor of Ottoman leadership, Canning had first to face the
fact that in 1844 he was still dealing with the same group
that had seized the reins a few years earlier. The membership
of the Divan constituted a reactionary bloc, and the sprinkling
of moderates among them were too disjointed a minority to
represent anything resembling a party.[4] The dearth of potential leaders outside that circle, however, made it mandatory
to whittle away at the predominance of the most reactionary
ministers by replacing them with those less rigorously inclined until a more balanced Divan should result. This was
but a continuation of the tactics he had been employing before
the apostasy crisis had erupted.

Canning's major aim was to restore Reshid Pasha to power
either as Grand Vezir or as the Foreign Minister (Reis Effendi). He turned his attentions to Rifat Pasha, the current
Foreign Minister. Knotty problems between the Greeks and
their former masters, a thorny dispute in the mountains of
Lebanon involving a triangular conflict between the Christian

Maronites, Moslem Druses, and the Turkish administrators of the province, a boundary disturbance on the Persian frontier—all kept the Elchi and Rifat in constant communication. Fortunately, in each instance, the British Ambassador found himself able to support the Turkish viewpoint. He was, therefore, able to demonstrate his devotion to justice on behalf of the Sultan just as much as he had previously been compelled to act against what the reactionaries claimed was their monarch's best interests. With his counsel and advice each of the issues was peacefully resolved in the course of the year to the satisfaction of all and to the increasing esteem of Rifat at home and abroad.

Interpersed among the official exchanges were frequent discussions of general problems facing Turkey, and Canning gradually sounded out the Reis Effendi's personal opinions. As he suspected, Rifat was more than sympathetic to reform but fearful that too rapid an extension would bring the whole structure down in collapse. In this the Pasha echoed the usual rejoinder of the Turkish dignitary but with an important difference: he was willing to discuss alternatives and to mull over hypothetical situations with an eye to the future. Inevitably the conferences broached the subject of the utilization of the talents of a man like Reshid, and Rifat readily agreed that they were being wasted in the civil administration of Adrianople. It would be impossible, however, he pointed out, to bring Reshid back into the government without provoking storms of the most serious kind. Canning happily concurred in this assessment because he did not want Reshid enmeshed in one of the lesser ministries and he could not ask Rifat to step down, much less propose the resignation of the Grand Vezir merely to open the way for the reformer.

Quite happily, the Presidency of the Council became vacant late in the year. Although the President of the Council was not a member of the ministry, the position was one of great influence in the hierarchy of the Porte. Its occupant could propose programs and policies for debate without having to initiate or support them as an executive or administrator. Thus, a competent man with a sense of timing could lead without the onus of partisan responsibility. The Elchi suggested to Rifat that he might justly seek the post. He had demonstrated his ability in the Foreign Ministry, and such a move could in no wise be construed as a demotion or mark of failure. Moreover, Rifat could be of immeasurably greater service to his country and his Sultan, Canning reassured him, by providing the leadership needed by the moderates.

The Ambassador also contrived to acquaint the Sultan with the desirability of such a move, and in due time Rifat Pasha became the President of the Council. Lest there be any suspicion engendered by the change, he was succeeded at the Foreign Ministry by an outspoken foe of Canning's, Shehib Effendi. And, to further cloak the pattern of succession, the dangerous Reshid Pasha was sent back to Paris as ambassador. The year 1844 drew to a close with the star of Stratford Canning ostensibly on the decline. Whispers were even circulated about the Porte that a cabinet change was impending in England and that the obnoxious Elchi would soon be leaving himself. Canning did nothing to dispel the rumors. He was reasonably sure they had their source in Riza Pasha, who had already made inquiries of the Ottoman Ambassador in London on the best method of securing Canning's recall.

While Canning was making these careful inroads at the Porte, he continued to encourage the Sultan on particulars of reform lest the momentum be entirely lost. Within two months of the close of the apostasy crisis, Abdul Medjid decreed the abolition of torture throughout the Empire and this was a boon to Moslem and rayah alike. Petty but oppressive irritants, such as distinguishing marks on Turkish merchant ships of Christian ownership, quietly disappeared. Canning also recommended an early end to the discriminatory *harach* (head tax) levied on Christians, and he painted for the Sultan a picture of the day when the *rayah* population must become the mainstay of the government and the army. If they were not engaged and trained in government service on a basis of equality, the future of the Empire would be endangered.

In order to protect what had been won, British consulates were put on the alert throughout the Empire and were under instruction to report to Canning any infringement of the newly recognized rights. The mere presence of a British representative in a courtroom helped to insure justice on more than one occasion. So commonplace did this habit of consular offices become that Turkish complaints of meddling and interference soon filtered back to the nervous ears of Lord Aberdeen in London. The Foreign Secretary reacted by sending a circular letter addressed to all consuls warning against undue interference in internal affairs of Turkish administration. The Ambassador dutifully forwarded the letter to all officers under his jurisdiction but appended to the directive a note assuring his agents that he never considered any action of theirs to have been contrary to the tenor of the Foreign Office instructions.[5]

As time went on his efforts in behalf of religious freedom brought him some embarrassment—in the form of scandalous conflicts among Christians. The Christian population of the Empire adhered overwhelmingly to one or another of the Orthodox sects, chiefly the Greek, Armenian, and Syrian Orthodox Churches, with a sprinkling of Roman Catholics and Maronites and smaller autocephalous groups scattered about. With the advent of "religious freedom" some of the smaller religious societies, along with Protestant missionary groups from England and America, attempted to begin activities. Sadly enough, their efforts ran into severe, and sometimes vicious, antagonism from their brethren in Christ. Like the major Christian communities, these minority sects appealed, in their turn, to Sir Stratford Canning. The situation posed a cruel dilemma for him. Personally, he was a convinced Anglican, and he dreamed of a united Christian church which would, one day, become irresistible in its attraction, even for the world of Islam. He had little sympathy,

therefore, for the type of Protestant fundamentalists seeking
entry into the fabric of Eastern Christianity. For the same
reason he abhorred any further splintering of the major
Orthodox churches. But at the same time he was doggedly
devoted to the idea of personal freedom, and though he detested the spectacle of Christian squabbling in full view of
Moslem hauteur, he found no real difficulty in giving priority
to that principle over his own sympathies. He solved the
personal dilemma by limiting himself to action in individual
cases according to their particular merits. On no account
would he present the Porte with a demand for a general
recognition of Protestantism as such, for to do so at this juncture in the over-all struggle would, in his opinion, result in a
general setback for Christianity. Accordingly, he sought
and obtained legal status for an Armenian Protestant group
and secured permission for the erection of a Protestant church
in Pera to serve the foreign Protestant community. He likewise requested the Sultan's blessing on the erection of an
Anglican hospice in Jerusalem and the establishment of an
Anglican bishopric there. Limited action of this type he
deemed sufficient for the times.

Secular aspects of the Sultan's regime interested the Ambassador no less than did the religious. Financial reform and
an efficient military organization were every bit as essential
to the welfare of the Empire as was legal reform. The Nizam-
Jedid of Selim III, resurrected by Mahmud after the abolition
of the Janissaries, aimed at a regular army, staffed by career

officers and maintained by the financial resources of the central government. Obviously, it was directly connected with the revenue system of the Porte; and here was the stumbling block, for, in spite of the tax system proclaimed in the Gulhane Decree, tax collection was still largely a matter of farming out the taxes. The net loss to the Sultan's government was enormous, and the opportunities for personal profit were in direct proportion. Invariably, the district tax collectors were the local beys and pashas on whose feudal-like local troops the Sultan's military power had formerly depended. That they should surrender the chief source of their income in favor of a system of direct taxation whose main purpose would be to reduce, if not destroy, the basis of their military responsibility and power was a "consummation devoutly to be wished" but obviously not one to be sought without trouble. The network of vested interests was widespread and the chain of corruption extended right back to the Divan, where the Seraskier, Riza Pasha, and the Finance Minister, Safti Pasha, were working hand in hand.

The foreign debt of the Porte had grown tremendously under the pressure of the Egyptian wars, and its credit had diminished to the danger point. Early in 1845, Rifat Pasha, freed from the restraint of ministerial responsibility, had begun to raise some searching questions as to the state of the Imperial Treasury. From a whisper the questions soon grew to a thunderous roar, and when the ensuing investigation revealed the extent of corruption that had damaged both the treasury and the army, the wrath of blame fell upon the respective ministers. Riza Pasha and his bedfellow, Safti Pasha, were summarily dismissed from office. Meanwhile the cry was being raised on all sides, from within the Council, from the associations of merchants and bankers, from reformers and patriots generally, for the return of Reshid Pasha as the one man best fitted to salvage the Porte's prestige.

So little did any of this appear to be the work of Sir Stratford Canning that the Sultan deemed it advisable to ascertain from the Elchi whether the British government would take offense at the appointment of the Ambassador to France as Foreign Minister of the Porte. When the necessary assurances that this would not be so came from the British Embassy without hesitation, Reshid Pasha was recalled from Paris and assumed the office of Foreign Minister on October 23, 1845. Stratford Canning had waited four years to see this day.

1. The more so because the Sheik-ul-Islam had not ratified the distinction pressed by Canning (Temperley, op. cit., pp. 26-28). But Canning was trying to push the Porte into a statement of principle from which escape would be difficult. It should be noted, therefore, to supplement Temperley's observation, that neither the Sheik nor the ulema denounced the distinction, so Canning was justified in applying the rule of silence.

2. Canning was neither shocked nor surprised, as some historians (e.g., Temperley, op. cit., p. 243) imply, when he had to face the fact that reform would be indefinitely postponed—a conclusion that is not supposed to have dawned upon him until the early fifties. As early as December 13, 1843, we find him writing to Aberdeen: "The plans of Reshid Pasha, the regulations of Gulhane, the improvements introduced from Europe went out of favor with the settlement of Egypt and the recovery of Syria and Candia. The Porte gradually relapsed into most of her old ideas . . ." (cf.

Bailey, *op. cit.*, p. 222 n. 73). And in October of 1845, he wrote to the Foreign Secretary: "If the principles now in requisition are found unequal to the process of restoration, what but despair can ensue . . . ?" (Lane-Poole, *op. cit.*, II, 110). And again, to Lady Canning, on July 20, 1846, he wrote: "I am sick of assurances, and believe nothing" (*ibid.*, p. 159). Disappointment, yes, but not shock.

3. Stratford Canning never claimed to be the "Reformer of Turkey," although the sobriquet was bestowed upon him by well-meaning friends and admirers, including his principal biographer, Lane-Poole. The substance of the reforms which Canning hoped to see adopted were not finally implemented until the Revolution of Mustapha Kemal succeeded in the early 1920's.

4. In or out of office, Reshid was the leader of the loosely knit liberal bloc, but as Bailey, *op. cit.*, p. 222, notes, "Reshid and his colleagues continued to work alone as individuals, rather than as leaders of an efficient organization or party."

5. Cf. Lane-Poole, *op. cit.*, II, 101.

XIV

SIR Stratford Canning had left England without his wife and family. So long a time had elapsed since his last previous residence in Constantinople that he wished to be sure the proper accommodations were available before sending for them. He had to be especially careful about arrangements because his young son, named George, for obvious reasons, had contracted an illness in Spain which had invalided him for life. The boy was never to follow in the footsteps of his famous namesake as his father had so fondly hoped. Lady Canning did bring the children out later on, but the weakness of the boy and the lack of proper medical facilities in Constantinople forced her to return to England early in 1845.

These periods of separation from his family were somewhat compensated for by the stimulating presence of a remarkable circle of men who were associated with him for varying lengths of time during this tenure of office. The days when the complexion of an embassy staff used to be largely of the ambassador's making had disappeared, and many an envoy was beginning to suffer under the curse of having to tolerate incompetent assistants foisted on him by the Foreign Office. Fortunately, Canning had little cause to complain in this regard, for among those who spent part of their apprenticeship under his tutelage were a number of men who went on to win their spurs in the field of diplomacy and statecraft. The more prominent among them were John Drummond Hay, Henry Wellesley, later Lord Cowley, and the Lords Stanley, Ampthill, Napier, and Zouche. In company with them were Charles Alison, the distinguished Orientalist, and archaeologists and historians Layard, Rawlinson, and Newton. With subordinates such as these at hand the Ambassador's burden was not nearly so heavy as it might have been, for, as noted previously, the concerns of the Embassy had grown tremendously, and Canning had been disturbed by a noticeable lack of efficiency when he had resumed office in 1842. These assistants were of a calibre to follow intelligent direction and to assume responsibility when it was given to them, and Canning gave them ample opportunity for both. At times each of these had felt the bite of his temper, but all testified, in later years, to the debt they owed him for his counsel.

With Layard and Rawlinson among the list of persons who were familiar figures at the Embassy, it was not unusual that Canning should choose as an avocation the growing science of archaeology, to which, on his own initiative and at his own expense, he was to make a contribution. At Budrun, in the far southwestern corner of Asia Minor, for example, there was a crumbling ruin that had excited the interest of antiquarians for some time. It was nothing but a nondescript crusaders' fortress, yet knowledgeable observers puzzled over the marble bas-reliefs of its massive walls. They had obviously been part of some ancient monument sacrificed to the needs of another era. Alison, sent by Canning to investigate the feasibility of extricating them, returned a favorable report, and the Ambassador made immediate overtures to the Porte regarding their acquisition. Abdul Medjid, in giving his assent to their removal, bestowed the sculptures as a personal gift from himself to the Elchi. When, after two years of patient excavation, the marble blocks were finally removed, the work involved in getting them out led to a discovery of their original use and the monument from which they had come. It proved to be none other than the tomb of King Mausolus erected at Halicarnassus by Queen Artemisia in 353 B.C., an edifice numbered among the Seven Wonders of the World. Canning, who had accepted the original gift in the name of the British people, presented all the finds to the Trustees of the British Museum, where they were eventually installed in a separate Mausoleum Room.

An even greater reservoir of knowledge, as far as history and archaeology are concerned, was tapped by the diggings of Austen Henry Layard at Nineveh. Layard, convinced that a series of mounds near Mosul covered long-buried secrets of ancient Assyria, had arrived at Constantinople in 1842, penniless after exhausting his own funds in fruitless effort. Canning accepted the logic of Layard's theories, and, being unable to procure government funds for the undertaking, he personally guaranteed the archaeologist a salary and advanced funds necessary to begin the work of excavation. Finances were only one part of the preparations, however, for in most cases the object of an archaeologist's search lay on the private property of powerful, and often greedy, landlords who bowed to nothing less than an imperial rescript. For Layard, and again for Rawlinson, who searched in the same regions, Sir Stratford Canning was always ready to ask for the requisite orders.

Canning was not a wealthy man; and, while it is true that these ventures were diverting to him, they cannot be regarded as the hobby of a dilettante. Here again, as in all things, it was to a great degree his sense of national pride that motivated his actions. He felt that England should be in the forefront of scientific achievement in the scholarly unearthing of the past, just as much as he considered it rightful for her to lead humanity to the glories of the future in a world of peace and enlightenment. But it was not until Layard had unearthed the royal palace at Nineveh, with its priceless records in clay and stone, that the British government and the British Museum moved to relieve the Ambassador of the financial burden involved.

The first bright results of these endeavors were coming to the fore in 1846, and they coincided, happily, with the promotion of Reshid Pasha to the office of Grand Vezir. To Canning it was a welcome sign of liberal strength in the Porte, and he felt that it would be a good time to take leave of absence. Reshid might do better if it were made absolutely clear that he was no tool of the English Elchi and could function on his own resources. Satisfied that much good had been effected, and feeling a need for a breath of English air, Sir Stratford Canning asked for an audience of leave-taking at the end of July, 1846. From the Sultan and from Reshid came sincere expressions of hope that the absence would not be too long and that he would return to them in health and safety. One misgiving marred the complacency of his departure, and that was caused by the knowledge that Riza Pasha had returned to the Divan as Minister of Commerce. This development could be an omen of ill, or it could be a smybol of Reshid's strength and self-confidence. Time would have to tell.

XV

THE England to which Stratford Canning returned after an absence of almost five years was undergoing some marked changes of her own. As a matter of fact, the whole continent of Europe was in a period of social and political transition. In England, the broad extension of the franchise effected by the Reform Bill had made Parliament more directly answerable to the country as a whole. The major parties, however, had been slow to adjust to the change, and their leadership, seemingly incapable of gauging the temper of the wider electorate, found it impossible to present more than a shadow of party unity on the great issues moving the mass of new voters. Both Tories and Whigs had been badly split in the thirties on the questions of Catholic emancipation and parliamentary reform. Now, in the forties, the same kind of cleavage continued over the issue of free trade and the corn tariff. The old party names were still in use, but the rampant criss-crossing of party lines was pointing to an inevitable realignment. Sir Robert Peel's ministry, for example, was Tory in name, but when Peel finally succeeded in repealing the Corn Laws in June of 1846, his Parliamentary majority depended heavily on the votes of Whig and Irish members. These same votes were denied him, however, in an ensuing motion of no confidence entered by rebels in his own Tory party led by Stanley and Disraeli, and the Peel government collapsed. The succeeding Cabinet was headed by Lord John Russell as Prime Minister, supported by his own Whig party and a mixture of Peel Tories and Radicals, the basis of the Liberal party of a later day.

Canning was really rather indifferent to the general confusion of party politics. What mattered most to him was the return of Palmerston to the Foreign Office, where he felt a strong hand was needed. The same currents that were breaking down traditional patterns in England were flowing even faster across the continent of Europe. But whereas public clamor had a constitutional outlet in England, it was stifled on the Continent. What passed as constitutional reform and social transition in England was looked upon as political revolt and the upheaval of established order in Europe. The Continental autocracies, almost without exception, were bent on maintaining the system of hereditary privilege and rank at all costs. Here was a hidden danger. What would happen if Europe were suddenly to explode in revolution? The French Revolution had been followed by almost a quarter-century of war and turmoil. It was not beyond the realm of possibility that a like eruption could occur again.

Men like Canning and Palmerston could not profess to foretell the future, but they knew that England had no policy to prepare her for these possibilities. Their number was dwindling, however, for in their preoccupation with their own affairs the English people had all but forgotten the rest of the world. Englishmen sensed that they were on the threshold of a new day, and the growth of political democracy was only one of its harbingers. The Industrial Revolution had progressed further in England than any other place on earth. The products of her new factories were being carried to every corner of the globe, and the vessels that carried them were returning swollen with fresh food for the machines and furnaces of the Midlands. The maritime supremacy of Britain, which had safeguarded her through the blackest moments of war, was now being used to corner world markets for her manufactures and to guarantee an unending backflow of raw materials. All this had come about in an era of uninterrupted peace that had settled over Europe after the Congress of Vienna. And as the prosperity and profits grew with each year of peace, who could be bothered contemplating the possibility of war? The new merchant aristocracy had no time for it. Let Palmerston and others of his quaint circle go on prating about coalitions and paramount interests, and play their games of treaties and notes and memorandums and the like. They were a carry-over from the past, and no one really paid attention to their antics. Macaulay was soon to bear scholarly witness to the popular fancy that nothing but un-

clouded glory lay in the future. "Optimism reigned throughout the land."[1]

Thus did the English seem oblivious to the ferment brewing beneath the surface calm of that continent which was
less than a day's sail distant. Except in France, the struggle
for personal political rights in Europe was still embryonic;
and the rising clamor of homogeneous racial and cultural
groups seeking national identity separate from the age-old
hegemonies which held them subject went unheard by the
bulk of Englishmen. Unmindful of the recent past, the
average Englishman no longer realized that the option of peace
or war might rest in the will of one man. Long accustomed
to popular control of government, they failed to realize that
it was not so everywhere. And if their new leaders acknowl-
edged the fact, they failed to remind their countrymen. The
aging Duke of Wellington fretted publicly about the woeful
state of England's defences, but few rallied to his side. What
need was there for armies? The world was on the march
toward unending progress.

Such was the atmosphere in which Stratford Canning spent
a quiet, relaxing year as a "simple householder," attending to
personal affairs, visiting the few old friends who remained,
and calmly planning his future. It was a year that wore
away all too rapidly; and as the summer of 1847 neared, he
began to prepare for a return to his station in Constantinople.
Because he was approaching his sixty-first birthday in an era
when longevity was the exception rather than the rule, he was
forced to examine the realities of the present and assess the

probabilities of the future. In deference to the desires of his family, he wished to set some terminal date to his public career, provided he could do so with the assurance that some gains had been cemented at the scene of his labors.

Since Reshid Pasha seemed to be securely in power, it was reasonable to conclude that the reform movement was in a strong position and that the time was ripe to push for practical implementation of, at least, the most important reforms. Sir Stratford was convinced that certain specifics could no longer be postponed lest they suffer cumulative deterioration and eventually atrophy from want of serious resolution. Accordingly, he wrote a long and detailed letter for Reshid's consideration in which he enumerated definite actions that must be initiated, and toward the completion of which he, Stratford Canning, was ready to spend a final eighteen months in the palace at Pera.[2]

The reforms he was now urging, the Ambassador reminded the Pasha, had long since been agreed to in principle. They included a revamping of the revenue system and a broadening of educational opportunities that would be of direct benefit to all subjects of the Sultan. Concerning the position of Christians, he demanded immediate abolition of the *harach* and the admission of Christian evidence in the courts of law. He mentioned the horror with which England regarded the forcible conversion to Islam of Christian children and pointed out that the Ottoman Empire could never hope for a real entente with England while such obnoxious practices continued. And the Sultan, Canning warned in this connection, might well need an English alliance in the near future. Events were to prove the foresight of this admonition, though no one then realized how soon the need was to arise. Finally, he alluded again to the impossibility of ever fostering a sense of patriotism and loyalty among the *rayah* population until its members were allowed to participate in government and military service on a basis of complete equality.

It is doubtful that the Elchi expected an answer in kind to this memorandum. He had submitted a statement of his conditions, and it was sufficient for his purpose. If Reshid could lead the Divan along in reasonable co-operation, it would soon be apparent for all to see, and then Canning would be happy to collaborate to the best of his ability. If, on the other hand, practical assurances were not forthcoming, he had resolved to give up his mission as a failure.

At any rate, the Ambassador had no further time for untrammeled thought. Lord Palmerston had decided to entrust him with two preliminary missions, one in Switzerland and another in Greece.

Switzerland was beset by religious strife, and outright civil war was in the offing. A few years earlier, all monastic establishments had been suppressed in the Protestant canton of Aargau. The bickering between Catholic areas and the rest of the country had grown until, lately, a resolution calling for the expulsion of the Jesuits had been passed by the Federal Diet in Berne. The reaction of the Catholic cantons had been severe, and seven of them had formed a protective league, the Sonderbund, which armed itself and was now defiantly challenging the power of the Diet. Purely political questions had become entangled with the original religious issue, with the Catholic league taking a position against a general constitutional revision being supported by the Liberal majority in the Diet. One canton, Neuchâtel, had officially declared its neutrality but succeeded only in incurring the enmity of the Diet because of that attempt. This was an added complication because the hereditary sovereign of Neuchâtel was none other than the Protestant King of Prussia, whose Hohenzollern family had never relinquished its original ties to that tiny princedom. The Swiss crisis, therefore, was dangerously near to inviting foreign intervention on a major scale both on religious and political grounds. The major powers, fortunately, were agreed on the necessity of antecedent mediation of a diplomatic nature, and Sir Stratford Canning, one of the chief architects of the federal system inaugurated in Switzerland thirty years earlier, was a logical choice as mediator.

Before Canning was able to reach Berne (December, 1847), however, an armed clash did occur, and it resulted in an overwhelming victory for the troops of the Diet. But the Diet, swelling with pride because of its easy victory, had assumed a vindictive posture toward the rebels. Not only did it carry through with the measures originally contemplated, but it imposed a punitive fine of one million francs on the former members of the Sonderbund and the monasteries collectively. The Diet also threatened to occupy Neuchâtel with Federal troops, whereupon King Frederick William of

Prussia, on behalf of Neuchâtel, and Austria and France, on behalf of the Catholics, entered forceful and ominous protests. The Diet curtly rejected the protests, and Sir Stratford presently found himself mediating between the Swiss government and the Continental powers. He did secure a commitment on the part of the Diet, in January, to refrain from occupying Neuchâtel, and a general amelioration of the punitive fines. Prussia was thereby satisfied and withdrew her active interest in the imbroglio, and France and Austria were soon to turn their attention elsewhere. The year 1848 had dawned and restless winds were blowing across the face of Europe.

Canning came back to London in February preparatory to returning to Constantinople by way of Greece where the situation was chaotic. Prince Otho of Bavaria, to whom the European powers had given the crown of Greece fifteen years before, had turned out to be a royal misadventurer. Ever since his arrival in Athens, early in 1833, he had carried on as though the Kingdom of the Hellenes had been erected for his personal pleasure and profit. Alien to the people over whom he ruled, Otho made not the slightest move to accommodate himself to their culture or to solve their problems. Consequently, the strife between parties and factions had never ceased. The sycophants who surrounded the King formed circles which succeeded one another from time to time in the guise of constitutional ministries, but they were governments in name only. And if its internal affairs were tragic, the relations of the Greek government with other states were almost ludicrous, since Greek envoys at foreign courts were chiefly concerned with transmitting information highly partisan to the interests of the King or were busy conspiring against him. Most embarrassingly for the Christian powers of Europe, Greece had completely failed to honor the obligation, imposed upon her by treaty, of indemnifying former Turkish owners for property expropriated at the time her independence was recognized. The British government's Foreign Office was determined to rectify the situation.

Palmerston proposed to Canning that prior to his return to Constantinople, he circulate through the courts of Europe and sound out the several governments on a solution to the Greek problem. It was his desire that Canning stop off in Athens and present Otho and his cohorts with a concerted ultimatum that they put their house in order or submit to forcible intervention of some kind. Canning was to work out the details according to the reaction he found en route.

What was to be a grand progress from capital to capital across the continent turned out to be a dismal first-hand observation of riot, misrule, and revolution. On his way back from Switzerland in February, Canning had stopped at Paris, where he had found the king confident of his close ties with the people, but within two weeks Louis Philippe and his court had been received as pitiful exiles in London. The Second French Republic had been born. Revolt spread rapidly, and within a month the turmoil was general throughout Europe. Though conservative fear described it variously as anarchism, socialism, hatred of the aristocracy, the movement was basically a not-to-be stilled public demand for constitutional democracy. Unfortunate excesses did occur but they were perhaps due mostly to muddled attempts to meet the popular upsurge with force of arms rather than reasonable compromise. The nature of the turbulence on the Continent is shown by contrast with the course that the Chartist movement took in England. Chartist leaders organized a popular meeting and issued threats and ultimatums. In a momentary fit of panic the Duke of Wellington was summoned to protect Government and Crown, but he wisely kept the regular troops out of sight and left the maintenance of law and order to a hastily erected organization of civil constables. On the day of the promised demonstration little happened beyond a quiet and dignified procession of three carriages leaving the meeting at Kensington with petitions addressed to the Commons. Not so on the Continent, where the Bourbons were ejected from France and the Second Republic arose from the barricades. In Vienna the Emperor Ferdinand was deposed and succeeded by the youthful Francis Joseph, while Metternich, who refused to bow to any semblance of democracy, was forced to fly in disguise. In Berlin and in a half-dozen lesser capitals of German states, kingdoms were shaken, but all weathered the storms by compromising to a certain extent with their subjects.

Nationalism, too, entered the picture. In Hungary, Poland, and northern Italy there were attempts, some concerted and successful, others sporadic and easily quelled, against the Hapsburg and Romanov overlordships. It was, as Canning himself described it, "the famous year of revolutions."

Needless to say, his tour met with little success under the circumstances. The question of Greece had receded far into the background for the embattled monarchs and their ministers, and Canning was left to his own resources to deal with the matter. Impatient of any further delay in picking up the reins in Constantinople, he had refused to alter his schedule and, as a mark of singular audacity, even allowed Mrs. Canning and his daughters to accompany him to the Continent. Fruitless as the journey was, he completed it as directed, and if nothing else was accomplished, he did acquire a fresh insight into the views and policies of the several powers.

He was quite understandably empty-handed, then, when he arrived in Athens, and though he listened patiently to all who approached him, there was little he could do with the intractable monarch save to deliver a frank and serious warning that the situation could not continue in a process of indefinite deterioration. Personally antipathetic to Otho, he nevertheless steeled himself to treating with the king as the legal ruler until events should determine otherwise. Curiously enough, this characteristic adherence to principle earned Canning the enmity of many Greeks and their English sympathizers who thought he should have been more forthright in his condemnation. But Canning felt that he was present in Greece as a judge for the European powers rather than a partisan of one faction or another. This adamant devotion to what he considered his sworn duty cost him the friendship of several Englishmen who had cast their lot with the Greeks since the days of Byron and who had become violently antagonistic to Otho. It was not the first time that Canning's strong will drove him in an opposite direction from his own sympathies, nor was it to be the last. Had he been less rigid with himself, less ready to sacrifice even friendship where duty dictated, he would not have been the man he was. He would have preferred to face Otho armed with definite directives and able to predict severe alternatives, but he was in no way so empowered nor could he make the slightest pretense of being thus commissioned.

The disappointment he suffered in Athens, where he had no direct and continuing responsibility, was trifling compared to the near disaster that threatened his inner hopes and his prestige in Constantinople. Revolution had not directly affected the Ottoman Empire, but it had galvanized the forces of reaction into seizing upon the opportunity afforded by the Elchi's absence to work on the monarch's fear and timidity. Shortly before the Ambassador returned in June, the conspirators had successfully effected the removal of Reshid, and a rigidly conservative cabinet was in the saddle.

Canning was overcome by feelings of rage and frustration. His wrath was directed no less at the combination of circumstances that had delayed him too long and at the intriguers who capitalized on it than it was at the obvious weakness of both the Sultan and Reshid. Had the times been normal, the patent inability of the Pasha to stand alone and the behavior of the Sultan, who wavered with every change of wind, might have caused Canning to throw up his hands in despair. But the luxury of petty recrimination and aggrieved pouting were not in the Elchi's repertoire, and this certainly was not the hour to include them, for the clouds on the horizon were too ominous to allow for such indulgence. The anger of the Ambassador caused shudders that vibrated in every corner of the Seraglio. Without waiting for the official audience of welcome, he made his views and his demands known at once. Abdul Medjid, already showing disappointing signs of dissipation, abjectly admitted that he had acquiesced to the exactions of an unworthy plot against his minister and restored Reshid to the Council immediately. Ali Pasha, who had been Reshid's foreign minister, was likewise reinstated and Rifat Pasha, who had gone back to the Foreign Office, pleaded that he had done so only to save what he could. Within two months of Canning's return Reshid Pasha was back as Grand Vezir (August, 1848), Ali Pasha as Reis Effendi, and Rifat returned to the Presidency of the Council. The celerity of the realignment was ample testimony of Canning's power. His influence was not being applied for motives of personal vengeance, however, but to prepare the Turks for coping with fresh disturbances in the Danubian provinces.

In the month of Elchi's reappearance at the Porte the air of revolution had blown as far as Bucharest, the capital of the principality of Wallachia where a popular uprising demanded, as elsewhere, universial extension of suffrage and, in particular, legal eligibility of all electors for the office of hospodar, or prince. The situation in this instance was uniquely complex.

This province, along with its sister state of Moldavia, enjoyed a semi-autonomous status under the sovereignty of the Sultan as a result of the Treaty of Adrianople forced upon Turkey to end the Turco-Russian hostilities in 1829. The clauses of the Treaty pertinent to these provinces guaranteed them complete internal freedom, but, in a vaguely stated article, Turkey and Russia jointly reserved the right to maintain law and order if they agreed such intervention was necessary at any time. To make the conditions even more complicated, the Czar was granted the protectorate over the Orthodox Church on the grounds that the population was preponderantly Christian and stood in need of such paternal guardianship. Thus Czar Nicholas I had sufficient legal grounds for concern in whatever transpired in these territories that stretched along the northern banks of the Danube and the western side of the Pruth, but he did not have the primary right to interfere, as it was expressly recognized by the terms of the Treaty that ultimate sovereignty over the territories was vested in the Ottoman Sultan. As practical recognition of that sovereignty, the hospodars were required to pay a yearly tribute to the Porte.

Autocrat of all the Russians by Divine Right and Supreme Head of the Orthodox Church, Nicholas I sincerely and firmly believed that the least questioning of authority was tantamount to political revolution and religious heresy. He regarded it as his sacred duty to crush revolution wherever it appeared, and he was in the forefront of those who proclaimed that sovereigns had the duty to support one another in defense of that principle. It was not surprising, consequently, that when the ugly demon appeared so close to his own sacred soil and within the shadow of the imperial eagles, he decided upon immediate annihilation. It made no difference to him that the hospodars were not hereditary sovereigns but elected princes, chosen for life by the aristocracy. An assault against them was an affront to the principle of absolutism which he could not tolerate, and he instructed his ambassador at the Porte to inquire, not about the advisability or relevancy of military occupation, which he took for granted, but about the method to be employed.

Upon receipt of this inquiry the Turks turned to Canning for advice. It was the first time he would be brought into direct conflict with the Czar, for despite years of cautious observation of Romanov pretensions, he had not yet found himself faced with an occasion to contravene Russian wishes. On the contrary, he often had acted in close co-operation with them: in the early years against the machinations of Bonaparte; in the days preceding and following Navarino; during the era of Egyptian expansion; in the Persian boundary dispute; on the apostasy question; and on a host of minor matters. It so happened that what was best for Turkey in each of these instances coincided, in his judgment, with the momentary desires of the Court of St. Petersburg, whatever its motives.

Canning saw beyond the façade of the issue of the Danubian principalities a wish on the part of the Czar to be within striking distance of Hungary where a determined effort of the revolutionaries was imperiling the hold of the Hapsburg dynasty. Now Sir Stratford had no sympathy for radicals and revolution as such, but the Hungarian uprising was nationalist in character, and many of the country's finest aristocrats and leaders were playing a decisive role in the struggle. They had already declared their independence of Vienna and had achieved striking success. Much as he realized the necessity of a strong Austria to preserve the European balance (and in this, of course, he but echoed Lord Palmerston), he could not look with equanimity on the prospect of a Russian army's moving up the Danube Valley to crush the rebellion from the rear. There was also the danger that a Russian occupation of the principalities would become a permanent one, which meant the possibility of a conflict with Turkish troops and further encroachment on Ottoman sovereignty. Thus he recommended to the Turks that they avoid the expedient of military occupation except as a last resort. He suggested that they advise the Czar to the effect that the Sultan, until he knew better, regarded the Wallachian insurgents as mere political reformers who could best be dealt with by a civil commission of investigation.

The Turks followed this advice, but in their simplicity did not sense the importance of strictly attending to it. On the fourteenth of July—and this was before Reshid was back in full control—a body of troops moved across the Danube to be in position should a summons come from the commissioner in Bucharest. They were in no sense an occupying force, but the bare movement was sufficient signal for the

Russians to take corresponding measures, and the next day several thousand Russians crossed the Pruth and took up stations in Moldavia. Incidents occurred between the local populace and troops of both armies. Headstrong nationalists provoked skirmishes whenever and wherever they could, and as the instances multiplied, the Russian demands increased in severity. The Czar wanted to make a terrifying example of the insurrectionists while the Porte held out for leniency and compromise. In response to popular demand the Sultan's government expressed the intent of incorporating some measure of redress in the general settlement; the Czar, by contrast, responded with an unqualified refusal to meet any of the demands made under the banner of rebellion.

There were few real secrets kept in the Seraglio, and the Czar was well aware of Canning's constant guidance behind the scenes. The intransigence of the Turks he attributed not to their own devices but to what he at first fancied, and later steadfastly believed, was a deep personal hatred for himself on the part of Stratford Canning. Nicholas concluded, with the agreement of his ministers, that this was so because he had not found other British statesmen with whom the Russians had contact subscribing to the inflexible policy of the Elchi.[3] It was not found at Whitehall, according to the Russian Ambassador to London, nor was it evident in the conduct and declarations of Canning's counterparts in Vienna or St. Petersburg. Thus the Russians must have decided that they could push with impunity, as Canning's position did not appear to have the backing of London.

In part they were correct. Canning knew that he and Palmerston did not hold the same views on the intermediate positions to be taken. Canning looked with apprehension at the presence of large Russian forces in the principalities, while Palmerston chose to ignore the immediate danger on the theory that the Czar was likely to overextend himself and become entangled in a web of his own spinning. But Canning was equally certain that there was no disagreement between himself and his superior on ultimate ends. This was an important distinction which the Russian government failed to make, and the error was to lead to a humiliation.

Correspondence between the two English statesmen at this time reveals that Canning was urging for more explicit assurances of support for the Turks from London. Obviously he was being pressured by his protégés for a defensive alliance as a price for continued Turkish resistance. He was supporting the request as being a measure within the confines of what the Turks might reasonably expect. Palmerston, removed from the daily immediacy of the problem and viewing it as part of a total European problem, looked upon compliance with such a request as something that would be needlessly provocative.[4]

The interchange of ideas, just as in earlier days, was largely academic, since the rapidly unfolding developments rarely allowed the anticipation of probabilities to keep pace with actualities. In spite of slow communications, nevertheless, each man was provided with a continued awareness of the final objectives. Hence, between Palmerston and Canning there was a mutual confidence regarding the other's instinctive reaction in the urgency of sudden crisis. In the ensuing year of 1849, a series of episodes proved that each man had been correct within the limits of his particular prognostication. True to Canning's fears, Russia showed no intention of withdrawing when the principalities were finally pacified. On the contrary, she proposed, in January, that a joint occupation of seven years be agreed to. In addition, she demanded permission for the passage of a punitive expedition into Hungarian Transylvania. The Turks rejected both proposals only to have the Russians defiantly ignore the objections by marching through the territory on a route of their own choosing.

Initially at least, Lord Palmerston's estimate of Russian capabilities proved to be true also, as the Hungarians, instead of being crushed, wheeled about and inflicted a severe defeat on the new enemy. The Russians fell back in the face of this unexpected blow, but the defeat, far from having the effect desired by Palmerston, only gave the Czar new grounds for prolonged operations. Nicholas rushed reinforcements into Moldavia, where bases and depots were established for a full-scale campaign in the spring. He increased his demands on the Turks for a convention or agreement of occupation and made it plain that, like it or not, they would face a large Russian army north of the Danube.

Palmerston reacted strongly to this turn of affairs and berated the Russian ambassador, Baron Brunnow, on the illegality of these measures. Unfortunately, because of the time-lag in communications, Palmerston's reaction came too late for the Turks. In light of his failure to extract the desired alliance from his home government, Canning was unable to hold the Turks in line any longer, and in April they entered into negotiations with a special envoy of the Czar.

Canning might have been expected to bow to the inevitable and remove himself from further participation in the affair, but he was under no illusion that this would be the end of the matter. On the contrary, he saw in the offing a new flood of Russian requirements awaiting only the conclusion of the campaign against the Hungarians. If he must accept the *fait accompli* of Russian occupation, he wanted to confine the legal limits of that occupation so that there would be no further usurpation of Turkish sovereignty. With some welcome assistance from the representative of the newly organized French government, he was able to induce the Turks to seek and obtain a softening of the harshest and most dangerous aspects of the Russian demands, and the resulting Act of Occupation stipulated that the armies of both countries would continue in the principalities for a time "for the maintenance of internal tranquillity and protection of the frontier." [5] The tenure of the hospodars was limited to seven years for the purpose of keeping them under stricter control of the supervisory powers, and the assemblies were suspended pending the study by civil commissions of an "organic reform" in the administration of the provinces.

The best Canning could say of the Act was that its terms "might have been worse," but in his foresight he had been able to keep out of the agreement any clause which might have legalized Russian activities against Hungary. By the omission of such a clause, Canning had gained two objectives: the preservation of the neutrality of Turkey should the insurrection in Hungary be successful and an independent state emerge, and, more important, the refusal to recognize the right of one state to cross the borders of a neighbor on the pretext of subduing rebellion in a third state. Canning, with regard to the latter objective, foresaw the eventual defeat of the Hungarians and the flight of their leaders. The Hungarian patriots and the Poles who had joined them had but one road of escape, and that was into Ottoman territory. If the Sultan had legalized, by his consent, Russian pretensions to enter Hungary by marching across his domain, it would be difficult to refuse to co-operate to the same extent should the remnants of the insurgent army retreat across his borders.

The wisdom of this move seems to have escaped the Russians in their haste for the immediate end they had in view, for although some minor figures of the revolt had already taken refuge in Ottoman territory, the Russian plenopentiary made no attempt to include this problem in the terms of the settlement. Canning did not think for a moment that the Russians intended to forgo punishment of the "criminals" and reasoned that they were counting on the ordinary procedure of extradition. He had so advised Palmerston and was equally certain that public opinion in England and the world would finally rouse itself from lethargy to protest.

Almost as predicted, the revolt was crushed, and through the weeks of August and September of 1849, several thousand refugees crossed the borders and sought sanctuary. They included Kossuth himself, Bem, Dembinski, and a score of other notables.[6] Within a matter of days the Austrian internuncio and the Russian ambassador at the Porte asked for their extradition as public criminals.

1. Churchill, *A History of the English-Speaking Peoples*, IV, 67. See also Yvonne Ffrench, *The Great Exhibition* (London: Harvill Press, 1950), pp. 3-6.

2. See the letter to Dr. MacGuffog, June 21, 1847, for relay to Reshid Pasha. (Lane-Poole, *op. cit.*, II, 160-62). Again, Canning's constant awareness of the real status of the reform movement is shown by his explicit reference to a time limit for his next residence in Constantinople: "It is agreed that I shall be free from the end of next year [1848], and much as I should be mortified in leaving Turkey for ever without the fulfillment of my hopes, I could not be expected to make a holocaust of all other views, and of the claims . . . of my family."

3. This is true. Palmerston was not aroused until the refugee crisis broke. (Cf. Temperley, *op. cit.*, pp. 259 ff.)

4. Cf. Lane-Poole, *op. cit.*, II, 182 ff.

5. *Ibid.*, p. 185.

6. See Temperley, *op. cit.*, p. 261.

XVI

THE legality of extradition, as it applied to murderers, brigands, and other criminals, had long been recognized by the law of nations. Turkey had specific treaty agreements with both the Austrian and Russian empires—an arrangement quite common between neighboring states—whereby the actual machinery of the process was formulated and defined. Tradition had limited the procedure to cases of ordinary criminals and offenders in time of peace, and no one in the civilized world considered Kossuth and his fellow patriots as falling within this classification. Thus the Turks sent a courteous note of refusal, phrased in consultation with the Elchi, to the Austrian and Russian representatives on the thirtieth of August. In it the Turks appealed to the requirements of their own honor as the determining criterion of their decision and pledged that the refugees would not be allowed to engage in any further conspiracy but would be disarmed and held to good conduct.

The guardians of absolutism had no intention of being so easily dissuaded from exacting cruel vengeance on those who had dared to take up arms against them. On the fourth of September a steamer entered the Bosporus from the Black Sea carrying Prince Michael Radzivil with an abrupt ultimatum from the Czar.[1] The Hungarians and Poles were to be surrendered at once or diplomatic relations would cease. Furthermore, pending their delivery to their masters, the escape of a single refugee would be taken as an act of war.

It was natural that the Divan and the Council should be panic-stricken. But the Buyuk Elchi was near at hand, and the inevitable call for help went out to his villa at Therapia. It was the moment of crisis when a resolute ambassador must be able to count on the backing of his superiors, and Canning knew well the fiber of the man who presided over the Foreign Office. He was confident that the might of Britain stood behind him and was able to instil this same confidence in the Sultan and Reshid. He assured them that if they were to be attacked for defending the interests of humanity, they could certainly count on the active aid of England. His French colleague echoed the same sentiments on behalf of France, and the Turks took heart.

Canning felt that a categorical refusal to comply with the ultimatum would have carried the most weight under the circumstances, but the Turks could not resist the temptation to evade. The Council, after several meetings, decided not to answer the envoys directly but to send a plenipotentiary to treat with the Czar himself. On September 10, they communicated this offer to Prince Radzivil for relay to St. Petersburg.[2]

Radzivil refused to receive the note, and there followed a week of ominous silence—a silence most unnerving to the Turks. It took all of Canning's restraint to hold them steadfast in their position, and even a mild threat that in yielding they might lose their close friendship with England. He put his assurances in writing the better to steel them and all but committed his country to war. He knew the Cabinet might repudiate him in spite of Palmerston, but had he not acted as he did, he knew the Porte would give in.[3]

The Russian answer came on September 17, when the flags were lowered at both the Austrian and Russian embassies and the missions departed without a farewell audience. On the very same day two urgent messages were dispatched from the Buyuk Elchi. One went to Admiral Sir William Parker, who commanded the Mediterranean squadron of Her Majesty's Navy, and warned him of the possible need for his fleet in the Dardanelles. The other message went to Lord Palmerston to apprise him of the newest move and ask for official endorsement: " . . . I felt that there was no alternative unattended with loss of credit and character," Canning wrote, "to say nothing of the unfortunate and highly distinguished men awaiting their doom . . . . The dishonour would have been *ours*, for everyone knows that even Reshid himself, with all his spirit and humanity, would not withstand the torrent without us . . . I am sure that you will feel the importance of coming to the rescue as far and as fast as you can."[4]

With that the Ambassador had gone to the limit of his authorization, indeed, a shade or two beyond it, and he thanked God that it was Palmerston with whom he was treating rather than the Earl of Aberdeen. Now he had to maintain an air of tranquillity for a minimum period of six weeks before he could receive a reply from London while at any moment the Czar might make a rash move. There were massive armies north of the Danube and a powerful fleet at Sebastopol within easy striking distance of the Bosporus and Constantinople.

Russian intemperance was not the sole danger he had to fear, for prudence required him to toe an extremely careful line with the Turks. Once he made a move such as he did, he found it necessary to exercise the utmost caution lest his nervous friends make more of it than was actually there. One day he would find them burrowing in the cushions, afraid to cast so much as a glance at the horizon, and he would have to remind them that he had summoned help. The next day they would just as likely be boasting of what they might do to the barbarian interlopers on their borders, whereupon Canning would have to give them strict warning that they do nothing rash that would rob them of English sympathy and destroy the possibility of assistance before the Western powers had time to assemble their forces.

His messages brought the instantaneous response he had hoped for. Sir William Parker, realizing the need for haste, weighed anchor at once and moved his fleet in the direction of the danger zone. He would not approach the Dardanelles without express orders from London, of course, but he advised the Admiralty that he would be in the immediate vicinity awaiting the necessary instructions. Ahead of him he sent his fastest frigate with a dispatch for Canning informing him of his action. The vessel arrived at the Bosporus on the third of October, when the suspense was becoming tortuous, and the news it brought was well timed to convince the Porte that the Elchi had not been chasing a will-o'-the-wisp.

In London, too, there was not a moment lost by Palmerston in translating the sympathy of people and government for the Hungarians and Poles into instantaneous action. The Cabinet of Lord John Russell ratified the proceedings without debate and sent immediate orders to Sir William Parker to move as directed by the Ambassador. Simultaneous response was sought for, and soon obtained, in Paris, and the two governments sent separate requests to the Austrian and Russian emperors that they desist in their pursuit of the patriots. Before sending these notes, however, Palmerston, leaving nothing to chance, sent his advices to Canning in triplicate by three separate messengers.[5] One of these left London on the second of October with immediate reassurances, another was directed to go by steamer from Marseilles on the seventh with further notices, and still a third was sent overland on the eleventh. All three messengers were ordered to use all possible speed on the journey, and the last one, the famous Captain Charles Townley of Byng Hall's *The Queen's Messenger,* rode day and night from Belgrade to Constantinople, 820 miles away, in five days and eleven hours. He was not the first to arrive, as the others had gotten through without mishap, but the speed of all three is indicative of the urgency impressed upon them by Palmerston.

By the end of October the two English statesmen, operating far apart from each other, had the situation well in hand. They now looked for the safest and quickest return to normalcy. They had not flinched from approaching the brink of war in order to preserve peace with honor, and their course was successful. Canning had made the emergency move on his own responsibility, and Palmerston had given him the fullest backing. Not only had he approved the action, but he had secured the support of the London Cabinet as well. Palmerston also had notified both Russia and Austria that England meant business, and in the face of this firmness the absolutist powers backed away from the precipice.

In St. Petersburg Nicholas I received Fuad Pasha with courtesy when the intentions of the English became known, and he indicated that a way could be found to solve the dispute. Later he was to withdraw the demand for extradition, but before his pacific mood became known at Constantinople an almost fatal slip occurred.

International treaty forbade the entrance of all foreign ships of war (except for dispatch vessels lightly armed) when

the Sultan was at peace.[6] For Turkey to disregard that convention would amount to a challenge to Austria and Russia.
Once the British fleet stood outside the Straits, Canning told
the Sultan and his ministers that they were not to ask for a
further approach unless the Russians reacted with force. On
the first of November a severe storm prompted Admiral
Parker to seek the permission of the Turkish authorities to
move his ships to a safe anchorage within the outer reaches
of the Dardanelles. The permission was given and Parker
moved in, with the doubtful assent of Canning. The Russian
ambassador, Titov, who was still resident in the capital despite
the rupture of relations, made a vigorous protest, and Canning
at once ordered Parker to withdraw. Palmerston subsequently
apologized to both Russia and Austria for the breach,[7] and
the incident was smoothed over.

What followed was largely anticlimactic, as the Czar
quickly lost interest in the refugees, and relations with the
Porte were renewed before the close of the year. Austrian
feelings were slower to soothe, and through the early months
of 1850 she still demanded virtual imprisonment of the
exiles, a demand which Canning refused to let the Turks
countenance. Eventually most of them returned home under
an Imperial (Austrian) amnesty while Kossuth and a few of
the leaders secured passports for admission to the United
States. They gradually departed from the scene.

Canning treasured a personal note he received from Kossuth
after the trouble was over:

I have my children again . . . .
They all find not enough words to praise the benevolent
kindness they met with at your Excellency's house. Myself
and my wife . . . will never cease to pray to God that
He may bless your noble lady, and you sir, for the consolation you afforded to our parental feelings.[8]

Palmerston drew an important lesson from the experience.
Previous to this crisis, he had continually counseled fore-
bearance in the matter of military support for the Sultan.
He feared that direct aid of this kind would tend to make
the Turks overreach themselves while it would, at the same
time, needlessly irritate the Russians. Now he was ready to
furnish the kind of help Canning had long been advocating.
He attested to this change of mind in a letter he sent to
Canning in October:

. . . Now is the time for the Turks to make all possible
improvements in their army, their navy, and their defences.
. . . If they wish for any British naval officers . . . , let
them ask and they shall have. . . . The considerations
which led me to think last year that it would be better
for them not to make such a request no longer exist, and
it might be well to strike the iron while it is hot. Upon
the same principle they ought to set to work and to put
the defences of the Bosphorus into good order without
delay . . . . [9]

1. In Temperley, *op. cit.*, p. 262, October 4 is the date given for
Radzivil's entry and October 7 for his audience with the Sultan. This
must be a printer's mistake, for a few lines further down the page we
find: " . . . the Turks remained firm so diplomatic relations were sus-

pended on September 17 . . . and Prince Radziwill steamed back up the Bosporus to Sebastopol."

2. Unknown to anyone, including Canning, the Sultan did actually send a representative, Fuad Pasha, to St. Petersburg.

3. Cf. letter from Palmerston, October 28, 1849, indicating the Foreign Secretary's awareness of Canning's position (Lane-Poole, *op. cit.*, II, 202).

4. Lane-Poole, *op. cit.*, II, 192.

5. According to Lane-Poole (*op. cit.*, II,194th n.), a Lt. Robbins left London on October 2, immediately after the decision of the Cabinet. Temperley (*op. cit.*, p. 263) says that notice was sent on October 7. It may be that the document dated October 7 is the one surviving in the archives.

6. Straits Convention of 1841.

7. Palmerston, by his apology, gained what he wanted: there was to be no interpretation of the Straits Convention by which a partial entrance would be permissible. Partial entrance by Russia would put her halfway down the Bosporus toward Constantinople. Better, in Palmerston's judgment, to have both ends completely sealed. (Cf. Temperley, *op. cit.*, pp. 266-67.)

8. Lane-Poole, *op. cit.*, II, 203.

9. *Ibid.*, p. 201.

XVII

THE eighteenth-month limit that Canning had set for his fifth residence at Constantinople had stretched into two years by the time the refugee question was settled. The final reforms he returned to accomplish were still as far off as ever.[1] But he had never completely abandoned his original objective even in the darkest moments of the preceding two years. In audience after audience he had hammered away on the same theme. Though he had to include reform as a secondary matter on these occasions and refer to it against the background of the international scene, he took advantage of every opportunity to allude to it. Sometimes he would hold it over their heads as the price of continued support; at other times, he would ascribe lack of energetic English assistance to Turkish failure to initiate those reforms desired by London.

He wrote to Palmerston that the Turks always listened avidly and promised much but did little. While they were engrossed, along with him, in the affairs of the Danubian provinces and terrified by threats of occupation, he could not wrest anything of consequence from them. Again and again Reshid and Rifat appealed to the existence of a revolutionary bloc in the shadow of the Seraglio itself led by no less a personage than Abdul Aziz, the brother of the Sultan. The island of reform was continually surrounded by a sea of enemies waiting to engulf it.

Despite the admitted resistance to innovation, the Elchi was convinced that with sufficient prodding the leadership of the Porte was strong enough to put at least some of the desired changes into effect. After the powerful demonstration of English support just given, he pressed on with renewed perseverance. At the close of the year 1850, he was able to look back on several distinct improvements. Four years after he had obtained some recognition for Protestant rights in 1846, he procured a firman, in November of 1850, which gave them legal status as a separate group and empowered them to name an agent to represent their interests at the Porte. The loathsome *harach* was partially abolished; instead of a head-tax on individuals, there was to be a tribute levied on religious communities as a unit. Mixed criminal courts were promised, in which not only Christian evidence was to be admitted but Christian magistrates as well as Moslem.

He was not exclusively concerned with the status of Christians. He secured another firman which forbade the transportation of Negro slaves in Turkish vessels. And in one of his letters he refers to the commencement of a system of macadamized roads as being of singular value in the good it could bring the internal administration of the Empire. The long list of benefits accruing to his mediation was something to be marveled at, but he found it personally disappointing that he had virtually to extort each one from unwilling fingers. "It is uphill work, requiring an immensity of patience," he complains in a letter to A. H. Layard, "and what is done bears no proportion to what remains to be done. . . . I would not lightly give up the task which Providence appears to have assigned to me. It seems, however, that the time is approaching when I shall either have obtained all the concessions which can possibly be obtained for a certain period, or be called upon to throw down my cards in despair." [2] The thought occurred to him that the Porte had been under too severe stress of late to undertake the broad social reconstruction entailed in his program and needed breathing space to assess its position and recast its plans for improvement. He suggested to Palmerston that the golden opportunity for a complete and fundamental renewal had slipped by and that for the present he would work for separate measures, leaving the whole in abeyance until the propitious time should present itself.[3]

The "golden opportunity" to which he referred was the excellent chance to nail down real reforms during the height of the Russian advance into the principalities. At Canning's prompting, the Sultan and Reshid had agreed then to sign a treaty of defensive alliance with England which would have included all the essential particulars of reform. But the Ambassador was rebuffed by London when he transmitted the offer, and, as the crisis dissolved, the convergence of circumstances necessary to pressure the Porte disappeared along with it. Six years, capped by a tremendous tragedy, were to pass before it became possible to exact similar arrangements.

The persistent roadblocks he encountered in Turkey were expected and bearable as long as he had support at the Foreign Office, and Palmerston was swinging more and more to a strategy identical to Canning's. The harmony was short-lived, however, for, once the emotional interest in the Hungarian refugees subsided, apathy toward foreign affairs again became the order of the day in England. Preparations for the Great Exhibition of 1851 absorbed the nation's attention to the exclusion of almost everything else. The Exhibition was the darling of the Queen, whose beloved Prince Albert was its guiding spirit, and it became the paramount interest of the Cabinet of Lord John Russell. Anyone who failed to share the enthusiasm generated for the new era, symbolized in the great Crystal Palace, was unwelcome in circles of influence and became the object of antagonism on the part of press and public.

Lord Palmerston was one of those whose fortunes thus went into decline. Although he tried to smother an actual antipathy to the commercial hysteria and its façade of international good will in deference to the Queen, he could not fully veil his opinion and seemed, at best, indifferent. When he expressed a concern that the influx of foreign visitors might include radicals and political malcontents capable of causing untold embarrassment to the Queen and her ministers, he was accused of trying to sabotage the whole project. The abuse to which he was subjected, as a result, caused the breach to widen between himself and the Prime Minister and led to his resignation in December of 1851.[4]

Palmerston's withdrawal from the government came at a time when the blue ribbon of the diplomatic service, the Embassy at Paris, was vacant. By all rights it should have been offered to Sir Stratford Canning, but because of his close connection with the discredited minister, it was not. To add insult to injury, the post was delegated to Lord Cowley, who had served his apprenticeship under Canning.

The injustice was glaring but might have been more palatable had it been allowed to pass without comment. On the contrary, it was sharpened by a weak letter of explanation from Lord Granville, who had taken Palmerston's place. The new Foreign Secretary felt a compulsion to acknowledge Canning's merited claim to the position but pleaded that the need for haste was the dominant reason for passing over him when the eligible candidates were being considered.[5]

Canning's natural impulse was to resign completely from the Foreign Service, but on reflection he felt that such a step would serve no purpose other than to close his career on an ignoble note. In addition to the considerations of his own dignity, he had too high a regard for the diplomatic service as a whole to degrade it to a level where it might appear subject to the whims of personal ambition or pique. Moreover, Canning was forced to admit to himself, he probably would have turned down the assignment rather than to abandon forever the possibility of carrying to a definite termination his still lively vision of Turkish reform and regeneration. His reply to Lord Granville was generous and open, frankly acknowledging that he would have welcomed the option of going to Paris as a mark of consideration deserved by him. Nevertheless, he pledged his continued loyalty and indicated his willingness to continue his service at the Porte.[6]

Ironically enough, the same delay in communications which was the alleged reason for his being passed over in the Paris appointment caused Granville's letter to reach him after the whole Russell government, the new Foreign Secretary included, had collapsed. There was no consolation in this, however, because this news contained an even crueller blow.

The evolving party realignments in Parliament had made it apparent for some time that the Whig government of Lord John Russell was living on borrowed time. Indeed, it had almost crumbled early in the preceding year (1851) but was saved by the indisposition of its presumed successors to be enmeshed in the nets of the Great Exhibition. Early in 1851, the leader of the Conservative opposition in Parliament, Lord Stanley, had written to Canning seeking to ascertain whether or not the Elchi would enter a Conservative Cabinet as Foreign Secretary should the change of ministry come to pass.[7]

In his reply Canning stated that he would regard the summons as a call to even greater duty than the sphere in which he was currently engaged. He made it perfectly clear that he understood the offer was provisional, being contingent upon the former's actual succession to office, and he signified his willingness to accept it should this come to pass.

For the reason stated above the Russell government survived for almost a year, finally collapsing in February of 1852, and Stanley, having succeeded to his father's earldom of Derby in the meantime, became the Prime Minister of the Queen. When the composition of the Cabinet was announced, the Earl of Malmesbury was named as the Foreign Secretary, although nothing had transpired to lead to the conclusion that Sir Stratford Canning had changed his mind.

Derby's letter of apology followed hard upon the bitter pill which Granville had awkwardly sent to the disillusioned statesman in Constantinople. The prescription was compounded of the same elements, and it had the same bitter taste. Time, the nobleman explained, was of the essence and "compelled me to apply at once to those upon the spot." Contrary to the usual procedure, the Earl indicated, the new ministry was formed and approved by the Queen within forty-eight hours of Derby's summons to the Palace, and the rapidity with which everything was accomplished produced, according to the new Prime Minister, "a most favorable impression on the public mind."

Regardless of the reasons, the rudeness of the double jolting could not be veiled, and Derby, sensible of the obvious hurt, sought to make amends by announcing to Canning that his first act as Prime Minister had been to propose to Her Majesty the elevation of her Envoy to the Sublime Porte to the peerage as a Viscount of the United Kingdom. Her Majesty, the Prime Minister assured Sir Stratford, had given her delighted assent to the proposal.[8]

There was, in this long-delayed honor, a possible hidden meaning which Sir Stratford Canning found quite inadmissible. Although he was uncertain in his own mind whether or not the multiplication of grievances was causing him to fancy another where none existed, he took pains, in his response, to dispel any illusions that might have arisen as to his future. He would accept the honor, he told Derby, as a reward for "past" service but certainly not as a substitute for "effective office," nor was it to be construed as "an honourable consignment to the shelf."[9]

Though he could be passed over at the pleasure of others, Canning had no intention of being retired against his own will. That decision, he had determined, would be one of his own time and his own choosing. The laurel wreath of the peerage was not to be looked upon as the conclusion of his public career, and he was fearful that an application for leave, submitted earlier to Granville, which Derby alluded to as having been already granted by Malmesbury, would be interpreted as signaling his readiness to retire. Canning suddenly found himself very unready to do so. A postscript to his letter of acceptance admonishes the Prime Minister that, should the occasion arise of referring to the matter in

Parliament, "His Lordship should place the matter before the public on its proper grounds."

Saddened by what he considered his failure at the Porte— though his departure brought tears to Moslem and Christian alike, both Turk and foreigner—and disheartened by a succession of false promises and shattered hopes, Stratford Canning left Constantinople, "perhaps for the last time," in June of 1852. The fact that he traveled under his new title of Viscount Stratford de Redcliffe[10] did not bring the satisfaction that should have attended it.

1. Cf. Bailey, *op. cit.*, p. 219: "The events of 1848, especially Russia's entrance into the Principalities while the rest of Europe suffered from national and social uprisings, tended to shift Englishmen from the thought of reform."

2. Lane-Poole, *op. cit.*, II, 213-14.

3. Letter to Palmerston, April 5, 1851, *ibid.*, p. 215.

4. See Ffrench, *op. cit.*, pp. 149 ff., for reference to Normanby incident.

5. Letter from Granville, February 5, 1852, Lane-Poole, *op. cit.*, II, 225.

6. Letter to Granville, March 4, 1852, *ibid.*

7. See correspondence between the two, March-April, 1851, *ibid.*, II, 220-22.

8. Letter from Derby, March 4, 1852, *ibid.*, 222-23.

9. Lane-Poole, *op. cit.*, II, 224.

10. From the Church of St. Mary Redcliffe in Bristol, which was built under the auspices of a fourteenth-century ancestor.

XVIII

QUITE unknown to himself, the curtains had already opened for the first scene in the climax of Stratford Canning's career. The players were remote from the central stage and the dialogue seemed unrelated to the whole drama, but the play itself turned on familiar themes: the conflict between absolutism and political freedom, the clash between autocracy and constitutional democracy, the struggle between oligarchic privilege and legal equality. Across the channel from England, the Second French Republic was being buried, and a Bonaparte was presiding over the obsequies.

Louis Napoleon, a nephew of the first Bonaparte, had been elected President of the Second French Republic after the Revolution of 1848. At the time he had given ample evidence of being a sincere and convinced believer in political democracy and republicanism. There is no question now, however, that from the very first he was intent on restoring the imperial glory of France under a Bonapartist dynasty, that he planned methodically and brilliantly to seize the power of France and make it his own. He frightened the conservative right, which was mostly monarchist in its sympathies, by continually unearthing "plots" and schemes of anarchists and socialists. He kept the republicans under his wing by appealing to the threat of a Bourbon restoration. Meanwhile he used with genius a small but disciplined island of Bonapartists to anchor himself in a sea of divergent parties and splinter causes. Slowly and quietly the Bonapartists were placed in key positions in the War Ministry, in the Ministry of the Interior, and in critical spots throughout the country. The favor of the anti-republican army, which had been roughly handled by the citizenry of Paris in '48, was carefully nurtured.

On the second of December, 1851, a cleverly planned coup d'état was executed with precision. Key members of any conceivable opposition were arrested and imprisoned; strategically located army units were moved into Paris; pressure was put on the remaining members of the National Assembly by the military; the constitution was duly suspended and martial law declared. All communications between Paris and the provinces were under the control of the Ministry of the Interior, and this ministry was safe in Louis' grasp. Proclamations of a gigantic plot against France were heard all over the country by the next day, and the necessity for M. le President to rule by decree was unquestioned.[1]

Of course, there was bloodshed in Paris as the tenacious and heroic people of that city recoiled from the bewildering shock, but the army was waiting and eager. Resistance was fierce but futile, and the blood ran in the streets to no purpose.[2] Before the month was over Louis Napoleon had been elected to a ten-year term as president, and a subsequent national plebiscite had restored the Empire of France. In deference to the wishes of his countrymen, Louis Napoleon consented to assume the imperial mantle of his uncle and to wear his crown. In a mark of respect to the memory of the tragic "eaglet," however, he insisted on being designated as Napoleon III. He began to reign, thus enobled, in December of 1852.

An absolutist requires personal glory and an emperor must needs have an imperial sway. If Louis Napoleon had laid his plans inside France with consummate care, he had not neglected to look outside as well. Ramifications of his coup were already being felt in the sphere of Stratford Canning. In the latter part of 1851, the French Ambassador at the Porte, De Lavalette, acting under instructions of President Napoleon, had suddenly suggested to the Porte the reactivation of a century-old treaty[3] appertaining to the shrines in the Holy Land, whereby Christians of the Latin rite were assured of free usage of the sacred places connected with the earthly life of Jesus Christ. Superficially considered, the request was simple and innocent and, in normal conditions, would have called for a proportionately simple affirmative response from the Turks. The circumstances, however, were far from normal.

In the first place, the original treaty had been concluded in 1740 with the France of Louis XV, and history has recorded the tremendous changes effected in century that followed. France moved from a monarchy with a state religion all the way to official atheism at the depths of revolutionary chaos, back to agnosticism and indifference. There was absolutely no interest shown in the shrines at the cradle of Christianity.

Russia, in the same century, had become an empire, and her concern for Christianity in the realms of the Sultan had increased in direct proportion to French neglect. More than that, the Russian state church was doctrinally and liturgically connected with the overwhelming majority of the Porte's Christian subjects, and from the time of Catherine the Great the rulers of Russia had claimed to be the protectors of the millions of Christians within the Ottoman Empire. Further still, by lack of counterclaim on the part of any other Christian power, this status had, at least, the force of immemorial custom. It had been recognized and acceded to by the Porte in countless instances,[4] and a long chain of imperial firmans and vezirial letters were extent in testimony to this fact. These decrees had gradually put the Holy Places in complete control of the Greek Church, and the small handful of Latin Christians in Jerusalem and the vicinity entered these shrines only at the sufferance of the Greek Patriarch and the monks who administered them. The Latin pilgrims who trickled in from western Europe were similarly

subject to the overriding convenience of the droves of Orthodox visitors whose needs and desires were given precedence.

This arrangement would be threatened if the terms of the
ancient treaty were to be enforced in compliance with French
demands, for it would entail a complete reversal and put the
administration of the Holy Places under control of the Latins
or, at best, make them coequal to the Greeks in a way that was
completely out of proportion to their numbers.

Now if this overturning of the existing situation affected
local sensibilities alone it would have been serious enough
for the Porte to grapple with, but it went far beyond that.
To acquiesce in French demands implied the annulment of
decrees and pledges made at the behest of a succession of Rus-
sion czars. In short, it involved a serious affront to the dignity
of Nicholas I, both as emperor and head of the Church.

It must be remembered that this proposition was advanced
when Nicholas had barely had a chance to recover from the
indignity of his defeat in the Hungarian refugee crisis. Only
the most naïve initiate into the European scene could have
contemplated his indifference to this added slap, and Louis
Napoleon was neither naïve nor a newcomer.[5] De Lavalette,
of course, took whatever pains were neecssary to be certain
that the Russian Embassy would hear of his demands and, to
no one's surprise, the Russian Ambassador entered a forceful
protest against any change in the status quo.

The poor Turks were in another quandary. They could
not placate France without offending Russia. They could not
bow to Russia without abrogating treaty obligations to France.

Canning was still resident in Constantinople when this freshest dispute had arisen, but he was momentarily expecting a summons to assume the direction of the Foreign Office. He was trying to conclude his affairs at the Porte and did not wish to add to his burdens. Moreover, as the motives behind the French request were hidden from him as much as from everyone else, he did not attach any great significance to the matter.

When, however, De Lavalette became somewhat menacing in his words and mentioned the possibility of French naval action along the coast of Tunis, it was quite natural for the Turks to seek the advice of the Elchi. Since there was a legal basis for the representations made by France, Canning saw no harm in concurring with the decision already made by the Porte to acknowledge their validity. A note was issued to the French on February 9, 1852, which granted to the Latin monks two keys to the main door of the church in Bethlehem and a key to the grotto of the Manger.

Sensing a probable Russian demurrer to this step, the poor Turks had a firman waiting to mollify the Czar. When the expected protest materialized, they blithely issued this document on February 15. It proclaimed that the privileges recently granted the Latins were in no way to detract from the existing status and administration of the shrines in question— a remarkable contradiction of the French note. The firman noted that an exhaustive study of all pertinent documents had been made—and there were many, going as far back as the

seventh century—and that the firman was the definite will of
the Sultan. The Porte also assured the Russian Ambassador
that somehow or other the Pasha of Jerusalem would avoid an
actual transfer of keys to the Latins!

A ready answer was at hand, too, for the certain storm of
protest to come from De Lavalette on this one. He was told
that although the firman was issued, it would not be read in
Jerusalem. A firman affecting a local situation was not considered to have the force of law until it was read to the pasha,
the cadi, and councillors of the place. "So the Latins had
received a key which was not to open a door, and the Greeks
had received a firman which was not to become law."[6]

By this time the Divan was deep in a morass of evasion.
Then the Sultan hit upon the scheme of moving the dispute
from his doorstep to the scene of conflict. He informed the
several ambassadors that a commissioner would be sent to
Jerusalem to confer with all concerned and arrive at a solution.

Canning hoped that the transfer of negotiations to the soil
trod by the Prince of Peace Himself would bring the two
Christian powers to their senses and put an end to the scandalous nonsense. Confident that good will would prevail, he
left Constantinople in June and returned to England and
peerage.

France kept up an incessant pressure, however. De Lavalette had hurried home for consultations after the Greek firman
and made his return passage up the Straits in a ninety-gun,
three-decker screw steamer, hardly within the classification

of a "lightly armed dispatch ship." The lesson was not lost on anyone, and Russia, Austria, and England all entered vigorous protests. France apologized according to form, but she had made her point. The Turks were quite impressed, not with the apology, but with the demonstration. The swift passage of the heavily armed steamship made them weigh the relative strength of France and Russia. Later on, in July, a French squadron appeared in the harbor of Tripoli (Syria) demanding the surrender of two deserters.[7] When the ships stripped for action, the Pasha meekly surrendered the pair, and another show of force paid immediate dividends.

The Turkish commissioner, Afif Bey, arrived in Jerusalem in October and late in the month assembled the disputants, including a Russian consul-general, in the Church of the Virgin at Gethsemane. The Russian official was on hand to certify to the reading of the firman, but instead of the firman the assemblage heard a speech permitting the Latins to celebrate Mass once a year in that shrine on condition that they make no change in the liturgical appointments of the altar. A cry of rage went up from the Latins over the impossibility of such a procedure, and a riot broke out. Afif Bey apparently gave up in disgust and left, hastening all the way back to Constantinople a few days later.

Whether the riot was provoked by Turkish design or not, the firman, at all events, had not been read, and in December the silver star of France was solemnly placed in the Church of the Nativity at Bethlehem, with local Turkish dignitaries very much in attendance.[8]   A set of keys was given to the Latin monks and the degradation of the Orthodox was a fact.

A constant flow of reports heaped one doleful notice after another on the desk of Nicholas I, and the growing weight became more than he could tolerate.   On December 30, he ordered two army corps to the frontiers of the Danubian provinces.   Count Nesselrode wrote to Baron Brunnow, who represented the Czar at the Court of Queen Victoria: "The mischief is then done . . . and there is no longer any question of preventing it.   It is now necessary to remedy it.   The immunities of the orthodox religion which have been injured, the promise . . . which has been violated, call for an act of reparation.   It is to obtain this we must labor."[9]   These were not empty words.   A new set of circumstances had emerged which the Czar and Nesselrode saw as being all to their advantage, and they were confident that Russia could gain the reparation that Nesselrode referred to.

The brightest spot on the Russian horizon was a ministerial change in London, where the Derby Cabinet fell in the same month of December.   The apparent successor was a ministry being formed by none other than the Earl of Aberdeen.   Now Aberdeen was a deeply religious man and a public champion of peace.   He was much to the Czar's liking.   More particularly appealing to Russian policy was the pointed relegation of Palmerston to a back seat in the Home Office.   As if this were not delightful enough, the news of the Cabinet change was capped by the dizzying revelation that Viscount Stratford de Redcliffe had seen the handwriting on the wall and had resigned his embassy to the Porte.

With Palmerston and Canning both removed from his path, Nicholas anticipated little difficulty in managing Aberdeen.[10] Brunnow had already reported to the Czar that Aberdeen was nervous about the intentions of the new French Emperor.[11] Thus Nicholas saw an opportunity to break England away from France, especially on the Eastern question.

By vagueness, if nothing else, Lord Aberdeen had already been instrumental in allowing Czar Nicholas to form a fixed misconception of English policy. Nicholas was a firm believer in personal diplomacy, that is, in his own personal diplomacy. He seems to have been unable to comprehend the difference between the personal assurances of an absolute monarch and the comments of a minister in a constitutional democracy.[12] He believed that he had a firm understanding with Aberdeen on the question of Turkey. The Czar's misapprehension arose in the course of a state visit he had paid back in 1844 to the Court of the youthful Victoria. In a series of talks with Sir Robert Peel, then the Prime Minister, Aberdeen, who was Foreign Minister, and the Duke of Wellington, Nicholas had aired his conviction that the Ottoman Empire was fast approaching dissolution. He suggested that there ought to be an agreement between Russia, England, and Austria as to what should take place in that eventuality—and he claimed to be speaking for Austria both by virtue of treaty obligations[13] and personal agreement between himself and the

Austrian emperor. Apparently he concluded that the English statesmen found no objection in principle to such an understanding, for his verbal approach was later put into writing and a memorandum was sent by Nesselrode to Aberdeen in December of that same year. In the Nesselrode Memorandum the Czar's position is reiterated in plain language, and this statement is found:

> This notion was in principle agreed upon during the Emperor's last residence in London. The result was the eventual engagement if anything unforeseen occurred in Turkey, Russia and England should previously concert together as to the course which they should pursue in common.[14]

Nothing had been done to counteract the impression left in Nicholas' mind that this "gentlemen's agreement" was binding. The recollection of these talks burned brightly in the Czar's mind as Aberdeen came to power, and he was to return to them again and again in the course of the coming year.

Another auspicious event coincided with this happy outcome on the London front. An outbreak of rebellion against the Turks in Montenegro was churning the waters in the Balkans. The usual barbarous excesses which resulted whenever the Balkan mountaineers and Turkish soldiers met in combat had compelled an Austrian intervention. Austria mobilized a small force on the border and was sending a plenipotentiary, Count Leiningen, to the Porte to mediate the dispute and seek restraint on the part of the Turkish soldiery.

Now if Nicholas had presumed to speak for Austria in his conversations with the English Cabinet in 1844, when the illustrious Metternich was still in the saddle, then he had assumed what amounted to a paternal responsibility for the young Francis Joseph after the revolution of '48. His intervention in the Hungarian revolt bears witness to this assumption of protective responsibility.[15] The prospect of unilateral Austrian intervention in the Montenegrin crisis at the beginning of 1853 was both inviting and somewhat disturbing. It was inviting because Nicholas could associate himself with the action and use it as a pretext for gaining the desired reparation of the insult he had just suffered over the Holy Places. On the other hand, he was disturbed by this unlooked for independence of action by Vienna. Such independence could threaten his presumption of primary responsibility for the Christian subjects of the Porte.

The question of these subjects was, of course, very much in his mind. The Holy Places dispute had raised it again, and the Czar was excited by the sudden emergence of support from an unexpected quarter. Reshid Pasha, formerly Stratford Canning's prize tool at the Porte, had begun to make secret overtures to St. Petersburg. He suggested to the Russian court that it might base its claims with respect to the Holy Places on certain articles in the old Treaty of Kustchuk-Kainardji. Those articles, Reshid intimated, gave the Russian

Czar a right to consider himself as the protector of all the Orthodox Christian subjects of the Porte.[16]

Without bothering to check the provisions of the Treaty carefully, Nicholas made up his mind to act. He decided to send a plenipotentiary to the Porte to back up the Austrian demands and to obtain redress on the matter of the Holy Places. The Imperial Russian representative was to secure a new firman guaranteeing existing Greek privileges. He was to offer to the Porte, if need be, a defensive alliance against French threats. Most important of all, he was to extract a second firman from the Sultan guaranteeing for the future full privileges to Orthodox Christians in the Ottoman Empire and acknowledging Russia's right to protect them. The right of protection was to be "embodied in a Sened, or Convention, having the force of a Treaty."[17]

To execute this plan Nicholas I chose one of his most trusted lieutenants, and one of the most devout Orthodox laymen, the Lord High Admiral, sometime Governor of Finland, his serene Highness, Prince Alexander Sergeievitch Menshikov. He was ordered to proceed to Constantinople in February and to leave it in three days if his demands were not met.

1. For a vivid account of Louis Napoleon's history and the details of the coup d'état see Kinglake, *The Invasion of the Crimea* (6 vols.; New York: Harper and Bros., 1864), I, 142-209.

2. Estimates vary from several hundred to several thousand dead. Temperley (*op. cit.*, p. 290) says merely that "the Paris boulevards were red with blood and the ablest Frenchmen were in gaol."

3. The Treaty of Capitulation of 1740, by which the Porte recognized the right of France to safeguard Latin rights in the Holy Land.

4. Principally, by the Treaty of Kustchuk-Kainardji, July, 1774. Russia's stand was based on an interpretation of Articles 7 and 14 of the Treaty, an interpretation that broadened considerably as the dispute progressed. (Cf. Hurewitz, *op. cit.*, I, 55 ff.)

5. French motives in raising the question at this time are a matter of some dispute. I have adopted Kinglake's view (as developed in his aforementioned work) that Napoleon wished to have an external irritant available in order to divert the French people from any subsequent reappraisal of his coup. Temperley's judgment that "the Prince-President would not have raised the question of the Holy Places at all but for his desire to secure the political support of the Catholics" (*op. cit.*, p. 280) seems to me an oversimplification. For it raises the question: Which Catholics? The French Church was badly split at the time on political, social, and ecclesiastical policies. It was rent by the ultramontanist-Gallican controversy, deeply divided on the matter of De Lamennais and his *Avenir* circle. To suppose that it could have suddenly formed a unity on such an obscure matter as the Holy Places seems unreasonable. An astute politician—and no one denies that Louis Napoleon was astute— would hardly have known which group to seek out. The only sources cited by Temperley are contemporary and local accounts which seem to be too full of anti-Jesuit bias to make them trustworthy. At the end of his notes on the matter Temperley seems to admit the lack of good sources when he says: "The French political side of the Holy Places dispute is hardly touched by Jean Maurain in 'La Politiqut ecclésiastique du second Empire de 1852-69,' Paris, 1930. But he leaves no doubt that the inspiration was Catholic and Jesuit."

Furthermore, Temperley's explanation glosses too easily over Napoleon III's relations with the Vatican, where he was most suspect. He had taken part in an early Carbonari insurrection against papal authority (cf. Sophie de Buxhoeveden, "Bonapartes and Carbonari," *Dublin Review*, April, 1944, p. 153 f.). He was known to be for a united Italy (under French hegemony if possible, but in any case to use against Austria), and it is highly doubtful that the Vatican would have listened eagerly to any scheme proposed by him. As a matter of fact, he was unable to persuade Pope Pius IX to come to Paris to place the Imperial Crown of France upon his brow. Temperley's readiness to interpret the affair as he does becomes even more mystifying when he adds (*op. cit.*, p. 284): "The

Pope . . . saw the need of conciliating the ultramontane party." The ultramontanists were the extreme supporters of papal supremacy so the Pope would hardly have had to conciliate them! Moreover, the Vatican had lately been making overtures to the Orthodox Churches in the interest of unity and would hardly have been willing to embitter them by taking part in such a silly dispute.

Finally, Temperley seems to contradict himself and to accept Kinglake's theory when he says: "On December 4, 1852, Napoleon attained the summit of his ambitions and was solemnly proclaimed Emperor of the French. He had no longer the same need to pursue a dangerous foreign policy" (op. cit., p. 297).

6. Temperley, op. cit., p. 291. Cf. also the account in Kinglake, op. cit., I, 46-55.

7. Temperley, op. cit., pp. 292-93, for an account of both incidents.

8. Cf. Kinglake, op. cit., I, 52-54.

9. Quoted in ibid., p. 54.

10. Cf. Temperley, op. cit., p. 299.

11. Ibid., pp. 298-99. The Czar, in fact, interpreted Aberdeen's fear of Napoleon III as a symptom of the cowardice and weakness of England.

12. See ibid., chap. x: "How Nicholas Negotiated."

13. Treaty of Munchengratz, September, 1833. Cf. Hurewitz, op cit., I, 107.

14. For the complete text, see Hurewitz, op. cit., I, 130-32.

15. It is worth noting here, in view of subsequent developments, that at the time of Russian intervention in '48, Metternich's successor, Schwartzenberg, said that "Austria will surprise the world with her ingratitude" (quoted in Vernadsky, op. cit., p. 154.)

16. It is not clear just what Reshid hoped to accomplish. Out of office, disillusioned over the failure of reform, and embittered toward those he felt responsible for the failure, he may have been seeking his own restoration by turning to Russia, or perhaps it was simple revenge. At any rate he had become personally weak and dissipated. Cf. Temperley, op. cit., p. 244.

17. Ibid., p. 306.

XIX

THE tempest brewing in the shadows of Hagia Sophia was not yet a matter of breakfast-table comment in England, but the Parliamentary murmur was beginning. The obvious disadvantage of feeble representation at the Porte was abundantly clear. An embassy under the direction of a chargé d'affaires could not claim to be heard with the consideration that protocol afforded to envoys enjoying higher status, nor could the Sublime Porte look upon a power thus represented in a moment of crisis as one which was greatly concerned about Turkish affairs. Already voices were heard in Parliament asking whether anyone but the Buyuk Elchi himself was fit to step in. The prospect was distasteful to the Cabinet, but the decision was unavoidable. Reluctantly, Lord Aberdeen and Lord Russell, the Foreign Secretary, requested Viscount Stratford de Redcliffe to forgo the pleasures of "honourable retirement" and to resume his post in Constantinople.

Canning had resigned his post in January, 1853, upon the accession of the new ministry. At the age of sixty-six he had no disposition to be treated like a schoolboy, nor did he relish the prospect of an open rupture with a government of the kind he felt Lord Aberdeen would lead. His retirement had been fortunate because when he was recalled to duty in less than six weeks he was able to respond on his own terms. The instructions which he received on February 25, 1853, were couched in his own language, for they were "largely borrowed" from his own memorandum.[1] The instructions were very general, and thus he had the latitude to choose his own method of operation. He was to strive for an equitable solution to the dispute of the Holy Places in a manner which he was to decide after he had acquainted himself with all points of view. In order to prepare himself more surely he was to travel by way of Paris and Vienna so that he might know the attitudes of the French and the Austrians. He was to refresh them, in turn, with a restatement of Britain's aim: the maintenance of equilibrium in the East.

To the Porte he was to indicate what co-operation was required in order that she might merit the friendly consideration of Europe. At the very least this demanded resolute and immediate reform along the lines laid down for many years: strict justice and equality for all its citizens so as to preclude forever the occasions for foreign intervention.

The only specific direction in the instructions stated

that in the event of imminent danger to the existence of the Turkish Government your Excellency will in such a case despatch a messenger to Malta, requesting the Admiral to hold himself in readiness, but you will not direct him to

approach the Dardanelles without positive instructions from
Her Majesty's Government.[2]

The annex is curious in that it supplied him with a pitiful
amount of pressure when compared with the tremendous
arrays at the disposal of Prince Menshikov and Count Leiningen. Later allegations represented this direction as an instrument of restraint imposed upon him to guard against any
impetuosity on his part. But this is unlikely, for then one must
assume that the Cabinet had entrusted a delicate mission to
one in whom they had little confidence. Actually it was
common in ambassadorial commissions and was most likely
inserted by mutual consent. Both Canning and Aberdeen
believed, at this time, that the whole problem was a minor
dispute that had, somehow or other, gotten absurdly out of
hand. All that was needed was a calming influence, and
neither considered fleet movements as necessary. Canning
had been armed with even stronger power in 1849 and had
usd it with consummate skill. He did not consider this crisis
nearly so dangerous.

Aberdeen and the Cabinet should have realized that it was
far more serious, for they had already received the first of
Sir Hamilton Seymour's urgent messages from St. Petersburg
and were in a position to interpret the Czar's mind more
exactly than Canning.[3] Certainly the Cabinet knew that the
Czar was thinking of more than the keys to the shrines in
Jerusalem. In that respect Canning went out ignorant of
the true nature of the enemy he was to meet.

He departed for Paris as quickly as he could, and further evidence that he viewed his assignment as temporary is the fact that Lady Stratford and his daughters remained at home. Otherwise his entourage included a formidable array of tried and trusted assistants: Alison, Pisani, and Layard, who, though a Member of Parliament at the time, begged to accompany the group as an observer.

In the midst of his conferences in the French capital he found time to write to Lady Stratford about the prospects for a settlement:

> France, I think, is inclined to move with us, and I question whether Russia even is ready to bring on a crisis, provided she be satisfied, which is by no means impossible, with respect to the Holy Places. . . . [4]

His confidence that the Czar could be placated arose, undoubtedly, from his exchanges with the newly crowned Emperor of the French. As he wrote in a memorandum to Clarendon:

> He spoke of the Holy Places . . . . He desired nothing better than to finish the affair. He was not disposed to make difficulties . . . and he would not object to the maintenance of the Sultan's firman [reaffirming Greek privileges], supposing France to retain what had been previously accorded.[5]

He felt that Louis Napoleon had derived satisfaction from being treated by England on a basis of equality with her

Queen and that the minutiae of a settlement in the East no longer concerned him. He wrote, on March 14, 1853, in a particularly shrewd report to Clarendon: "The impression left upon my mind . . . is that Louis Napoleon, meaning to be well with us, at least for the present, is ready to act politically in concert with England . . . . " But then he added a prophetic note of caution:

> As it appears, moreover, that the maintenance of his own personal position is the mainspring of his policy, . . . he [cannot] be expected to abstain from any attempt required in his judgment by the circumstances of the time to consolidate his power or to avert any danger that may threaten its continuance. It may, therefore, be doubted whether his coöperation even in the East can be accepted by us without some shades of caution; nor would it apparently be safe to rely upon his goodwill . . . . [6]

His misgivings about the dependability and direction of French policy were soon to receive a rude confirmation, although some time was to pass before he learned it. When he left Paris for Vienna he was necessarily out of contact with events. Telegraphic communication was just linking major cities at the time, and there were no intermediate exchanges on his route. A railway breakdown, adding to the normal delays caused by late winter snows, impeded his journey across southern Germany, and it was nearly the end of March when he arrived in Vienna. He felt this absence of news keenly, too, as witnessed by a letter to his wife written during one of these delays:

As for me, when I am not reading or sleeping, and at times
when I am, my thoughts are divided between London and
Paris, Vienna and Constantinople. . . . I am very anxious
to know more and to be on the spot. At Vienna we shall
probably get some further intelligence.[7]

The "further intelligence" which he anticipated would be
forthcoming at Vienna was, initially at least, most welcome.
Despite some smoldering resentment over the "Kossuth affair," his reception at court was hospitable and courteous,
and he was pleased to learn from the Emperor, Franz Joseph,
and the Foreign Minister, Count Buol, that the Montenegrin crisis had been satisfactorily settled. The facility with
which the Porte and Vienna had come to terms, incidentally,
strengthens the conjecture that the Hapsburg court was already looking askance at the extension of Russian interest in
the direction of the western Balkans, an area which Austria
regarded as being exclusively within her own sphere of influence. The sending of Prince Menshikov to the Porte,
ostensibly to back up the mission of Count Leiningen, implying that Austria lacked sufficiency of strength and purpose
to bear her own burdens vis-à-vis the Porte, apparently did not
sit well with the Austrians, either. All in all, it appeared to
Canning that Czar Nicholas had unwittingly, by his forward
action, hastened a *modus vivendi* in Montenegro. One of
the avowed grievances of the Menshikov mission was thereby
disposed of.

But this welcome turn of events was counterbalanced by
a disturbing communication from Lord Clarendon in London.

The Foreign Secretary reported that the Porte had suddenly been seized by some fright upon the arrival of Menshikov in Constantinople and had asked for an appearance of French and British warships at the entrance to the Dardanelles. The British chargé d'affaires, Colonel Rose, had presumed to transmit this request to the British admiral at Malta who, wisely, had refused to move except upon express orders from London. These orders, of course, were not given, but the French fleet did sail to the Bay of Salamis. Clarendon described the French decision as "precipitate": obviously, it would ruffle the Czar's sensibilities. There was no doubt in the Foreign Secretary's mind that the development was, in some way, connected with Menshikov, although he discounted the seriousness of the situation: "After all the solemn and personal assurances given to us by the Emperor of Russia, . . . we do therefore believe that the independence and integrity of the Turkish Empire are not endangered by the mission of Prince Menshikov."[8] Canning was urged to proceed posthaste to Constantinople.

Canning was now in a quandary. In the first place, he knew nothing of the "solemn and personal assurances" given by the Czar in connection with the Menshikov mission. These assurances, of course, were being given to Sir Hamilton Seymour, the British ambassador in St. Petersburg, and they were being kept secret by London. Yet it was obvious that there was more involved than what met the eye. Secondly, he could not divine the motives of Napoleon III. Thirdly, he feared a grave mistake on the part of his own government in

London in that Clarendon was apprehensive over future Russian moves *only* as they might come in reaction to the French
naval display. Canning was beginning to sense that Russian
plans were quite independent of any other events. In a reply
to Clarendon he echoed the Foreign Secretary's dismay over
the provocative act of the French but coupled with it an al-
lusion to ulterior Russian motives:

> Russia, without meaning downright mischief just now, is
> probably seeking to restore her old prepotential influence,
> and unfortunately France has given her the opportunity.
> She has the vantage ground with respect to the Holy Places,
> and there would be little wisdom in tempting her further.[9]

Canning was not even sure where the final sympathies of
Aberdeen and Clarendon would lie, but he added the last
sentence because of an editorial in the London *Times* which
he saw in Vienna and interpreted as a possible expression of
support for Russia in the matter of the shrines. He added
this searching comment, as if to evoke some response: "She
[Russia] will, however, in my humble judgment, require to
be closely looked after, especially as she has found so able an
advocate in the *Times*."

He spent no more time than protocol demanded in Vienna,
and heedless of the deep snows, the sixty-six-year-old diplomat
journeyed across the Alpine passes to take ship at Trieste.
He crowed rather triumphantly about this: "I am too old and
tough to be the worse from this, but younger constitutions
find it trying."[10] By the time he boarded H.M.S. "Fury" in

Trieste on Wednesday, March 30, 1853, much of the mystery
had been cleared away, for Stephen Pisani had come to meet
him from Constantinople and was able to report that Menshikov was demanding more than a mere settlement of the Holy
Places dispute. The Porte had admitted this much though
it refused to tell the dragomans the exact nature of the demands. Canning felt a kind of kinship to David on his way
to meet Goliath, as he indicated to his wife in this final letter
of the journey:

> The Russian demands and accompanying demonstrations
> seems to mean the acquirement once for all of a preponder-
> ating influence . . . or some act of territorial encroach-
> ment by way of substitute. . . . The prospect is more than
> enough to make one nervous; but there is hope to be de-
> rived from the best of books, and possibly a pebble from
> the brook by the wayside may be found once more the
> most effectual weapon against an armed colossus. My pebble
> is the simple truth . . . . [11]

On the morning of April 5, 1853, the "Fury" dropped anchor
off the Golden Horn and the Elchi, Viscount Stratford de
Redcliffe, was back at the palace of the British Embassy. As
one historian has put it, "It was the angry return of a king
whose realm had been suffered to fall into danger."[12]

---

1. Lane-Poole, *op. cit.*, II, 234, quoting Clarendon. The instructions
were signed by Clarendon because he had replaced Russell in the Foreign
Office in the interval between Canning's summons and the date of the
instructions. Lord Russell remained in the Cabinet as a minister without
portfolio.

2. *Ibid.*, p. 235.

3. Cf. chap. XXI below, on the Seymour Correspondence.

4. Lane-Poole, *op. cit.*, II, 236.

5. *Ibid.*, pp. 236-37.

6. *Ibid.*, pp. 238-39.

7. *Ibid.*, pp. 240-41.

8. *Ibid.*, p. 240.

9. *Ibid.*, p 244.

10. *Ibid.*

11. Letter to Lady Stratford, April 4, 1853, *ibid.*, p. 244.

12. Kinglake, *op. cit.*, I, 128. Temperley says that Canning still knew of no Russian danger. Not from his London advices, it is true, but the dragoman had brought him disturbing news, as the letters to his wife show.

XX

PRINCE Menshikov had arrived more than a month prior to Canning's appearance. Ostentatiously following in his train, and to all intents and purposes under his direct command, was a large staff of military officers including the commander-in-chief of the Black Sea fleet and the chief of staff of the army group poised along the Pruth. Whatever his diplomacy was to be, it would be highly colored by military hues.

In order to give an immediate and forceful demonstration of his determination, he brushed aside the nicety of protocol that required him to wait upon the convenience of the Reis Effendi and demanded an immediate audience with the Grand Vezir. The Turkish ministry at this time was led by Ali Pasha with Fuad Pasha functioning as the Foreign Minister. Fuad, bristling with anger at the direct insult, offered his resignation to the Sultan. It was an opportunity for Abdul Medjid to insist upon the etiquette of his court and thereby take some of the wind out of the Russian sails. Unaccountably, and to

the panic of the Divan, the Sultan accepted the resignation
without comment, thus indicating to his shocked advisers that
he was already frightened into a state of abject compliance.

It was the urgency of this fear that had sent the Grand Vezir
flying to the haven of the British Embassy evidencing symp-
toms of total collapse,[1] and this, in turn, which prompted
Colonel Rose to summon the Mediterranean fleet. The highly
imaginative Turks had become convinced that by some means
unknown to them Prince Menshikov had contrived to threaten
the Sultan with instantaneous attack, and they managed to
communicate this fear to the British chargé.

Although the summons was nullified by London, it had not
been entirely futile. The transmission of the request for a
movement of the fleet gave the Turks a breathing space in
which they could recover their composure. And the denial
of the request by London had a good effect in St. Petersburg,
for Czar Nicholas took it as added proof that his high-level
negotiations with London were bearing fruit. Aberdeen's un-
hesitating disavowal of Rose's impulsive gesture was ample
confirmation of the Czar's fixed conviction that England would
avoid any and all recourse to force. Consequently, Prince
Menshikov did not receive any orders to quicken the pace of
his proceedings and lapsed into a policy of persuasive diplomacy. He had lost the hoped-for imbroglio in Montenegro as
a main bargaining point and was thrown back on the sole
matter of the Holy Places as far as public issues were concerned. His utterances on this matter became mild and con-

ciliatory, and he coyly hinted that he had much to offer the Porte. Before he would expatiate on the hidden proposal, however, he enjoined the need for absolute secrecy on the Grand Vezir and on Rifat Pasha, who was once more the Reis Effendi, following Fuad's withdrawal. He told them he had a secret treaty to offer in the name of the Czar, but that should its terms be revealed to either England or France, he and his mission would instantly quit Constantinople.

The necessity for such clandestine agreement lay, he asserted, in habitual English jealousy and in the bellicose aggressiveness of the upstart imitator who grandiloquently described himself as the Emperor of the French. Russia well knew, he intimated, the straits to which the Porte had been driven by the pressure of France, and for that very appreciable threat the Czar was ready to conclude a treaty of defensive alliance with the Sultan, guaranteeing him an army of 400,000 men and the whole of the Black Sea fleet against any power or combination of powers. The *quid pro quo* sought in return was a Russian protectorate, with the Greek patriarchate and the whole of the Orthodox community under the guardianship of the Czar.[2]

This entailed far more than recognition of the Czar's right to intervene on behalf of his coreligionists for that was already established by custom and precedent. Moreover, it had been exercised constantly. Heretofore, however, there had never been even an implied doubt as to where legal jurisdiction lay. The Czar's intervention, when it occurred, always cast the

Russian sovereign in the role of *amicus curiae,* never as the legal magistrate. The appeal was made to the Sultan as the constituted authority, and it was made in behalf of subjects owing allegiance to the Sultan as their lawful sovereign.

The background of this custom arose from the social and political structure of the Ottoman Empire whereby non-Moslems were arranged in religious or racial groupings—the *millet* system. The *millet* system had a twofold origin. On the one hand, it was an adaptation of the original Islamic society which was a tribal society, where tribal decision, tribal custom, was law. When the first Islamic empire swept over non-Arab peoples and into urbanized societies, it encountered the highly developed civilization of the Byzantine state. Tribal law could not administer complex urban societies nor could Islamic law countenance non-Moslem law.

Fortunately the Romano-Byzantine law already possessed a traditional dichotomy which could be successfully adopted by Islamic law to take care of the non-Moslem. For Roman law had long recognized the difference between civil law and tribal or group law. As the Roman Empire extended over the Mediterranean world and northwards into Europe, the distinction between the *gens Romana* and the *nationes* generated the distinction between the law for Roman citizens, the *jus civile,* and the law for subject peoples, the *jus gentium.* The priority of Roman law was never questioned, but the national or group law was considered fully binding upon those who came under its sway. Hence the refusal of Pilate, for example, to interfere in the religious trial of Jesus. Conversely, the appeal of the Roman citizen, Paul, to the higher jurisdiction of Rome as opposed to a local court functioning under local law.

Thus the Islamic state found a convenient legal system, completely compatible with the demands of Islam, to take care of the practical administration of non-Moslem peoples. These people had no Islamic legal entity, but they had their own scriptures and laws to live by. The tribal aspect endured in that the recognized head of the community of non-Moslems was responsible for the behavior of his group or millet.[3]

When the Ottoman Turks swept across the corpse of the last of the Paleologues in the dust of Constantinople, the only centers of authority left there were the patriarch and the bishops of the Greek Church. To them was given the responsibility of the Christian millet. It bears repeating that as far as Islam was concerned the Christian millet had no rights in law. Its members lived by sufferance rather than by right. The Sultans did not concern themselves with the individuals of the millet, but dealt only with the patriarch and the bishops.

At the zenith of Ottoman glory this was quite sufficient. Additionally, it was a source of revenue, as appointments to bishoprics and to the patriarchate could be purchased. Largely, however, the Orthodox were left to their own laws. When Ottoman power began to decline in relation to the West, the power of the patriarchs increased in the same proportion. When they felt injustice was being done, they naturally ap-

pealed to one or another of the Christian powers for intervention in their behalf. (The predominance of Russian intervention can be explained by the fact that the Greek Orthodox Church and the Russian Church were closely related.)
By the nineteenth century this was a common practice.

This clarifies the perpetual insistence of Canning and the
reformers for a code of law that would equalize Moslem and
Christian subject alike. Only such equalization would do
away with the appeals for outside help, and without such
appeals the grounds for foreign intervention would disap-
pear.[4]

Up to this time, to reiterate, the legal sovereignty of the
Sultan had never been called into question by the intervening
power. The European powers had sought leniency or justice
for his subjects, not for theirs; they demanded equitable adju-
dication of problems under his jurisdiction, not under their
civil codes. No matter how forceful their representations had
been, even to the extent of war, there had never been any
attempt to destroy his sovereign rights.

Now it became the definite, declared intention of imperial
Russia to overthrow and eradicate once and for all this cen-
turies-old legal tradition. By the stroke of a single treaty the
Czar seemed to be asking the Sultan to surrender irrevocably
all semblance of authority over more than fourteen millions
of his subjects. The nomination and investiture of all patriarchs and bishops was to be the prerogative of the Emperor
of Russia, as head of the Orthodox Church. Their police and

civil powers, their magisterial tribunals, the property holdings of the Greek Church—all were to be under his direction and his alone. In short, Nicholas was demanding what seemed to amount to extraterritorial sovereignty over a vast segment of the Ottoman Empire.[5]

The Turkish ministers were stunned when the true purpose of the Menshikov mission was finally revealed to them, but they listened to Prince Menshikov in silence and agreed to give some time to serious study of the project. What the Russian plenipotentiary did not know, of course, was that the news had come to them, and it was welcome to even the most reactionary members of the Council, that the Buyuk Elchi was wending his way across Europe and would soon be at their side. They could temporize until he came, and the Russians seemed confident enough to be patient for their answer. Turkish hesitancy in responding did not imply in the slightest an inclination to bow before these demands; the Turks were merely searching for the best possible means of refusal.

Curiously enough, when Canning did arrive, they were not completely frank with him, and although they entered into immediate discussions with him, they failed to relate the full scope of the transactions. Whether they were trying to observe as far as they were able the secrecy stipulated by Prince Menshikov, or whether they feared to admit to the Elchi that they had so much as listened to the Russian, is difficult to ascertain. They did seek his advice on a hypothetical situation somewhat akin to the real one without admitting that this situation had already been thrust upon them.

Canning, from his own reflections and from subsequent conversations with the Embassy staff, had succeeded in forming a fairly accurate idea of what was behind the Russian mask, but before he could commit himself to a proper diagnosis he had to know precisely what was at stake. In the meantime the Embassy dragomans had become quite certain that the Russian position had been committed to writing and handed to the Porte. These emissaries were flatly refused when they ventured to ask for a copy to show their master, whereupon Canning sent word to Rifat that the Porte could hardly expect guidance on a matter whose details were unknown. On April 7, 1853, the Grand Vezir sent word that the Elchi would be furnished a copy as desired, and by the eleventh of April, Canning was able to transmit the substance of the Russian project to London.[6]

Now he could set to work in earnest and employ all his skill to meet the enemy head on. As he reviewed the picture the following facts stood out: Ostensibly, Prince Menshikov had come to Constantinople to obtain redress for the alleged insult suffered by the Czar as a result of developments in the Holy Land. That was the public issue. Secretly, it was but a lever that the Czar wished to use to force his will on a far greater matter. Undue intransigence on the part of the Turks regarding the Holy Places would serve as a public pretext for the Russian legions to march, and in the current state of opinion, especially in England, the balance of justice would be awarded to the Czar. If the Czar were to march on this issue, he would accomplish his ulterior goal either through direct surrender or as a result of internal collapse in Turkey. This result would appear to have come about as a matter of course rather than by design. If, however, the public issue could be successfully settled, it would leave the Czar without a pretext, and then he would have either to abandon his ultimate aim or be cast in the role of an aggressor. This, Canning was sure, would not be appealing to the Czar, who was well aware that the other powers would not stand idly by.

The question naturally arises, then, of why a public presentation of the case was not immediately made, and the answer is that such a disclosure might have forced the hand of the Czar and compelled him to set his armies in motion or face an intolerable loss of prestige at home and abroad. And in April of 1853, as far as anyone could tell, the Czar could have acted with impunity since no one else was ready, England least of all. It was Canning's hope that, having been informed of the serious nature of the crisis, the Aberdeen government would see the handwriting on the wall and look to its defenses.

There was never any doubt on Canning's part that the Czar could eventually be checked by England alone or by a coalition of interested powers, but it would take a war to do it and before the coalition could be organized the Ottoman Empire might be destroyed. This is what he hoped to avoid. The chances for an awakening of the powers were immeasurably greater if, in the face of a peaceful solution to the dispute of the shrines, the Czar reopened negotiations for the treaty alone or, by failing to demobilize, hinted at action still to come. It was necessary to bring Austria, at least, into concert with England and France, and that could be done only if the intrigues at St. Petersburg could be clearly revealed, as Vienna felt that Russia was justified on the public issue.

His instructions to the Turks, then, were to keep the particulars of the Holy Places entirely separate from the terms of the treaty.[7] They must be courteous, he told them, and sympathetic to Russian religious sentiment on the matter of the shrines. Above all, they must be definite in their proposals with regard to the details of the shrines, discussing even doors and cupolas, sanctuary lamps and altar decorations. Meanwhile they could plead for patience on the treaty as a whole, promising nothing, refusing nothing.

He turned his personal attention to the Prince, and the hapless Russian was no match for the shrewd Elchi. Initially, their conversations ran to generalities, until they gradually came around to the central issue of the Russian complaints. By patient listening and a few sympathetic comments Canning led Menshikov to believe that England had been won over to the inherent justice of the Czar's stand. The English government felt that the traditional arrangements in the Holy Land should not be altered in any substantial way and was prepared to use all of its good offices to support the moderate and just demands of the Czar. It was fortunate, Canning intimated, that from the vantage point of a secure and stable dynastic history both the Queen and the Czar could appreciate the pretty actions of Napoleon III and could afford to be generous and condescending. England was counting very heavily on the reiterated pacific intentions of the Czar to lead the way to a solution that would be just and at the same time offer a measure of recognition to the French Emperor.

Canning was receiving a stream of assurances from London that such was the declared position of St. Petersburg, as communicated to Sir Hamilton Seymour by Count Nesselrode and the Czar himself, and he was most happy to show them to Prince Menshikov. Imperceptibly he maneuvered the Prince into the position of either acceding to a negotiated settlement of the Holy Places dispute or contradicting the assertions of his master.

While he convincingly cajoled the Prince, he could not afford to ignore the pressure from the French end of the line, but here he was tangibly aided by the freshness of his own personal contacts with Louis Napoleon. In a parallel series of conferences with De la Cour, who had succeeded De Lavalette at the Porte, he advanced the suggestion that the dignity of France had already been deferred to in the matter of the star and the key and that the majesty of the French Emperor did not depend on needless hair-splitting that could block a desired conclusion. He persuaded De la Cour that his Emperor was not disposed to prolong the debate so long as what was granted was not withdrawn. Finally, he asked the Frenchman to imagine how absurd Menshikov would appear if, after all his labors, he went home with nothing to show but a firman redefining what Russia already had. If it was important to Russia, it was little short of comical to the rest of Europe, and it was all to French advantage to treat it as such, for which treatment they would merit the gratitude not only of the Porte but of England as well.

With the French and Russian envoys now disposed to accept his point of view, Canning's next step was to offer his services to Menshikov in the matter of procuring from the Porte a firman that would precisely delineate Greek precedence in each and every particular brought forth in the Russian agenda and a similar decree that would unmistakably confine the recent gains of the French. "I thought," he modestly reported, "it was time for me to adopt a more prominent part in reconciling the adverse parties."

By the nineteenth of April he had brought Menshikov and De la Cour to agreement on the text of the firmans that were to be addressed by the Sultan to the Turkish authorities in Jerusalem. The major points, picayune as they actually were, covered a number of items. As to the French privileges they were to remain as granted; that is, the Star of France would remain in the Grotto of the Nativity and the key to the main door of the church would remain in the custody of the Latin Monks. However, a Greek priest would remain as the actual doorkeeper with no right of preventing entry to any and all pilgrims. The custody of the key did not confer ownership, and no change was to be made in the appointments of the sanctuary to impede the proper celebration of the Greek liturgy. The repairs on the shrine were to be made by the Sultan, but under the direction and supervision of the Greek

Patriarch of Jerusalem. The crowning genius of the arrangements, however, was the solution reached for the vexing
problem of precedence. Here priority was given to the
Greeks, but it was declared to be a temporal precedence alone,
based not on inherent right nor on greater intrinsic dignity
but established solely as an accommodation to the difference
in canonical hours of the respective rites. Since the Greeks
had always celebrated the Divine Liturgy at a much earlier
hour than the Latins did the Mass, neither side could take
umbrage at a continuation of their respective customs nor
could either claim a signal victory.

In fifteen days of unremitting labor Canning had solved
an argument that had arisen eighteen months previously. It
had not been easy on the veteran diplomat, as he testified
to his wife: "I am well, thank God! but my brain is half on
fire, and my fingers worn down to the quick. I get up at five;
I work the livelong day and I fall asleep before I reach my
bed . . . . "8 It was not yet over, however, for on the very
day the firmans were being drawn up the whole apple cart
was very nearly upset.

It will be recalled that the French fleet had moved from
Toulon to the vicinity of Salamis in mid-March. It is not
known exactly when the Czar became cognizant of this fact,
but at any rate it is certain that when he did the intended
irritant must have been weakened somewhat by the knowledge
that England had already thwarted any idea the French had
entertained of joint action. As he had declared in a message
to Lord John Russell: "When we are agreed, I am quite with-

out anxiety as to the rest of Europe; it is immaterial what the others may think or do."

Although the French move must have rankled considerably, the confidence that he was walking arm in arm with England allowed Nicholas to stifle any hasty response to this sword-waving. When, however, to cap this insolence, he had to suffer the re-emergence of Stratford Canning, and when it become very plain that the Menshikov mission had ground to a halt, undoubtedly against this same hated barrier, he turned back to the French move and seized upon it as the occasion to order the Prince to press for the treaty without delay.

The new orders reached Prince Menshikov in almost the final hours of the preceding negotiations, and the plenipotentiary was at a loss as to what he should do. The pace the English Ambassador had set for all concerned had left no opportunity for Menshikov to communicate with St. Petersburg quickly enough to submit the terms of the proposed settlement before his acceptance of them on behalf of the Czar. Moreover, there appeared to be no necessity for doing so, as Lord Stratford seemed to be winning more in the matter of the Holy Places than the Czar himself had dreamed possible. Now he was ordered to return to the peremptory language and behavior that had marked the start of his embassy. Yet Menshikov knew that it was possible to lose what he had gained by an overextension of effort at this stage.

In his dilemma the Prince chose an alternative that was most foolish for him, and most fortunate for the Elchi. He was not so naïve as to suppose that Canning knew nothing of the additional project, for the Englishman had alluded, more than once, to the rumor of ulterior proposals, but in each reference the English Ambassador himself had been quick to dismiss the reports as baseless since they were in direct contrast to the pledges the Czar was making to Lord Aberdeen.[9] These dismissals Prince Menshikov had avidly concurred in, and to corroborate his agreement he had gone so far as to acknowledge that he was empowered to enter into treaty discussions, but they were to relate to nothing more than a reaffirmation of existing generalities, and the question of peace or war did not depend on their conclusion. At most, a refusal on the part of the Porte might lead to a temporary strain, but nothing more than a break in negotiations.

Since he had not found Lord Stratford to be the demon he was made out to be, Menshikov decided to discuss with him the treaty the Czar was desirous of making. That he did so was an indication, first of all, that he himself did not see the full force of the consequences of such a proposal and, secondly, that he had resigned himself to the fact that ultimately he would be dealing with Canning anyway. He might receive the formal replies from the Grand Vezir or from Rifat Pasha, but the actual acceptance or rejection was the Elchi's, and since he had found him amenable thus far, he might as well have the treaty in such a form as to merit acceptance. His duty was to effect an agreement, and if by prior consultation with the Elchi he could speed it up, there was no harm done.

Now it was Canning's turn to be in a quandary. He could not, of course, signify assent, but, on the other hand, an abrupt rejection would spoil everything. He needed Menshikov's public acceptance of the forthcoming firmans before all else. Then let come what may. He engaged in a classic equivocation that took the poor Russian in completely. Without commenting on the treaty as a whole, he did, after reading it over, question whether the language used in reference to the patriarchs would be considered admissible by the European powers. He went so far as to suggest some alteration in the language of this section before it was submitted to the Porte. By so concentrating on this single item, he let Menshikov draw the conclusion that he had no serious objection to the engagement as a whole.[10] His success can be gauged by the lengths Menshikov went to later on to show that Canning at first approved the treaty and then reversed himself after the agreement on the shrines was concluded. But there is not a single item on record other than Menshikov's unwarranted inference that this was so.

Regardless of Menshikov's subsequent recriminations, the strategem worked, and the altered draft was presented to the Porte with the assumption that it had been approved by the Elchi. Meanwhile the firmans were completed and accepted by all parties, and the dispute over the question of the Holy Places was over in the manner planned by Canning, and just seventeen days after he had returned to Constantinople. Prince Menshikov, not realizing that the rug had been pulled out from under the Czar's feet, avidly tendered his public gratitude to the Elchi. The Czar was left without a pretext, and what was to come all depended on his mood and purpose.

"But we are not yet out of the wood," Canning admitted sadly to Lady Stratford. "Russia wants what the Porte cannot give, and it remains to be seen whether Menshikov will be satisfied with what I may conscientiously advise the Turks to give him. . . . I am, so far, on good terms with all the world."[11]

1. See Kinglake, *op. cit.*, I, 81-82.

2. See Temperley, *op. cit.*, p. 315.

3. With regard to the relation of the millet system to a Romano-Byzantine legal heritage, Toynbee (*op. cit.*. VII, 291) quotes from Goldziher as follows: " 'It was quite natural, from the changed conditions after the conquests, that the formation of law . . . was greatly influenced by what the authorities on the development of law in Syria and Mesopotamia were able to learn of Roman law, sometimes of the special law for particular provinces.' " Toynbee himself states more specifically (*ibid.*, p. 258, n. 3): "Moreover, the capitulations, as well as the millets, had been a going concern in the parochial states whose place the Ottoman Empire had taken."

4. "The more the Turkish Government adopts the rules of impartial law and equal administration, the less will the Emperor of Russia find it necessary to apply that exceptional protection . . . . " (Lord John Russell to Sir Harrison Seymour, in Hurewitz, *op. cit.*, I, 140).

5. Temperley emphasizes (*op. cit.*, pp. 315-16, 320, 332) that the proposed treaty included laymen as well as clergy. Rifat Pasha said that "it would give a foreign power the right of mixing in our internal affairs and protecting our subject peoples" (*ibid.*, p. 316).

6. Cf. Lane-Poole, *op. cit.*, II, 251-53.

7. Temperley (*op. cit.*, p. 317) says: "It has been absurdly suggested that Stratford deliberately separated the question of the Holy Places from

the other disputes in order to put Russia in the wrong." I am not sure to which part of the proposition Temperley ascribes the absurdity. If he means that it is absurd to state that Canning's motive was "to put Russia in the wrong," I agree with him. His motive was to remove Russia's legitimate grievances on the matter of the Holy Places. If, after that was accomplished with justice, Russia persisted in unreasonable demands, then she would have to answer for her own actions. On the other hand, Temperley means that Canning did not consciously strive to separate the two questions, I disagree. Cf. Canning's instructions to his chief dragoman, April 23, 1853 (Lane-Poole, *op. cit.*, II, 258): " . . . what I have so often urged, the importance of keeping the question of the Holy Places apart from that of the Protectorate."

8. Lane-Poole, *op. cit.*, II, 260.

9. See Kinglake, *op. cit.*, I, 97-98.

10. Canning was not simulating. He believed the controversy could and would be settled. Menshikov had agreed to delete the clause creating the patriarchs for life. (Cf. Temperley, *op. cit.*, p. 317.)

11. Lane-Poole, *op. cit.*, II, 260.

XXI

THE Aberdeen government was well satisfied with Stratford Canning's handling of the Holy Places dispute. Lord Clarendon described the Ambassador's action as being "most judicious and pacific."[1] But at the same time the Cabinet was falling victim to an inertia and blindness which ultimately eroded the chances for peace and set in motion the drift toward war. Advices had been coming from Sir Hamilton Seymour, their ambassador to Russia, which should have opened their eyes to the realization that the matter of the Holy Places was not the sum of the Czar's interests.

The content of this correspondence from Seymour was not to come to light until almost a year later, and it was only by chance that it was made public then. On February 17, 1854, when it was generally thought to be a matter of a few days before war was declared, Lord John Russell rose in the House of Commons, and, speaking in behalf of the government, he laid the entire blame for the coming conflict at the door of

Czar Nicholas I. Lord Russell accused the Czar of having misled the English Cabinet with regard to his intentions. This speech evoked a bitter countercharge which was carried in the semi-official *St. Petersburg Journal* of March 2, 1854. The Russian reply claimed that the English government had received ample information from the Russian court with respect to its views on the Turkish situation, and that the transmission of these views had begun when Lord Russell himself was still Foreign Secretary (January, 1853), "before ceding to Lord Clarendon the direction of foreign affairs."[2] Moreover, the same article noted without reservation, the Russian position was stated by Czar Nicholas himself and was forwarded to the Aberdeen Cabinet by Sir Hamilton Seymour at the Czar's own request.

So grave was the Russian charge, implying a deceptive silence on the part of Lord Aberdeen's ministry, that the Earl of Derby saw fit to ask the Prime Minister for an explanation, and to produce the alleged documents for Parliament. Whether Lord Aberdeen would ever have seen fit to publish them is a moot point for, in response to this demand, the papers were laid before Parliament. It seems eminently fair to say of the Seymour Correspondence that, at the very least, the exchanges should have put the Cabinet on guard. The crisis was deeper than a dispute over church keys.

Two facts must be kept in mind during this review of the record. One is that the Nesselrode Memorandum of 1844, implying an understanding among Russia, Austria, and England on the future of Turkey (see Chapter XVIII above, p. 241), had never been disavowed. The other is that the Foreign Minister who, according to the Czar, by his tacit acceptance had approved the generalities of the memorandum was now the head of the English government. Czar Nicholas saw a close connection between these widely separated events. He met Seymour at a party in the palace of the Grand Duchess Helena in St. Petersburg on January 9, 1853, shortly after the formation of the Aberdeen Cabinet. After requesting that his good wishes be conveyed to Lord Aberdeen, the Czar launched into a discussion of the European scene and dwelt on the necessity for English and Russian co-operation.

> "When we [Russia and England] are agreed (d'accord), I am quite without anxiety as to the west of Europe; it is immaterial what the others may think or do."

Then, according to Seymour's summary, he turned specifically to the matter of Turkey:

> He said . . . "The affairs of Turkey are in a very disorganized condition; the country itself seems to be falling to pieces . . . it is very important that England and Russia should come to a perfectly good understanding upon these affairs . . . . "

And the Czar, Seymour reports, characterized Turkey as "a sick man—a very sick man."

Seymour concluded the report of this initial meeting with a succinct comment on the policy difference between England

and Russia. After offering his advice on the necessity of an understanding, he wrote:

> The sum is probably this:—That England has to desire a close concert with Russia, with a view to preventing the downfall of Turkey; while Russia would be well pleased that the concert should apply to the events by which this downfall is to be followed.[3]

This dispatch was received at the Foreign Office by Lord Russell on the twenty-third of January. It was followed by another message in which Sir Hamilton reported what transpired when the Czar, as he had promised in their first meeting, sent for him. This was five days later, (January 14, 1853). Seymour recorded the Czar's recurrent theme:

> "Now, Turkey . . . has by degrees fallen into such a state of decrepitude, that, as I told you the other night, eager as we all are for the prolonged existence of the man . . . , he may suddenly die upon our hands . . . ; and I put it to you, therefore, whether it is not better to be provided beforehand for a contingency, than to incur the chaos, confusion, and the certainty of a European war, all of which must attend the catastrophe if it should occur unexpectedly, and before some ulterior system has been sketched? This is the point to which I am desirous that you should call the attention of your government."

Seymour ventured an immediate response:

> "With regard to contingent arrangements, her majesty's government, as your majesty is well aware, objects, as a

general rule, to taking engagements upon possible eventualities, and would, perhaps, be particularly disinclined . . . in this instance. . . . [A] great disinclination (*répugnance*) might be expected in England to disposing by anticipation (*d'escompter*) of the succession of an old friend and ally."

"This rule is a good one," the emperor replied . . . ; "still it is of the greatest importance that we should understand one another, and not allow events to take us by surprise . . . . "

. . . .
His imperial majesty then alluded to a conversation which he had held the last time he was in England with the Duke of Wellington [the circumstances culminating in the Nesselrode Memorandum] . . . ; then, as now, his majesty was, he said, eager to provide against events which, in the absence of any concert, might compel him to act in a manner opposed to the views of her majesty's government.

The Russian Emperor then turned to the events of the day for a moment, and assured Sir Hamilton that no troop movements had yet taken place over the Holy Places dispute; this was a patent falsehood since Seymour had already been able to report the flow of troops to the Danube. However, the Emperor warned that if there was any French movement of a military nature, he would unhesitatingly send his forces into Turkey, and

that if the result of such an advance should prove to be the overthrow of the Great Turk, he should regret the event, but should feel that he had acted as he was compelled to do.

The Czar ended the conversation with a request that Seymour communicate "What has passed between us to the queen's government, and you will say that I shall be ready to receive any communication which it may be their wish to make to me upon the subject." Seymour concluded the dispatch with a recommendation phrased in plain language:

> I would now submit to your lordship that this overture cannot with propriety pass unnoticed by her majesty's government. . . . . the conversation held some years ago with the Duke of Wellington proves that the object in view is one which has long occupied the thoughts of his imperial majesty. If, then, the proposal were to remain unanswered, a decided advantage would be secured to the imperial [Russian] cabinet, which, in the event of some great catastrophe taking place in Turkey, would be able to point to proposals made to England, and which, not having been responded to, left the emperor at liberty, or placed him under the necessity of following his own line of policy in the East.[4]

To this second report, received in London on the sixth of February, Seymour appended a note, stating that before sending the report on to London in accordance with the Emperor's wishes, he had made a separate visit to Count Nesselrode to make sure that he was giving his own government "a correct summary of the conversation." Seymour recognized the gravity of the Czar's words respecting the probable effect of a military advance by Russian troops into the Ottoman Empire. He had also advised London that Russian mobilization was in process north of the Danube. Surely, with Count Nesselrode's confirmation that the report represented the mind and policy of the Czar, Seymour expected a reaction from the English Cabinet. Of course, he practically goaded Russell into a reply, and he received one, but it was hardly the kind he expected. On February 9, Lord John Russell sent the British representative a response remarkable for its several unusual distinctions as to what the Cabinet considered to be internal Turkish affairs and what they did not. Lord Russell seemed to be arguing that the troubles vexing Turkey were really matters that were problems to neighboring countries and not signs of malaise at the Porte:

> The question raised by His Imperial Majesty is a very serious one [though not serious enough to be brought to Lord Stratford de Redcliffe's attention a few days later]. It is . . . "whether it is not better to be provided beforehand for a contingency than to incur the chaos, confusion, and the certainty of a European war . . . . "
> In considering this grave question, the first reflection which occurs to her majesty's government is, that no actual crisis has occurred which renders necessary a solution of this vast European problem. Disputes have arisen respecting the holy places, but these are without the sphere of the internal government of Turkey, and concern Russia and France rather than the Sublime Porte. Some disturbance of the relations between Austria and the Porte has been caused by the Turkish attack on Montenegro; but this, again,

relates rather to dangers affecting the frontier of Austria
than the authority and safety of the sultan . . . .

The Czar did not have to wonder very long about the mean-
ings hidden in this bit of logical dexterity, for when Lord
Russell went on to discuss the proposal for an arrangement
of the kind the Czar was seeking, he seemed to object not
to the injustice inherent in such a project, but rather to the
difficulties involved in keeping it secret and to the embarrassment that would accrue to England and Russia once it were
known:

> In these circumstances it would hardly be consistent with
> the friendly feelings towards the sultan which animate the
> Emperor of Russia, no less than the Queen of Great Britain,
> to dispose beforehand of the provinces under his dominion.
> Besides . . . an agreement made in such a case tends very
> surely to hasten the contingency for which it is intended to
> provide. Austria and France could not, in fairness, be kept
> in ignorance . . . . It is to be inferred that as soon as
> Great Britain and Russia should have agreed on the course
> to be pursued, . . . they should communicate their inten-
> tions to the great powers of Europe. An agreement thus
> made, and thus communicated, would not be very long a
> secret; and while it would alarm and alienate the sultan,
> the knowledge of its existence would stimulate all his
> enemies to increased violence and more obstinate conflict.

Instead of the forthright and vigorous rejection of any plan
of partition or disposal of the Ottoman Empire that Sir Hamil-

ton Seymour hoped to be able to show to Nicholas, the
Aberdeen ministry seemed to object only to the timing and
mechanics of the proposal. Indeed, who could blame the Czar
for such an interpretation when he found, a little further on,
the assurance that the English government "will enter into
no agreement to provide for the contingency of the fall of
Turkey without previous communication with the Emperor
of Russia"?[5] To a man of Nicholas' frame of mind the English
reply was not in the least a negative one. It questioned only
the imminence of Turkish collapse and the prudence of an
immediate understanding. Lord Russell promised, on the
other hand, that England would, indeed, enter into a discussion with the Czar if and when conditions should point
to an imminent collapse.

Seymour had to make the best of this reply when he
brought it to the attention of the Czar on the evening of
February 20, 1853, at a soiree. The conversation was brief
and informal, but the Czar directed his remarks to the
question of the imminence of the Turkish downfall and
expressed his doubt that the English government had reliable
information:

> " . . . I will tell you that, if your government has been
> led to believe that Turkey retains any elements of exist-
> ence, your government must have received incorrect in-
> formation. . . . "

So insistent did the Czar seem to have become on the subject
of an imminent fall of the Ottoman regime that Seymour

injected his own opinion by way of a warning to London and an implied suggestion that the Foreign Office should consult Austria about the possibility of an Austro-Russian agreement:

> It can hardly be otherwise but that the sovereign, who insists with such pertinacity upon the impending fall of a neighbouring state, must have settled in his own mind that the hour, if not of its dissolution, at all events for its dissolution, must be at hand. . . . I reflected that this assumption would hardly be ventured upon unless some, perhaps general, but at all events intimate understanding, existed between Russia and Austria.[6]

Seymour reported this brief but important exchange immediately, even though he was scheduled to meet the Czar in a formal audience the next day. According to Sir Hamilton, the meeting on the following day lasted for one hour and twelve minutes. In the course of it the Czar amplified his proposals in order to meet what he considered to be an English reluctance to make positive commitments:

> . . . the emperor observed, that her majesty's government did not appear to be aware that his chief object was to obtain . . . some declaration, or even opinion, of what ought not to be permitted in the event of the sudden downfall of Turkey.

When Seymour asked for some concrete examples of what he had in mind, the Czar was at first reluctant to express himself, but then he went on to specify that he would not tolerate the occupation of Constantinople by any foreign power, including Russia; that he would not allow the restoration of a Byzantine empire or the expansion of Greece; still less would he suffer the "breaking up of Turkey into little republics, asylums for the Kossuths and Mazzinis, and other revolutionists of Europe." Later on in the conversation the Czar went on to suggest that

> . . . it might be less difficult to arrive at a satisfactory territorial arrangement than was commonly believed. "The principalities [Moldavia and Wallachia] are," he said, "in fact an independent state under my protection; this might so continue. Servia might receive the same form of government. So again with Bulgaria. . . . As to Egypt, I quite understand the importance to England of that territory. I can then only say, that if, in the event of a distribution of the Ottoman succession upon the fall of the empire, you should take possession of Egypt, I shall have no objections to offer. I would say the same thing of Candia [Crete] . . . I do not know why it should not become an English possession."

As for the position of Austria with regard to Eastern affairs, a question put by Seymour had, much to his surprise, caused the Czar immediately to reply:

> " . . . you must understand that when I speak of Russia I speak of Austria as well . . . ; our interests as regards Turkey are perfectly identical."[7]

The separate reports of these conversations, the one of the evening of February 20 and that of the daytime audience

of February 21, were both received in London on the sixth
of March. In the light of all this intelligence at their disposal,
one can only wonder how Aberdeen and his Cabinet were
interpreting the total situation. They were sending Stratford
Canning back to the Porte to take a hand in the negotiations
about to begin between Prince Menshikov and the Turks,
but they told him nothing of these dispatches from St. Petersburg. Did they see no connection between the two sets of
circumstances? Or did they fear that the added burden of
such knowledge would needlessly complicate his position?
In either case, they were sending a negotiator who was
dangerously ignorant of the total position of one of the parties
to the dispute.

One might argue that Aberdeen and his advisers felt bound
to observe an honorable secrecy concerning these dispatches
from Sir Hamilton Seymour on the grounds that they represented the private confidence of a friendly sovereign. It is a
reasonable conjecture, but they were guilty of staggering
ineptitude once they had knowledge that the Czar claimed to
be speaking for Austria, and they had that knowledge well
before Canning reached Vienna, where he was officially
charged to ascertain the posture of the Austrian government
relative to the Holy Places dispute in particular and the
Turkish situation in general. There were ample means at
the disposal of the government in London to find out, without
violating any confidences, whether or not the Czar of Russia
was empowered to speak for the Emperor of Austria in regard
to either or both of these matters. It could have been done

through Lord Westmoreland, the English ambassador to Vienna, or through Canning himself. No attempt was made to confirm or give the lie to this claim of Nicholas.

Sir Hamilton Seymour had seen the need for some definite clarification from London once the Czar had declared himself on specifics, and at the conclusion of the last-mentioned report he asked for "some expressions . . . which might have the effect of putting an end to the further consideration . . . of points which it is highly desirable should not be regarded as offering subject for debate." In spite of this plea London allowed almost three weeks to pass before it responded. When a reply to the Russian overtures was finally sent—from Lord Clarendon on the twenty-third of March—it was verbose, repetitive of the first reply, and consequently open to serious misconstruction:

> The generous confidence exhibited by the emperor entitles his imperial majesty to the most cordial declaration of opinion on the part of her majesty's government, who are fully aware that, in the event of any understanding with reference to future contingencies being expedient, or indeed possible, the word of his imperial majesty would be preferable to any convention that could be framed.

Clarendon then expresses agreement with the negative propositions put forward by the Czar with the qualification that such pre-determinations, of themselves, would not constitute a guarantee against a conflict among the powers should the

contingencies under discussion actually come to pass. The
Foreign Secretary also disavowed any ambition, on the part
of England, for territorial aggrandizement as a result of
previous partition plans and indicated that England would
look askance at the enrichment of any other power by such
means. This was the closest he came to rejecting any of the
Czar's overtures, and it was hardly the categorical type of
response called for. And even this weak rebuff was further
eroded by Clarendon when he expressed the general feelings
of the English government:

> They feel entire confidence in the rectitude of his imperial
> majesty's intentions, and, as they have the satisfaction of
> thinking that the interests of Russia and England in the
> East are completely identical, they entertain an earnest hope
> that a similar policy there will prevail, and tend to strengthen
> the alliance between the two countries . . . . [8]

No other document of any significance came from London
after this, and the correspondence was concluded by a trio of
messages from Seymour. They relate the final understanding
left in the mind of the Czar by Clarendon's reply, and the
last of them, sent from St. Petersburg on April 21, 1853,
picks up the Foreign Secretary's use of the word "alliance,"
which Nesselrode, speaking for Nicholas, refers to:

> His majesty congratulates himself on perceiving that his
> views and those of the English cabinet entirely coincide

on the subject of the political combinations which it would
be chiefly necessary to avoid . . . .
. . . .
He readily accepts the evidence offered by the British cabinet of entire confidence in the uprightness of his sentiments,
and the hope that, on this basis, his alliance with England
cannot fail to become stronger.[9]

On that note the Seymour Correspondence was closed and
consigned to the files. There was nothing sinister in the
Czar's efforts; they were a frank expression of policy. But
the policy was clear, and the Cabinet of Lord Aberdeen did
not see it. The ambiguity of the English government's replies
was freely accommodated to his own desires by Nicholas I,
who was convinced that he knew Aberdeen well enough.[10]
He became certain that England would never go to war, and,
although he drew more than he should have out of the
exchanges, the Aberdeen Cabinet was greatly responsible for
his mistake.

1. Temperley, *op. cit.*, p. 317.

2. For the complete article see Henry Tyrrell, *The History of the
Present War with Russia* (3 vols.; London and New York; London
Printing and Publishing Co., n.d. [*ca.* 1855-57]), 83-84.

3. *Ibid.*, pp. 85-86. Tyrrell quotes the whole of the Seymour Correspondence; Hurewitz (*op. cit.*, I, 135-41) includes only what he considers
to be the most important documents.

4. Tyrrell, *op. cit.*, I, 86-88. In his commentary introducing the
Seymour Correspondence, Hurewitz (*op. cit.*, I, 135) says that insofar as
it illumines the respective policies of Britain and Russia, its importance
"can hardly be exaggerated." As does Temperley, he relates the Seymour

Correspondence and the Nesselrode Memorandum as a link in the chain of Nicholas' diplomacy.

5. Tyrrell, *op. cit.*, I, 88-89.

6. *Ibid.*, p. 90.

7. *Ibid.*, pp. 91-93. Cf. also Temperley, *op. cit.*, p. 461, n. 410, for partition plans.

8. Tyrrell, *op. cit.*, I, 96-97.

9. *Ibid.*, pp. 100-101.

10. Cf. Temperley, *op. cit.*, p. 299.

XXII

THE secret exchanges between London and St. Petersburg had concluded on a theme that was entirely satisfactory to the Czar. The evolution of negotiations in Constantinople stood in sharp contrast to his own personal success. The futility of further dickering at the Porte presumably led the Czar to order Prince Menshikov to bring his mission to a successful conclusion or to break off talks and depart.

To return to the chronology of the negotiations in Constantinople, then, it will be recalled that Prince Menshikov had assumed agreement between himself and Lord Stratford de Redcliffe on the substance of the proposed convention between the Porte and Russia. On the nineteenth of April, accordingly, he forwarded to Rifat a draft which he thought would be acceptable. Confident of the outcome respecting this part of the discussions, he gave his assent, on April 22, to the compromise solution of the Holy Places question. When the new instructions came from St. Petersburg and

nothing seemed to be issuing from the Porte, Menshikov once
again began to exert pressure on the Turks.

On the fifth of May he sent to Rifat Pasha another draft
of the desired treaty together with a stern note that required
an answer within five days. Failure to comply, the Prince
said, could be taken in no other light than "a want of respect
toward his Government, which would impose upon him the
most painful duty." The meaning of the ultimatum was
plain, and the object of the divisions concentrating along
the Pruth was clear. Clear also was the next move of the
Turks, and the Reis Effendi was not slow in appealing to
Lord Stratford for advice.

The new move was ample evidence that the Czar intended
to push to the utmost in an effort to accomplish his end, and
although the Elchi did not pretend to have certain knowledge
as to how far that was, he was sure that sooner or later powers
other than Turkey and Russia would become involved. It
was important, then, to allow the Russians to propel themselves as far as possible into such an advanced position that
their aggressive and imperialistic aims would be manifest to
all of Europe. It would require all the patience and restraint
he could muster from the Turkish ministers to keep the
negotiations going on until they were ruptured from the
Russian side.

His advice to Rifat, therefore, was to continue the courteous
and dignified tactics he had been using all along, admitting
what was admissible, deferring to the wishes of the Czar

where it could be done without sacrificing the dignity and sovereignty of the Porte. Canning analyzed the Russian note in a lengthy memorandum.[1] He saw it as containing three elements, two of which were merely reaffirmations of traditional arrangements, and these he thought could be the substance of a new firman, for "a readiness ought to be shown to remove any abuse and redress any grievance." What was objectionable, of course, and hence inadmissible, was the treaty arrangement which would give Russia the legal right to interfere anytime a Greek cleric might complain of injustice or even inconvenience. Moreover, the language of the proposed agreement implied that the privileges of the Greek Church were being renewed solely as a result of Russian intervention, thereby derogating from the authority of the Sultan and the historic fact that these had been granted before Russian interest had reached the current proportions.

On the eighth of May he took it upon himself to address a private letter to Prince Menshikov begging that plenipotentiary to soften his demands and bring them into accord with the temperate and pacific language emanating from the Czar himself. The Western powers, the Elchi asserted, were in complete sympathy with the Russian desire to better the lot of the Orthodox Christians, but they could not countenance a situation in which Russia would have the right to interfere in the internal affairs of the Ottoman Empire by treaty arrangement. It was a letter which evoked the peaceful character of Nicholas' quarter-century reign on the throne of

Russia and his repeated declarations in favor of tranquillity among nations. Although it was written in the sincere hope that it might bear fruit, it was also framed with the realization that the Russian position was firm. He knew that Menshikov's answer must either express a disposition to soften his demands in the face of concerted opposition or reveal the final aims of the Romanov government with respect to Turkey. The answer indeed confirmed his worst fears: Russia could no longer be content, the Prince replied, with *une position secondaire* in Ottoman affairs. The pretext of the Holy Places was gone; the pretext of Montenegro had ceased to exist; there remained only the question of paramount influence at the Bosporus.

It was critically necessary, as the Elchi saw things at this period, that the position of the Turks be just as clear as Russia's so that the world might compare the morality of their aims. That very same night, with no doubt as to what Menshikov's answer would be, Lord Stratford departed from protocol and visited the villa of the Grand Vezir on the Bosporus. He had learned from the French Ambassador, earlier in the day, that there seemed to be some weakening in the Porte's willingness to withstand Czarist pressure. He found the Reis Effendi and the Seraskier there in conference with Ali Pasha, and once more he urged them to hold the door open for negotiations in their reply. He advised that as a substitute for the treaty they promise a firman guaranteeing complete religious freedom to be sent not only to Russia but to all the five major European powers. The Turks listened and gave ready assent to all the Elchi's words of wisdom, but the true extent of their fear was revealed when the Grand Vezir asked if they could look forward to the approach of the English fleet to counterbalance the Russian threats. "I replied," reported Canning, "that I considered the position in its present stage to be one of a moral character, and consequently that its difficulties or hazards, whatever they might be, should be rather met by acts of a similar description than by demonstrations calculated to increase alarm and provoke resentment."[2]

It would have been very easy for Stratford Canning to tell the poor Turkish ministers that he was empowered to alert the English fleet at Malta, but he did not want them to proceed on that basis. He was certain that all the powers would recognize the justice of the Porte's position, and he desired, above all else, that the Porte reject the Russian demands on the basis of their intrinsic injustice rather than look to outside help as the condition for continued resistance to Russian pressure. He wanted to lay the groundwork for international censure of Russia rather than let it appear that England would proceed alone. After the Divan signified its conviction that this was the course it would follow, he asked for an audience with the Sultan on the following day.

On the morning of the ninth of May, the Reis Effendi conducted him to the apartments of Abdul Medjid and then withdrew. The Elchi and the Sultan faced each other at a precarious moment in history. To the north powerful armies were poised to strike; at Sebastopol a battle fleet was armed and manned to sweep down to the Golden Horn. Behind the Sultan was the decaying power of a once great nation, while the Ambassador knew he spoke for a government that did not know its own mind and shrank from the very thought of conflict. To oppose the Russian juggernaut Stratford Canning had nothing but the words "moral resistance."

He reviewed the whole situation calmly and congratulated the Sultan on having ministers who stood ready to defy the Czar on the grounds of strict justice. He frankly admitted that to spurn the overtures of Prince Menshikov would be to invite a rupture in relations between the Porte and St. Petersburg which, quite possibly, might result in an occupation of the Danubian principalities. Even in that event, though, "I conceive that . . . the true position to be maintained by the Porte is one of moral resistance to such demands as are really inadmissible on just and essential grounds, and that the principle should even be applied under protest to the occupation of the Principalities, not in weakness or despair, but in reliance on a good cause, and on the sympathy of friendly and independent governments."[3]

When the Sultan expressed, in return, his reliance on the Elchi and on the English people, then, as if in reward for his faith, Canning confided to Abdul Medjid that in the event of imminent danger he was empowered by his government to instruct the English admiral at Malta to hold his squadron in readiness. The power in the Elchi's hands was

not extended to anything more concrete, but the effect of
this information, imparted in the given circumstances, was
the same as if he had spoken of huge armies in motion. The
Ambassador knew, moreover, that the renewed faith of the
Sultan would be quickly transmitted to his advisers and would
thus have a far greater psychological effect than if it had been
announced to them in the course of ordinary proceedings.

Canning was not surprised, then, when the Turkish reply
was delivered to Menshikov on the following day. It was
courteous—deferring to Russia in the matter of privileges and
precedence at the Holy Places, reaffirming traditional guarantees relative to the position of the Greek churches, but politely
and definitely negative with respect to the protectorate
envisaged by the proposed treaty. On the eleventh of May,
Prince Menshikov angrily replied that he could not accept the
decision of the Divan as their final answer and gave them
three days in which to reconsider. Their failure to do so,
he threatened, would compel him to acknowledge that his
peaceful mission had come to an end and leave him no alternative but to depart from the capital with all his delegation.
The responsibility for the consequences of such a move, he
warned, would rest with the Turkish ministers and not with
himself.

Notwithstanding the extension of the time limit he gave
them to answer his note, he importuned one Turkish official
after another to pay heed to the dangers on the horizon and
finally demanded an audience with the Grand Vezir on the
afternoon of the thirteenth. Then he committed an unfor-

givable breach of etiquette by failing to keep the appointment. Instead, he brusquely pushed himself into an audience
with the Sultan at ten o'clock that morning. Abdul Medjid
received him, which was wrong, but simply referred him to his
ministers for action on his requirements; and for Menshikov
this was tantamount to throwing him back upon the wiles
of Stratford Canning. But to have allowed Menshikov to
force an audience was an unfortunate manifestation by the
Sultan of lack of confidence in his ministers, and the Cabinet
thereupon resigned. The Sultan allowed the resignation in
a forlorn attempt to mollify Menshikov.

One might hazard the guess that the resignation of the
ministry was a ruse seized upon by the Divan to prolong the
negotiations, for the new ministry was not such as to be
any more obsequious to the overbearing Russian.[4] Actually
it was little more than a reshuffling; the former Grand Vezir,
Ali Pasha, became Seraskier, and was succeeded as Grand
Vezir by Mustapha Pasha, who had been President of the
Council. That office, in turn, was assumed by Rifat Pasha,
who moved over from the Foreign Office to make way for
none other than Reshid Pasha. The new ministry was in
office on the fourteenth, the day appointed by Menshikov
for Turkey's final answer, and Reshid asked for a few days
delay so that the new government could study the problem.

Menshikov was in a real dilemma. He had apparently
received orders to terminate his mission at once, yet courtesy
and circumstances demanded that he wait until he was sure
there was no change of heart. At any rate, he replied, on the

fifteenth, that his mission to the Porte was at an end and that there could be no further communication of an official nature between the Seraglio and himself. He intimated, however, that it would be a few days before he could leave Constantinople and thus left the door open for the Turks to bend to his imperial master's will.

In spite of the official break in relations as announced by the Prince, Reshid Pasha made one last attempt to stay the Russian's hand. He made a personal visit to him on the eighteenth and reiterated Turkish willingness to satisfy the Czar's concern for his coreligionists in the Ottoman Empire and to guarantee Russo-Greek privileges in the Holy Land, but at the same time he told him that the Council had again overwhelmingly rejected the treaty proposal.[5] A written Russian reply, delivered that same day, once again declared that negotiations were at an end, that Russia had received fresh injury, and that the refusal of the Porte to give the guarantees in the form demanded left the Emperor of all the Russias no alternative but to seek the desired end in his own way and through his own power. Any infringement on the rights of the Eastern Churches would be regarded as an act of hostility. And, finally, Menshikov declared that both the extraordinary mission headed by himself and the regular staff of the Russian Embassy were departing with him.

On the next morning, the nineteenth, the English Ambassador assembled the envoys of Austria, France, and Prussia at his home. It was now time to establish a four-power united front against the Czar. Stratford Canning was certain that there would not be a war—not that he believed the Czar was incapable of going to war against the Turk, but that in face of a coalition of the powers, Nicholas would back down. It was the first order of business to give him the chance to retreat without public humiliation.

The representatives of the powers were unanimously agreed that the conduct of the Porte had been rigorously correct, and each attested to the fact that the projected treaty arrangement would be frowned upon by his own government. They jointly designated their Austrian colleague, consequently, to approach Prince Menshikov for yet another attempt at reconciliation. This was done on the twentieth of May. The Prince finally made a change in his demands. If the major objection of the powers was to the word "treaty," he would accept the guarantees in the form of a note or declaration. This offer was to be transmitted to Reshid Pasha by the conference of ambassadors. Actually the same demands were there, to be promised just as solemnly as they would have been in a treaty, and the several ambassadors could see no substantial alteration. They therefore advised Reshid that they considered him the best judge of what should be done with this amended demand. It was not answered; and on the twenty-first of May, the Russian arms and flags were removed from the embassy building, and the entire Russian mission steamed up the Bosporus for Odessa.

Stratford Canning had come back to Constantinople on the fifth of April under instructions to mediate the dispute that had arisen regarding the Holy Places in Jerusalem. This

he had done to the declared satisfaction of all the parties
involved. When, in the course of effecting this settlement, he
had ascertained the broader aims of the Russian government
and its Emperor, he had determined that if he held the Turks
to a policy of just amends then any further Russian project
would be answered by the world.

When Prince Menshikov left for Odessa on the twenty-
first of May, he did so with the strong disapproval of all the
major powers represented at the Porte. There was a four-
power European front in being, and it seemed amply capable
of bringing the Czar to an abrupt halt.

1. Lane-Poole, *op. cit.*, II, 264-65.
2. Kinglake, *op. cit.*, I, 115; see also Temperley, *op. cit.*, p. 322.
3. Kinglake, *op. cit.*, I, 116; Temperley, *op. cit.*, p. 323.
4. Temperley says the ministers were dismissed at the behest of
Menshikov, who wanted Reshid back in the Foreign Office. Reshid's
appointment was certainly not at the behest of Canning, who had virtually
lost all faith in the Pasha.
5. The vote of the Grand Council was 42 to 3 against submission.
(Temperley, *op. cit.*, p. 327.)

XXIII

THE summer of 1853 has been described as the season of a continent-wide diplomatic ball game, "whereof," in Stanley Lane-Poole's words, "the exact name and rules were apparently not understood, at least by the players. There were four corners to this game: one was Paris, another was London, a third Vienna, and the fourth Constantinople: indeed, Berlin considered itself a fifth, but this was premature. The object was to throw a ball,—which they called by various names, as Note, Project, Declaration, Convention,—from Constantinople to the goal at St. Petersburg. But the most extraordinary accidents happened on the way. Sometimes the ball, after being thrown from corner to corner, got hopelessly lost. Sometimes, after much careful preparation, it never started on its way at all. But most often two balls were projected from opposite corners at the same instant, and meeting in mid-air broke each other in pieces. About a dozen of these missiles were flying about Europe in the summer of 1853, and the strangest part of the performance was that each was so timed as to arrive at its destination (if it did not burst on the way) exactly at the moment when another missile had been sent off. One only reached the Petersburg goal in safety, and that was found to contain some explosive matter, and was hastily dropped by the players.

" . . . It would be hard to discover in the history of diplomacy a more painful example of good intentions egregiously, we had almost said ludicrously, foiled by their own superabundance. Every Great Power, as represented by its Foreign Secretary, was laudably eager to have its share in the work of healing, and managed its contribution so skilfully that it was certain to be neutralized by some other prescription." [1]

The foregoing description, for all its irony, does not strain reality. To attempt to find some direction or coherence in this maze of diplomacy—with its futile digressions, reversals, and blind alleys—is almost impossible. For those who would pursue all the details there is an excellent account in the second volume of Lane-Poole's oft-cited work (pages 276-338). Kinglake, also, in his first volume, provides an exhaustive account (running from page 127 to page 142 and from page 214 to page 298), but that historian's editorial rhetoric must be carefully separated from his presentation of factual material. His propensity for the rhetorical style is, in the opinion of Temperley, responsible for much of the adverse criticism to which Stratford Canning has been subjected by later observers who failed to sift fact from flights of purple prose. Though it was far from Kinglake's purpose, his glowing description of Canning's power and influence lends credibility to the thesis advanced by many of his contemporaries that Stratford Canning, by failing to stem the Turks at the later moments of the negotiations, suffered the war to happen, so to speak. This thesis has now been discredited, even though it was held by Queen Victoria herself and stated by others in private correspondence. The record indicates that such accusations were nothing more than an attempt to find a scapegoat for the tragedy that ensued.

In demonstration of this assertion we shall try here to follow the thread of the negotiations; but before doing so, several propositions ought to be stated which suggest this writer's interpretation of the events leading to the Crimean War.

First and foremost of these is the incontrovertible fact that, at the moment of Prince Menshikov's departure from the Golden Horn, Canning had achieved unanimity with respect to the four major powers who were not parties to the direct dispute. This unanimity progressively diminished in direct proportion to the degree in which negotiations were removed from his direction. Secondly, the chances for peace were lost as the direction of the plans for peace came under the control of men who could not comprehend the totality of the situation. That inability stemmed both from the lack of a *Weltanschauung* proper to the times and from wishful thinking that peace could be maintained so long as it was desired. Thirdly, general war resulted because the Aberdeen government could not, or would not, opt firmly either for peace or for war. Had the English government made clear its readiness to go to war, the Czar of Russia would have backed down.[2] On the other hand, had it firmly advised its Ambassador in Constantinople that the Porte could not look to England for support, the Turks would either have given in to the Russian demands or engaged in a limited, though futile, war.

The immediate reaction of the Aberdeen government to Menshikov's departure was to give vigorous support to its Ambassador at the Porte and the ministers who had been following his advice. On the twenty-sixth of May, Lord Clarendon informed the Elchi that it was "indispensable to take measures for the protection of the Sultan, and to aid his Highness in repelling any attack that might be made upon his territory," and that "the use of force was to be resorted to as a last and unavoidable resource for the protection of Turkey and in defense of her independence which England is bound to maintain."[3] Corresponding orders went to the fleet commander at Malta to consider himself under the orders of Viscount de Redcliffe. At the same time, the Foreign Secretary sent a dispatch to Sir Hamilton Seymour in St. Petersburg which stated the views of the Cabinet in

unequivocal terms: "No sovereign, having a proper regard
for his own dignity and independence, could admit proposals
so undefined as those of Prince Menshikov, and by treaty
confer upon another and more powerful sovereign a right
of protection over a large portion of his own subjects."[4]

Similar expressions of reproof came from Paris, Berlin, and
Vienna, signifying that the concert of the four ambassadors
in Constantinople had resulted in a superior coalition on the
part of their respective governments. The Porte, meanwhile,
went ahead with plans for a new decree guaranteeing freedom
to all its Christian subjects and this firman, or *hatti-sherif*,
was duly circulated among all the European chancelleries on
the sixth of June.

This declaration of intent notwithstanding, the Russian
government countered with a note from Count Nesselrode to
Reshid Pasha demanding compliance at once under pain of
Russian occupation of the principalities. The Turks were
given eight days to consider the consequences of their action.
The Turks, of course, refused, but their reply was still
couched in terms of courtesy and bespoke a readiness to do
everything possible to maintain peace with honor.

At this juncture there occurred the first in a long series of
contradictory moves made by London. After having placed
the disposition of the Mediterranean fleet in Lord Stratford's
hands, the Cabinet unaccountably bypassed him and, at the
instance of Paris, suddenly ordered the naval forces to proceed
to the vicinity of the Dardanelles in company with a French

squadron.[5] Not only was it needless sword rattling and an unnecessary challenge to the Czar, but, more importantly, it was the beginning of a series of independent military moves by France and England which derogated from the international coalition then crystallizing. Additionally, the martial spirit implied by the move was consistently belied by the irenic utterances of Lord Aberdeen and his subordinate ministers. Just as in the case of the Seymour Correspondence, the Czar chose to believe only what he could interpret to his own liking.

The Anglo-French naval movement was followed almost immediately by the long-threatened invasion of the principalities, an operation that was completed early in July.[6] It would be difficult to prove that there was a cause and effect relationship involved here, for the two moves seem to have been made independently. Yet it is obvious that it would have been increasingly difficult to return to a peaceful atmosphere after these steps had been taken.[7] And a moment's reflection will show how difficult this action made Canning's efforts to maintain the peace.

The Elchi had already warned the Sultan that the invasion was most likely. He had appealed to the Turks to restrain themselves on the occasion of this warlike move and continue in their position of moral resistance. The Divan had gone along with him thus far; its members had reaffirmed the position and privileges of the Orthodox Church; they had reasserted the Sultan's desire for justice to all non-believers;

they had done all that human patience could have expected of them. They now had to suffer an invasion of their domains, an affront to their sovereignty and dignity. Just when the Turks were beginning to seethe under the lid of restraint imposed by the English Ambassador, the government in London chose to adopt the forward position of a naval movement that implied gathering strength for the Sultan's cause. If the Czar could choose to attend only to the pacific utterances of London, the Turkish extremists could, with equal logic, choose to observe nothing but the martial display of the same government. So, while Canning was pressuring Reshid for a continued attempt at rapprochement with the Russians, the English government sharpened the ardor of the reactionaries by weak compliance in the wishes of the French to move the fleets closer to the scene of action. The effect this move had on the Turkish war party is manifest, for, on the seventh of July, the Sultan precipitately removed Mustapha and Reshid from office. They were the ones, the Grand Vezir and the Reis Effendi, who were following Canning's instructions. It is unfortunate, from Canning's position as interpreted by some of his detractors, that there was not more public notice of this incident, for it would have undoubtedly revealed the pressures he was fighting at the Porte itself. Had there been a ministerial crisis or interregnum at the time, it might have brought home the fact that the desires of the Turks had to be considered in the subsequent negotiations. But so great was the crisis as

Canning saw it that he leaped in immediately, and the deposed ministers were reinstated on the following day. It proves beyond shadow of doubt that Stratford Canning was working for peace so long as it could be maintained with honor, but he made so little of this ministerial fluctuation in his dispatches that it was passed over without notice at home and has been lost sight of in subsequent histories. It is most probable that had he remained aloof from this cabinet change the Turks might have begun hostilities forthwith along the Danube.

Canning was hoping, however, that the Russian occupation would provoke an Austrian protest, for that was the one power above all others who could not look on complacently while Russian legions established themselves along the lower Danube and threatened further incursions into the Balkans. The Czar's actions did produce the Austrian reaction hoped for by Canning, and, at the time, Prussia was following the lead of Austria. The Austrian foreign minister, Count Buol-Schauenstein, gave vent to strong expressions of Austrian displeasure, and significant reinforcements were sent to the frontier garrisons. Buol announced, moreover, that Austria was of one mind with England and France on the matter of the dispute, and, in a move to cement the relationship, he summoned the several ambassadors to a mutual consultation in Vienna.

This was all desirable from the point of view of unanimity, but the net effect of the resulting Conference of Vienna was deleterious in that it removed the pivotal negotiations from

the more informed and skilled hands at Constantinople and
deposited them in less capable hands at Vienna. By this time
the powers were all sufficiently aroused to the dangers threatening European peace to the extent that each cabinet began
to scramble for a means to preserve peace and prevent Russian
hegemony over the European portion of the Ottoman Empire.
The various peace plans referred to at the outset of this
chapter began to emanate from the several capitals, one after
another, before any single plan could be digested and assimi-
lated; and although all the governments entered wholeheart-
edly into the Vienna proceedings, none of them had the
patience to wait for that Conference to produce something
substantial. There was indeed unanimity of purpose to be
found through the summer of 1853 but absolutely no agreement regarding the means to achieve the end in view. Above
all, the busy searchers for peace seem to have become oblivious
to the fact that the Porte was a party to the dispute and in
effect so proceeded as to intimate that the Turk would have
to be content with whatever scheme was agreed upon by the
mediating powers. The Western ambassadors in Constantinople were put in the position of having to inform the Porte
of decisions made in Vienna or Paris or London involving
sovereign prerogatives of the Turks.

These were the general conditions which led to the failure
of the Vienna Conference, and their application to the circumstances of the famous "Vienna Note" affords an example of
the workings of the Conference which was typical of all its
well-intentioned effort.

Canning had welcomed the union in Vienna, never sup-
posing that it was to supersede the close association of the
ambassadors in Constantinople, but rather that it would rein-
force the work begun at the Porte. By the end of July he had
drawn up what was to be a final Turkish offer to appease the
sentiments of Czar Nicholas. The offer went as far as possible
in its efforts to satisfy Russian claims but also noted that if
Russia failed to agree and to withdraw her forces from the
principalities, the Turks would have no alternative but to
reassert their authority in the principalities and move to eject
the Russians by force of arms. The "Turkish Ultimatum," as
it was called, was a mild one, which looked for confirmation
in Vienna.[8] It arrived in Vienna at a time when the diplomats
working there had just concluded a peace plan of their own
which was to be known as the "Vienna Note." The note
which the Elchi submitted had already been approved by
the Porte and was to be transmitted to Russia by the Vienna
Conference in the name of the Sultan and—it was hoped
at the Porte—with the unanimous recommendation of the
powers. Canning and his diplomatic colleagues had every
reason to feel that it would be agreed to by St. Petersburg,
especially if the respective allied cabinets would add their
own words of warning in their separate recommendations that
it be adopted.

The men in Vienna, however, presumed to interpose themselves between the Porte and St. Petersburg, for they had
contrived to draw up a solution which took into account only
the grievances of Russia. The Vienna Note, which they

forwarded to the Czar in place of the Turkish Ultimatum, while it did not allow the treaty provisions specifically demanded by the Menshikov mission, did, nevertheless, grant the same ends. It did so by binding the Sultan anew to respect the stipulations of the former treaties of Kustchuk-Kainardji and Adrianople, and the language in which this promise was stated was open to the interpretation that these agreements gave the Russians the same right to interfere that the Turks now refused to grant. Secondly, the language of the Vienna Note implied that whaever privileges the various Christian communities presently enjoyed in the Ottoman domains were a result of Russian intervention rather than a Turkish desire for justice. The intrinsic injustice of this implication seems to be borne out by the fact that the Vienna Note was accepted eagerly by the Court of St. Petersburg. Unfortunately, the Turks had not been consulted, and they found both of these points inadmissible. They did agree to the Note, however, with some amendments of language which served to remove the questionable interpretation noted. There were three such clarifications inserted, and they read as follows (the text of the Vienna Note is given first in each instance, followed by the Turkish alteration, which I have italicized): [9]

1. If at all times the emperors of Russia have shown their active solicitude for the maintenance of the immunities and privileges of the Orthodox Greek Church in the Ottoman Empire, the sultans have never ceased to confirm them . . .

This language, in the view of the Porte, implied that the sultans acted only in response to Russian initiative, which, according to the Turks, was historically incorrect. They therefore proposed the following wording:

> If at all times the emperors of Russia have shown their active solicitude for the *worship of the Orthodox Greek Church, the sultans have never ceased to watch over the maintenance of the immunities and privileges of that worship and of that Church in the Ottoman Empire and to confirm them* . . . .
>
> 2. The undersigned . . . declare . . . the government of the Sultan will remain faithful to the letter and the spirit of the stipulations of the treaties of Kustchuk-Kainardji and of Adrianople relative to the protection of Christian worship . . . .

Here the phraseology left in doubt to whom these treaties give the right of protection, and the Divan desired an amendment:

> The undersigned . . . declare . . . the government of the Sultan will remain faithful to the letter and the spirit of the stipulations of the *treaty* of Kustchuk-Kainardji, *confirmed by that of Adrianople,* relative to the protection *by the Porte* of Christian worship . . . .

The following quotation completes the declaration begun in Number 2.

3. . . . and that His Majesty regards it as a point of honour with him . . . to allow the Greek worship to participate . . . in the advantages conceded to other Christians by convention or special agreement.

In this passage there were two ambiguous elements calling for modification. For one thing, the Turks thought it somewhat hazy as to which "His Majesty" the language referred. Secondly, the Porte could envision the Russians demanding for the Orthodox Greeks privileges accorded to chapels in diplomatic embassies, for example, privileges amounting to the extraterritorial sovereignty demanded by the Menshikov mission. They sent this wording back to Vienna:

. . . and that His Majesty, *the Sultan,* regards it is a point of honour . . . to allow the Greek worship . . . *the advantages accorded, and which may be accorded, to other Christian communities, Ottoman subjects.*

It is chiefly with regard to the controversy over these passages in the original text of the Vienna Note that Stratford Canning has been blamed for the downfall of peace negotiations. Nothing could be further from the truth, and the charge contradicts the record and sequences of exchanges, as well as the testimony given by the subsequent behavior of all parties to the proceedings.

The Turkish Ultimatum, it will be remembered, was sent to Vienna before the text of the Vienna Note was known at

the Porte. It arrived in Vienna, by courier, the day after the
Vienna Note had been sent to St. Petersburg and Constanti-
nople. The Vienna diplomats decided to suppress the Turkish
Ultimatum because they had already ascertained Russian
willingness to accept the Vienna Note. Moreover, Lord
Westmoreland (the British ambassador in Vienna) had
Lord Clarendon's approval of the Note. Unfortunately,
Vienna had telegraphic communication with London whereas
Canning did not (either with London or Vienna), but Westmoreland had the good sense and courtesy to send immediately to Canning a copy of Clarendon's approval of the Vienna
text. This relay from Westmoreland reached Canning on the
ninth of August. The record shows that on the fourth of
August, *after* he had received the text of the Vienna Note
but *before* he knew of the suppression of the Turkish Ultimatum and the substitution of the Note for it by the Vienna
Conference, Canning sent a response to Lord Westmoreland. His explanation is ample evidence that there was not
the slightest chance for Turkish agreement to the Note even
had they known it had the approval of London:

> There is an old proverb . . . about broth suffering from
> the zeal of too many cooks, and I hope we are not about to
> have a new proof of its truth.
> Reshid Pasha told . . . [us] that the Porte will hear of
> nothing but the Ultimatum, which has probably been in
> your possession since Monday, and which goes on to St.
> Petersburg—if, as I trust, you send it on,—uniting all voices
> here and all chances in its favour with the advantage of
> springing . . . out of Clarendon's instructions to me.

He then added a private opinion on the Vienna Note:

> The Convention [Vienna Note], even if it had arrived in time, would not have been accepted by the Sultan's ministers. I am free to say, between ourselves, that even to my humble judgment, it does not seem to be a *safe* form of arrangement, if taken seriously, as Russia would necessarily understand it. Excuse all this and let me live in hope that the Porte's "Ultimatum" will be accepted with your assistance.[10]

On the twelfth of August Canning received the disappointing, but official, instruction from Clarendon to urge acceptance of the Vienna Note upon the Porte. Simultaneously the news arrived in Constantinople that the Note had been approved by Czar Nicholas. Without hesitation the British Ambassador sought an audience with Reshid Pasha in the course of which he followed his instructions:

> I called the attention of Reshid Pasha to the strong and earnest manner in which the Vienna Note was recommended to the acceptance of the Porte, not only by her Majesty's Government, but also by the Cabinets of Austria, France, and Prussia. I reminded him of the intelligence which had been received from St. Petersburg, purporting that the Emperor of Russia had signified his readiness to accept the same Note. I urged the importance of his engaging the Porte to come to a decision with the least possible delay. I repeatedly urged the importance of an immediate decision, and the danger of declining, or only accepting with amendments, what the four friendly powers so earnestly recommended and what the Cabinet of St. Petersburg had accepted in its actual state.[11]

Reshid listened graciously to the Elchi but informed him that sentiment was already in favor of rejecting the Note. He promised, however, to relay the Elchi's words to the Council of Ministers at their meeting scheduled for the fourteenth of August. At this meeting of the Divan there was stormy discussion, with the Grand Vezir, Reshid Pasha, and one other minister arguing for acceptance of the Note with suitable modifications (those later entered by the Porte). Eight other members, including Rifat Pasha (the powerful President of the Council), Ali Pasha, the Sheik-ul-Islam, and the Ministers of Finance and the Navy, refused to countenance the Note in any form, while five ministers abstained from voting. The meeting broke up without any decision.[12]

On the following day Reshid Pasha informed Canning that there was no hope of obtaining a majority vote in the Council to accept the Note as it stood, and no certainty that it would be accepted even with due amendment. Even here the Elchi had not exhausted all means of following out the instructions of the London Cabinet. He suggested to Reshid that the Porte could accept the text of the Note as it stood, signifying, at the same time, the construction it put upon the questionable passages, and rely for its security on the support and guarantee of the four powers which supported the Note. This assurance, he promised on his own certainty, would be readily forthcoming.

In spite of the Elchi's personal guarantee, nothing could sway the adamant majority of the Council. It would have been better, Reshid told Canning, for England to have abandoned the Porte at the outset than to have carried her thus far only to desert at the last moment. The patience of Turkish patriotism and Islamic ardor had gone as far as it could go without an explosion.[13] The best Reshid could do was to secure the permission of an expanded Great Council of the Empire, including, in addition to the Divan, all important persons of the ulema, the aristocracy, merchants, etc., to return the Note to Vienna with the modifications already noted above. This was done on the twentieth of August.

The shock of the Turkish rejection had, at least, the effect of returning some semblance of reality to the Conference of Vienna. After the initial chagrin over the unlooked for "obstinacy of the Turks" had passed away, the assembled diplomats were able to take a second look at the Turkish modifications and appraise them in the light of the immediate past. When that was done they were seen to be not unreasonable, and, on the twenty-eighth of August, they were dispatched to the Czar with the recommendation that they be accepted. If nothing more, they could be the basis for further negotiation.

If the Conference of Vienna could be described as being shocked by the refusal of the Porte to accept the Note, then the Czar and his ministers can safely be pictured as shuddering with rage. They categorically rejected the amended document and ranted at the Turks and all the warlike influences at work in the Seraglio (among which they undoubtedly included Stratford Canning). In fact, they went too far in their recriminations, far enough to reveal that the Turkish objections were well founded. In an imposingly titled "Analysis of the Three Modifications Introduced by the Ottoman Porte into the Vienna Note," delivered to the Austrian Ambassador at St. Petersburg for transmission to Count Buol-Schauenstein, the Russian foreign ministry implicitly admitted what Canning and the Turks feared about the Vienna Note. After rejecting the thesis that the Sublime Porte had, of its own volition, watched over the immunities and privileges of the Orthodox Church, Count Nesselrode, either unthinkingly or in desperation, unveiled the true Russian objective: " . . . It is precisely the reverse of what is thus stated," he says of the Turkish alteration, " . . . which has compelled us to apply a remedy to it, by demanding a *more express* [my italics] guarantee for the future." In other words, the promise of the Sultan is insufficient for the future. He goes on to say, further, that "there is an appearance of throwing a doubt upon the *right* [my italics] we possess of watching over the strict fulfillment of that promise."[14]

These baldly stated remonstrances prove that Russia would be satisfied with nothing less than the right by treaty of intervening in the internal affairs of the Porte whenever and wherever she judged such intervention to be warranted. The truth was out, at last, and Tyrell quotes the London *Times* (no date is given) in this wise:

It cannot be denied that in this matter of the Vienna Note
there had been a singular amount of diplomatic blundering.
Four trained diplomatists had drawn up a document to
secure a certain object, which object such document left
substantially unsecured; and, what is more, the oversight
remained undetected by their respective governments, and
even unappreciated after its detection by Turkey, until Russia herself came forward with a demonstration of the fact
. . . All that can be said is, that when the mistake became
apparent they did their best to remedy it . . . . This course
the governments of France and England adopted, and while
still earnestly advocating a pacific settlement, they resolutely
backed the Porte in its rejection of the Vienna Note.[15]

When the news of the Russian refusal to accept the
compromise note submitted by the Porte reached Constantinople (September 25), it was apparent that only a miraculous
reversal of events could prevent the outbreak of war between
Russia and the Ottoman Empire. Still, Canning tried again.
He again appealed to Reshid and the Divan to accept the
original Note along with a guarantee from the four powers.
But the specter of revolt from below had already made itself
felt within the confines of the Seraglio, and the appeal was in
vain. On the twenty sixth the full Grand Council of the
Empire, 172 members strong, examined the Koran and the
facts and decided that there was no choice but to go to war.
The determination of the date for the proclamation was left
to the Caliph himself, but it was a decision he dared not
ignore. As Charles Alison described it in a letter to Lady

Stratford, " . . . It was a hint which the Sultan dared not throw away, for they would very shortly have produced another text, such as, for instance, 'and when one of the rulers of the faithful shall incline his ears unto the counsels of the ungodly, slay him, lest he be thereby perverted, and save his soul to the Lord.'"[16] Alison, the Orientalist, who had been through it all with the Elchi, knew whereof he spoke.

1. Lane-Poole, *op. cit.*, II, 276-77.
2. Temperley, *op. cit.*, pp. 337-38, 509. The Dutch minister was certain this would have occurred.
3. Kinglake, *op. cit.*, I. 127.
4. Tyrrell, *op. cit.*, I, 33.
5. Temperley, *op. cit.*, p. 333.
6. *Ibid.*
7. *Ibid.*, pp. 333-34.
8. *Ibid.*, p. 324: " . . . the phrase 'Turkish ultimatum' was unfortunate."
9. The French text may be found in Kinglake, *op. cit.*, I, Appendix 2, the English text in Tyrrell, *op. cit.*, I, 36 ff.
10. Lane-Poole, *op. cit.*, II, 289-90.
11. Letter to Clarendon, August 13, 1853, Kinglake, *op. cit.*, I, 229-30.
12. See Lane-Poole, *op. cit.*, II, 292.
13. Cf. Temperley, *op. cit.*, p. 348: "That feeling, and not Stratford's influence, was the true reason for rejection."
14. Tyrrell, *op. cit.*, I, 37-38.
15. *Ibid.*, p. 40.
16. Lane-Poole, *op cit.*, II, 301.

XXIV

THE ill-fated Conference of Vienna was a noble attempt to save the peace of Europe. Rather than a gathering of victors united to dictate the terms of peace, like its more famous predecessor, the Congress of Vienna, it was an attempt to prevent war and may be fairly said to have contained in embryo the peace-maintaining machinery of the United Nations: a collective effort to persuade diverse parties to compromise their differences. The Vienna Conference cannot be condemned because it ultimately proved incapable of its purpose; more than a century later and after more horrible conflicts, the several nations have not yet devised a method of preventing war between major powers. The European unanimity which found expression in Vienna through the summer and fall of 1853, a unanimity which Stratford Canning prayed for and worked for, did actually delay the outbreak of general war for more than half a year after the nations began to totter on the brink. Why, or how, did it finally fail?

Certainly, it did not founder because of any intrinsic imperfection of concept. As long as the idea of united action prevailed, it was successful. It was only when this unity suffered damage by peripheral actions that the central theme was lost sight of and was buried in confusion and contradiction.

When, after Nesselrode revealed Russia's aims in his interpretation of the Vienna Note, Czar Nicholas I realized that he faced the possibility of a united four-power coalition ranged against him, he did indeed waver and soften. He met the Austrian emperor at Olmutz and disavowed the interpretation that had been put upon his minister's comments. He expressed a willingness to accept the substance of the Turkish amendments in the form of an international agreement that such was the understood meaning of the Note.[1]

The Russian softening came too late, for jingoism had been born in England.[2] Within days after the publication of Nesselrode's analysis, Aberdeen had lost the press and the public. He was even losing his Cabinet whose members had shortly before been ready to recall Viscount Stratford de Redcliffe on the mistaken notion that he had been responsible for Turkish rejection of the Vienna Note. Palmerston had not been part of this; he had long been for close action with France even if it meant war, which he did not think it did. Now Russell swung toward Palmerston, and Clarendon wavered and gave up hope for peace. There remained only the Prime Minister himself, and Gladstone, still looking for peace. Aberdeen was now at a loss, and instead of attempting to lead he became a follower.

The leadership was provided by France, and the Cabinet insisted that the Prime Minister follow. It has already been noted (page 306) that England and France, while supporting and participating in the inchoate alliance in Vienna, engaged nevertheless in a series of independent moves of a military nature. These moves were always instigated by the French government, and Austria and Prussia were never consulted nor were they invited to participate. The idea naturally grew in the minds of the Germanic ministers that the western maritime powers were quite prepared to be the military executors of the four-power association. Hence Austria and Prussia wondered if they were to be dispensed from the obligation of following their word with deeds.

The question of French motives is not germane to this study. The fact is that the moves were made, often impulsively and at critical moments. The motives might have been very high-minded and the maneuvers might have been salutary as far as warning the Czar was concerned, but any possible beneficial effect was weakened by the continued assurances of English statesmen that war was out of the question. In his innermost thoughts the Czar could not believe, until the very end, that Aberdeen would take England into war. It is also worth noting that when, in June of 1853, the French and English fleets were transferred to Besika Bay at the mouth of the Dardanelles, the Czar was, in effect, publicly challenged. He could not suddenly exhibit fear by pulling his forces back from the principalities without suffering irreparable loss of prestige. More than that, he knew from the Seymour Correspondence that the English government was unable to abandon the Sultan without reason. He might well have decided, therefore, that the fleet movement was a gesture and nothing more, and thus did not substantially alter the situation.

On three successive occasions before the outbreak of hostilities, the Paris government urged England to join with it in sending the fleets up the Dardanelles to the Bosporus.[3] This would have been a direct violation of the Treaty of 1841 by which the five major European powers pledged themselves to respect the inviolability of the Straits except when the Sultan was at war. On the thirteenth of July, Napoleon's Minister of Foreign Affairs declared to the London Cabinet that if the Russian occupation of the Danubian principalities continued, the French fleet could not long remain at anchor in Besika Bay. Again on the nineteenth of August, when the Sultan rejected the Vienna Note, Paris advised London that it was absolutely necessary that the fleets proceed up the Straits. True, the Aberdeen Ministry did not succumb to these entreaties, but neither did it reject them as being inconsistent with the aims of the Vienna Conference. On the contrary, it allowed itself to be drawn into expressions of special unity with the Emperor of the French, so much so that the Queen in her speech at the close of the Parliamentary

session of 1853 in August, spoke of being "united" with the
Emperor of the French whereas there was a weaker expression
of association with the procedures of the Vienna Conference.

In this same month of August, when both governments
were officially supporting the Vienna Note, Stratford Canning's French colleague at the Porte, De la Cour, was also
consulting with the Turks as to the best landing places for
French troops should the need arise. On August 18, and
again on the twenty-second, "he asked Reshid Pasha to give
instructions to the Pasha of the Dardanelles to let the French
fleet pass up, should Admiral Hamelin so desire, without
reference to any corresponding movement on the part of
Vice-Admiral Dundas [British naval commander]."[4]

But Canning continued to fight for peace. However, his
restraining influence, as we have seen, faced an increasingly
complex mixture of patriotism and fanaticism in Constantinople during the month of September. It is not surprising
that as this ardor grew in intensity there were public demonstrations demanding that the Sultan go to war. There is no
question that the demands became insistent and inflammatory,
nor that they eventually influenced the Grand Council to
vote for war; but when theological students began pasting
up placards calling for "holy war," the French Ambassador
panicked and telegraphed his government that unless something was done the lives of all Christians in the capital would
be in danger. This was on the twentieth of September, before
the final Russian rejection of the amended Vienna Note was a
certainty, and before the Council had decided on war. On

receipt of this information the French foreign minister for the third time implored London to move at once to protect the lives of its own subjects and the countless *rayahs* in the capital.

Although Lord Clarendon had some misgivings, apparently, since he had heard nothing of the kind from Lord Stratford, nevertheless both he and the Prime Minister gave way before the onslaught of French insistence, and on the twenty-third he dispatched an order to Canning to summon the whole fleet to Constantinople. The Russian Ambassador in London, Baron Brunnow, informed the government at St. Petersburg at once and at the same time protested vigorously to the Foreign Office that the order was a clear violation of international agreement.

This was the only instruction Canning disobeyed. He knew the facts, both with regard to the spirit of the Moslem populace and the legality of the situation. He had, indeed, anticipated the possibility of intermittent riot and a display of public emotions which might get out of hand by sending for three small steamers in accordance with recognized diplomatic privilege. By the time the orders reached him the popular disturbances had quieted down (the Council had already bowed to the inevitability of war), and he was able to write Clarendon on the fourth of October:

> I fear that nothing can now prevent the declaration of war. There is just the possibility of something coming through Vienna . . . before the formal declaration is pub-

lished. But the better chance is that after the declaration
no actual hostilities will take place . . . and that a strenuous
interposition of the *Four* [powers], if that be possible, may
produce a reconciliation while blood is still undrawn.

We have nothing to apprehend from disturbances *here,*
and I regret that the French have shcwn so little disposition
to send away their extra force when the danger has passed
away. I make no comments on M. de la Cour's telegraphic
despatch . . . .

The French would seem to have some motive of *their own*
for bringing up the squadrons. . . . and are ever and anon
endeavouring to carry out some by-object of their own under
pretence of acting for the common cause.[5]

His resignation to the declaration of war lay in the publication on the same day of a proclamation by Abdul Medjid
which stated that the continued occupation of the principalities was a *casus belli* and gave notice that the Turkish general
in the area, Omar Pasha, was instructed to notify the Russian
commander, Prince Gortchakoff, to this effect. Omar was to
give the Russians fifteen days to initiate the withdrawal of
their troops and upon conclusion of that period, or upon
receipt of a negative reply, was to commence hostilities.

The tremendous strain and labor that this situation involved
for the aging diplomat—he was nearing his sixty-seventh birthday—is attested to in a note that he "scribbled" to his wife:

We have narrowly escaped a sanguinary revolution, and
we have escaped it only to go full tilt into war. The Sultan
and the General Council have resolved upon war, and the
Russians will soon be summoned to march out of the prov-

inces, preparatory to hostilities if they don't, as they won't, comply.

This is an awful prospect . . . . I have done what I could to avert it, but circumstances swollen by mismanagement have carried all before them . . . . My feet are literally sore with standing at the upright desk for the last eight hours. I shall be asked to bring up the squadrons, and feel embarassed beforehand . . . .[6]

Despite the growing probability of a state of war between Russia and Turkey, he was still hopeful of containing the war, and he was unwilling to do anything that might widen its sphere. That is why he did not obey Clarendon's order to bring up the fleet: he was certain the Czar would not willingly engage in a general war and was unwilling to force it upon him. If England and France moved too hastily, there could be no turning back. On the other hand, as long as they observed the strict letter of international agreement, there was yet chance for peaceful "interposition." Once the state of war actually existed, the Sultan could legally invite the fleets to enter, and Canning's original instructions were to summon the fleet only to "protect" the person of the Sultan if the need should arise. "I wished to save her Majesty's Government," he amplified his explanations to Clarendon on the sixth of October, "from any embarrassments likely to accrue from a premature passage of the Dardanelles."[7]

Again the Elchi's estimation proved to be the correct one in that he divined exactly what was going on in the minds of the Russians. When the time limit of the Turkish ulti-

matum expired, the Sultan declared that a state of war existed
between him and the Czar of Russia. Russia, protesting that
war was declared by the Sultan and not by its government,
circularized the European governments to declare that

> . . . we shall content ourselves with maintaining our posi-
> tion there in the Principalities, remaining on the defensive
> so long as we are not forced to abandon limits within which
> we desire to confine our action. We will await the attack
> of the Turks without taking the initiative of hostilities. It
> will then entirely depend on other powers not to widen the
> limits of the war, if the Turks persist in waging it against
> us, and not to give to it any other character than that which
> we mean to leave to it. After the declaration of war, it is
> not to Russia that it belongs to seek for new expedients, nor
> to take the initiative in overtures of conciliation. But if,
> when better enlightened as to its interests, the Porte shall
> manifest a disposition to propose or receive similar overtures,
> it is not the emperor who will place any obstacles to their
> being taken into consideration. . . . They [our intentions]
> furnish an additional proof of the desire of our august master
> to limit as much as possible the circle of hostilities, if they
> should unhappily take place, and to spare the consequences
> of them to the rest of Europe.[8]

These protestations of restraint and injured innocence were
by no means haphazardly chosen. The Czar had lately concluded a week-long meeting with the young Francis Joseph
of Austria at Olmutz; and despite the deep personal affection
between the two men, Austria's increasing objection to the
amassing of Russian armies on or near her frontiers was made

unmistakably clear. Austria pointedly warned that she would consider the outbreak of war in the Danube a menace to her own peace and tranquillity. The Czar was faced not only with ominous naval mobilization on the part of France and England but with land mobilization by Austria as well. Indeed, the time was ripe for the "strenuous interposition" of the four powers to which Canning had alluded on October 4.

Diplomacy had not yet surrendered to the god of war, and Stratford Canning was busy framing a new note which would, first of all, call for an armistice, then a meeting of plenipotentiaries at a neutral place, then negotiations on the basis of a collective European guarantee of the privileges of the Eastern Church as outlined in the Sultan's latest firmans. At the same time he was under increasing pressure to bring up the fleet—a move he resisted until the very end (i.e., until the fifteen days of the Turkish ultimatum expired). Actually, the state of war existed before this, for Prince Gortchakoff had curtly refused to withdraw and that refusal, of itself, was sufficient to legalize the state of war.

Even at this late date Canning extracted a promise from Reshid for a ten-day delay in the opening of hostilities. It was, as he described it, a "forlorn hope" but one he felt in duty bound to attempt. The Porte agreed to his note, Clarendon agreed to it, but the French pressure for entrance into the Dardanelles and their threat to enter alone (and thus undermine the concerted action he deemed necessary) forced his hand, and he agreed to the summons on the twentieth of

October. But he resolutely refused to sanction a passage into the Black Sea as being entirely uncalled for. The presence of the English fleet at the Golden Horn was sufficient guarantee of the Sultan's safety.

Stung by this action the Czar naturally ordered the Sebastopol fleet to put to sea to interdict Turkish commerce. Now the instructions to the British admirals and to the Ambassador were to the effect that if this occurred then the fleets were, in fact, to enter the Black Sea. Again this explains Canning's reluctance to summon them at all, for he knew the Czar would be constrained to take countermeasures. Yet there was nothing to be done but follow the orders from home. Curiously enough, it was now France's turn to hold back: their ships were not seaworthy enough to face the winter storms that buffeted that landlocked body of water. So the fleets rested at anchor while the Russian ships ranged over the eastern and southern shores.

Stratford Canning implored the Turks not to send their fleet out to a hopeless contest just yet, and they listened to him.[9] They kept their heavy ships in the anchorages about the capital but unfortunately allowed some of their lighter vessels to cruise along the Asiatic shores. On November 30, a trim Russian squadron appeared off the coast of the minor naval base at Sinope and completely destroyed a Turkish squadron at anchor there. Those Turkish ships that did not sink burned until they were charred wrecks, and at least two thousand Turkish seamen perished.

When the news reached Constantinople, the Turks were in a fury, at the Russians, of course, but also at their purported protectors whose ships remained serenely at anchor. They would have no more of diplomacy, and once again there was near revolt. The latest peace plans were lost in the excitement.

The news hit London like a thunderbolt about the tenth of December. Lord Palmerston resigned from the Cabinet, ostensibly in protest over the weak policies of Aberdeen, Clarendon, and Gladstone.[10] For ten days he remained outside the government and re-entered only after waging a vigorous campaign at public meetings to meet fire with fire. A warlike rage swept through London and the other cities. The Ministry wavered, then gave in. Palmerston returned to the Home Office which he had held, but on his own terms: that the Cabinet place England in resolute, united action with France to curb the crimes of the Czar.

The disaster at Sinope had indeed delivered a mortal wound to peace, but the diplomats tried anew to ply their trade. On the fifth of December, through a protocol suggested by Stratford Canning and approved by Clarendon and the Conference of Vienna, the four powers declared that the existence of Turkey in the limits assigned to it by existing treaties was necessary for the maintenance of European peace. Again, however, the French interfered. The French government, on receipt of the news of Sinope, reversed the decisions of its admirals in the Levant and proposed to London that the combined fleets enter the Black Sea. France also proposed that the two governments inform the Russian government that all Russian ships would be forcibly limited to the waters adjacent to Sebastopol and, furthermore, that any attempt or act of aggression against Ottoman territory or against the Turkish flag would be repelled by force. It was tantamount to a defensive alliance with the Turks and could mean nothing but war at this stage. Aberdeen saw it as a chance for peace, and agreement to it was Palmerston's price for returning to the government. Agreement was given, and the appropriate orders and notes were sent forth from London.

This was while the protocol of the fifth of December, strengthened by the incorporation of a request for a ten-day cessation of hostilities—Canning's "forlorn hope" of mid-November—was being studied at St. Petersburg. There was every reason to feel that the Czar would assent. The rising pressure of concerted opposition was unnerving him, or, at least, his generals. Russian honor, moreover, had been vindicated by the victory at Sinope and minor success in Asia. The time was once more propitious.[11]

On January 4, 1854, the Anglo-French fleet moved into the Black Sea, and on the twelfth the Czar was ordered by France and England to keep his warships in their anchorage or risk their destruction. He sent orders to his ambassadors at London and Paris to close their embassies and come home. By the twenty-first of February diplomatic relations between

France and England, on the one hand, and Russia, on the other, were completely broken.

1. I do not think too much should be made of Nicholas' pacific protestations at Olmutz. He had little choice, as Austrian "ingratitude" (see above, chap. XVIII, n. 15) was already evident. Austria was demanding evacuation of the principalities.

2. See Leon Dennen, *Trouble Zone* (New York: Ziff-Davis., 1945), p. 15: "In the 1850's the word 'jingoism' was born in the London music halls, and good Englishmen sang: 'We don't want to fight, but, by jingo, if we do,/We've got the ships, we've got the men, we've got the money too.'"

3. For a discussion of the various fleet movements see Temperley, *op cit.*, pp. 350 ff.

4. Lane-Poole, *op. cit.*, II, 306.

5. *Ibid.*, pp. 302-3.

6. *Ibid.*, p. 302.

7. *Ibid.*, p. 308.

8. Tyrrell, *op. cit.*, I, 44-45.

9. The Turks had proposed to send their line-of-battle ships on a sweep around the full perimeter of the Black Sea (see Temperley, *op. cit.*, p. 369).

10. Palmerston actually resigned over a domestic dispute but was content to let the press interpret it as a foreign policy dispute.

11. The Turkish leaders were favorably inclined, but the rush of events swallowed that chance for peace.

XXV

FROM this point on it is almost impossible to write a separate diplomatic history of the events that finally culminated in the Crimean War. In the first place, the remaining diplomatic activity is overshadowed by transactions of a military nature. Secondly, there was little initiative left to diplomacy, and whatever took place was little more than the backwash of efforts previously set in motion and still floating about, aimlessly subject to the incoming tide of war.

As for Viscount Stratford de Redcliffe, he was too much of a realist to suppose that he could do anything more to stem this onrushing tide. He could hope only that it might be effectively channeled and blocked by the barrier of the still-enduring quadripartite association functioning in Vienna. With the rupture of relations between the western European powers and Russia, all further overtures in the direction of St. Petersburg were, perforce, abandoned to the agency of the central European powers, and this meant, for all practical purposes, to the initiative of Austria.

If in retrospect one tends to dismiss the prospects for thus containing the impending disaster, one does so at the cost of ignoring the realities of the then current conditions. For the Austrian government still expected to be called upon to fill the role her own interests logically destined for her. On February 22, 1854, her foreign minister declared to the French ambassador: "If England and France will fix a day for the evacuation of the Principalities, the expiration of which shall be the signal for hostilities, the Cabinet of Vienna will support the summons."[1] These words were quickly relayed to London and Paris where their meaning must have been amply clear. Austria had mobilized, and increased her military appropriations; Prussia had done likewise. And each had informed the Czar of its complete support of the Anglo-French position in the crisis.

Napoleon III had already sent a personal letter to the Czar (January 29), in which he presumed to speak for the Queen of England as well as for himself, asking a Russian evacuation of the principalities in return for Anglo-French evacuation of the Black Sea.[2] Since the answer to that letter was negative, although not conclusively so, the French seized upon the Austrian suggestion at once, and the French Foreign Minister, Drouyn de Lhuys, pressed London for an immediate response. The two governments should, he argued, contact Nesselrode without delay and press for an immediate withdrawal, to be concluded at a given time, "say the end of March."[3] Now here, above all, was the opportunity of sending a joint draft to Vienna for concurrence, and for subsequent dispatch from there to St. Petersburg. That, surely, was the intention of the Austrian invitation. Unaccountably, no such obvious step was taken. Instead, each government drafted separate, though nearly identical, notes and sent them to the Czar not through the medium of the Vienna Conference but through their chief consular agents remaining in the Russian Empire. The notes demanded an affirmative answer, within six days of their receipt, that such withdrawal would be concluded by the thirtieth of April. Failure to reply, or refusal to comply, would be considered a cause for war.

The Czar could scarcely have been expected to bow to such ultimata; and on March 19, Count Nesselrode informed the same consuls that Nicholas I refused to answer such a degrading summons. On the twenty-fourth, Russian troops crossed the Danube and pushed south into Ottoman territory.

On March 27, the sovereigns of England and France announced in separate addresses from the throne that they were now in a state of war with the Czar of Russia for the defense of Turkey and justice. On the tenth of April, France and England concluded a treaty of alliance by which they bound themselves to use all the land and sea forces necessary to re-establish peace and set free the dominions of the Sultan. They pledged themselves to refrain from a separate peace and to withdraw from Turkey as soon as that peace and the independence of the Ottoman Empire were secured. Turkey, of course, became a party to that same treaty, but Austria was not specifically asked or invited to do so. Indeed, through May and June she still stood ready; and notwithstanding the

separate military moves of France and England, she maintained her mobilized forces on the frontier and repeatedly
demanded Russian withdrawal.[4] Those demands, coupled
with the gathering of French and English armies in the East,
finally swayed the Czar, and in the summer the Russian
armies did retreat.

When the withdrawal came, it should have been another
opportunity for peace, but by that time jingoism was in
sway. That is a story that anticipates somewhat the military
history of the war and will be treated below. It is mentioned
here to conclude the dismal account of how the English
government drifted into war, and the lengths to which Austria
went to implement the four-power concept of Stratford
Canning.

The portents in the sky had been sufficient to warn
Canning that he must look ahead to the war that was coming
and the demands that would be made upon him. In mid-
January he had written to his wife:

> The importance of the work in hand goes on increasing.
> It is like the cloud on the horizon, no bigger than a man's
> hand at first, but destined to cover the whole vault of heaven
> . . . . If we have war, as I expect, it will be a war of giants
> . . . and we must make the sacrifices necessary for success,
> and obtain results equal to the sacrifices. . . . it was exactly
> because I foresaw the depth and extent of the contest that
> I was against having out the squadrons in the first instance,
> that I was for peace if attainable with safety and honour to
> the Porte, and endeavouring to obtain peace by confronting
> the danger at once and imposing on Russia the necessity

of either giving way to European principles, clearly and stoutly asserted, or of throwing off the mask and picking up the gauntlet without further prevarication.

What might and ought to have been done more than six months ago is now at last in operation, but under circumstances which make arrangement far more difficult, and a war, more or less general, far more probable.

Yet, in spite of his resignation to the inevitability of war, he obviously thought, as the last sentence quoted implies, that the diplomatic coalescence achieved at Vienna would be carried over to the military operations. In this respect he saw the possibility of much good coming out of the evil, for it presaged a wide and final settlement of the Eastern question:

I always thought that the great struggle of the East would not be in my time, and that I was destined only to fall in the ditch that others more fortunate in later times might pass over with less difficulty. It seems to be otherwise ordained, and with Heaven's grace I accept my lot, and will apply what little remains of me to reach the promised land.[5]

This cautiously expressed optimism respecting the final good to be achieved was perhaps the only mistaken estimate he formed during the whole of the crisis, but even Stratford Canning was human and had to have hope that there was still some good to be attained. If humanity had not yet found the way to peace through reason and good will then, at least, there were ends worth fighting for, and he now made it his resolve that those ends be realized.

That it was his place to begin to hold up these ends for all
to see is, perhaps, an indication that in his heart he had
already begun to fear that all was not well in this respect. On
all sides there were signs that less noble, less ideal goals were
coming to the forefront, that farseeing people and groups
were already jockeying for positions whereby they could reap
the benefits of the suffering bound to ensue. The war party
was naturally in the ascendant in the Seraglio, and it was a
party to whom patriotism was equated with extreme nationalism and reaction. The Turkish mobilization had already
brought a host of primitive recruits and tribal irregulars into
the otherwise respectable ranks of the Sultan's army. Extremists in the ulema had long been crying for a jihad, or holy
war, and these inflamed irregulars had already begun to hurt
the Sultan's cause by their violence toward the innocent
rayahs among the Sultan's subjects. These crimes naturally
met with forceful resistance on the part of Greeks living in
Thrace, Macedonia, Thessaly, and Epirus, and the budding
spirit of revolt was aided and abetted openly by the Greek
government at Athens. The confusion was compounded when
still more of the irregulars (Bashi-Bazouks) were hurriedly
moved out against the revolutionaries, and any Greek, peaceful or otherwise, became fair game for their cruelty ("If they
were paid by Russia they could not serve her cause better,"[6]
the Elchi wrote at the time).

While the English government was even then "muddling
through" (the Cabinet asked for increased military appropriations only at the beginning of the new session of Parliament

in January), the French were hard at work preparing for the future, both politically and militarily. As early as November of the preceding year, they had replaced their ambassador at the Porte, De la Cour, who, though an experienced diplomat and loyal servant of his Emperor, was not warlike enough to suit the realities of the situation. In his place Napoleon had sent a general, Barraguay d'Hilliers, who came for no other purpose than to prepare the way for the French army, which was to follow. His main concerns, and they were honest and intelligent in view of the facts, were to secure adequate camp sites; demarcate landing areas, supply depots, and the like; and stockpile fodder and materiel. But even a soldier-diplomat must be a full diplomat at times and this D'Hilliers was not. He was demanding and offensive in his mode of requisitioning and in his interference with internal matters of the Turkish government. On one occasion, he even threatened to break off relations with the Porte when his demands were not satisfied. For a time Canning was as much engaged in keeping peace between the Porte and the French ambassador as formerly he had been in striving for peace between Turkey and Russia. Underneath the French brusqueness he saw hidden an intense jealousy of the position he and, through him, England had already secured in the councils of the Seraglio.

Nevertheless, France was preparing and England was not, neither so far as a definite policy for the future was concerned nor for the immediate needs of a gathering army. Whereas France sent out a general and a staff of militarily skilled

men, the English government, without even the formality of
definite instructions, left to their Ambassador, who had never
been in an army uniform, all the details necessary to provide
for an army that was beginning its long march from home.
"I completed my treaty for the reception of the Allied armies
last night," he wrote to Lady Stratford on March 13, 1854,
" . . . twelve hours passed at Reshid Pasha's! I went out
at 8 [in the evening] and returned after 9 this morning—no
bed, no dressing, and I have scribbled ever since."[7]

Stanley Lane-Poole describes the burdens of the sixty-seven-
year-old statesman in a passage that is worth quoting at
length:

> When it was known at Constantinople that England and
> France had declared war against the Czar and were pre-
> paring an expedition for the succour of the Sultan, Lord
> Stratford discovered that he had suddenly changed his pro-
> fession. For many months he was no longer to be the diplo-
> matist, the statesman, the guide of the faltering Turks, and
> the no less hesitating English ministers. He was now ap-
> parently Commissary-General, head of the Intelligence De-
> partment, Quarter-Master-General, Director of Transports,
> and provider-in-chief of everything that the British war
> departments had forgotten to supply for the use of the ex-
> pedition. He was even credited with the function of Surgeon-
> General to the Forces. Such at least is the impression
> produced by a study of the various demands made upon him
> by officials of every rank and description. At one time it
> is the Duke of Newcastle, who wants Lord Stratford to
> find boots to go over the trousers of 30,000 British soldiers,
> and who apparently expects that the bazaars of Stambol will
> furnish an admirable supply of Wellingtons. Then it is

Lord Raglan, who depends upon him, not only for reinforcements of Turkish infantry and artillery, but for planks for the hutting of the troops, and warm winter clothing for their comfort. Or again it is the London newspapers, who angrily ask why the ambassador has not had the forethought to store up a sufficient quantity of lint and physic and bedclothes for the sick and wounded at Scutari. . . .

As one reads these multifarious demands, one wonders whether an ambassador is supposed to be a man or a god, that he should do all these things. One who has served his country . . . in the strict career of diplomacy, . . . who has guided nations with his pen, but has not once controlled a busy executive department,—is suddenly called upon to supply every deficiency that a notoriously defective public service has overlooked. The British army goes forth to the Crimea, practically in the clothes it stands up in, and when the men are shivering for want of blankets and huts, and the wounded are lying on bare floors for want of beds, and the investing lines before Sevastopol are exposed on their flank for want of reinforcements, a universal cry arises . . . and Lord Stratford is to find the clothes and boots and blankets and huts and beds and reinforcements without a moment's delay. And if it chance that the markets of Stambol and Brusa and Adrianople and Salonica do not possess the articles required . . . there goes forth a general groan of indignation against the callous Elchi who has the misfortune to own but one brain and two hands with which to do the work of fifty experienced army officers . . . . It was not till the middle of 1855, when the war was almost over, that Lord Stratford obtained the valuable assistance of General Mansfield as military adviser; and till then the same staff which hardly sufficed to carry on the ordinary work of the Embassy in time of peace . . . was expected to add to their . . . labours the work of saving the British army from the consequences of the blunders of an unprepared War Office and Horse Guards! [8]

The foregoing is not a flight of literary fancy; it is but a brief summary of the miserable and deplorable conditions under which England went to war. It naturally brings up the question of how this came about. The answer is not only a fact of history—for the past is finished and unalterable—it also points to the duty of a peace-loving government to keep a military apparatus in being and to provide it with skilled, competent, and trained leadership. The tragedy of the Crimea, no less than the failure of diplomacy, is the tragedy brought about by the delusion that peace and goodness are served by a mere desire for them.

1. Kinglake, *op. cit.*, I, 292.
2. Tyrrell, *op. cit.*, I, 56-57.
3. Kinglake, *op. cit.*, I, 293.
4. Austrian intentions were sufficiently clear to Russia to force the Czar eventually to evacuate the principalities. And the subsequent engagement entered into by Austria with the Porte explicitly states: "His Majesty, the Emperor of Austria, engages to exhaust all the means of negotiation and all other means to obtain the evacuation of the Principalities by the foreign army which occupies them, and even to employ, in case they are required, the number of troops necessary to obtain this end" (Article I, Austrian-Ottoman Convention, June 14, 1854, in Kinglake, *op. cit.*, I, Appendix III). Some Russian historians credit Russia's military defeat in the Crimea to the necessity of keeping her main armies on guard against Austrian attack (cf. Vernadsky, *op. cit.*, p. 155).
5. Lane-Poole, *op. cit.*, II, 341-42.
6. *Ibid.*, p. 345.
7. *Ibid.*, p. 343.
8. *Ibid.*, pp. 350 ff.

XXVI

THE first elements of a completely inefficient English army had begun to filter through Gibraltar even before the declaration of war, and they began to reach the environs of the Turkish capital about the first of April. However, as noted above, there had been precious little arrangements made for receiving them. Above the regimental level there was no organization or over-all command until the first general officers started to arrive upon the scene. These men, unfortunately, had last witnessed large-scale operations in the closing days of the Napoleonic Wars, forty years earlier, and none had ever seen active service above the lowest commissioned grades. Some had been under fire in various Indian campaigns, but those experiences hardly fitted them to lead untrained troops in a major European war. Though they tried to whip the growing mass of men into brigade and divisional order, they had to occupy themselves chiefly with procuring basic supplies of food and shelter—and the small transport which were needed to move any such supplies they might lay their hands on.

By the time Lord Raglan, the designated British commander-in-chief, and his French counterpart, Marshal St. Arnaud, reached the area at the beginning of May, confusion was widespread and sickness had already begun to take its toll of the gathering forces. A plan of action had been agreed upon, meanwhile, and it called for removal of "combat-ready" troops to the Danubian theatre where it was hoped they would deliver a quick and stunning defeat to the Russian armies. Units already riddled by camp illnesses were crowded aboard transports and warships, where the fevers rapidly spread under ideal conditions for contagion. With even less planning they were disgorged at Varna, in Bulgaria, where the summer heat was turning the whole Danube estuary into a steaming marshland. There they were marched inland to higher ground in the hope that the fevers would abate in a better climate, but the marching under full knapsacks in the heat weakened the disease-struck ranks even more, and the military cemeteries grew almost as rapidly as encampments for the living.[1] The ill-used troops were not even to have the opportunity for the glory of quick victory, for on June 24, Czar Nicholas, bowing to Austrian demands, announced that he would withdraw his troops from the Danubian principalities.

The major threat to Turkey was thus removed, and it should have been the ideal time to reopen negotiations. But the war hysteria had reached a fever pitch in London and in Paris. The lust for martial glory demanded far more than such a disappointing climax to the gathering of the legions. Even if the most foolhardy seeker after glory recognized the impossibility of a full-scale invasion of European Russia, there was still an inviting target nearby. All eyes turned toward the Russian naval base at Sebastopol in the Crimea. That was the arrow continually pointed at the heart of the Ottoman Empire. The decision was made in London that the Czar's Black Sea stronghold had to be destroyed.

Accordingly, the weakened soldiers in Bulgaria were marched back to the coast during the latter half of July and the first part of August and packed anew aboard ship. More thousands of newly arrived contingents were sailed up from Gallipoli, and a vast armada grew and waited about the mouth of the Danube until final orders and arrangements were made. Illness was rampant in the over-crowded vessels, and the only bright spot was the adamant refusal of the British naval commander to allow his warships to be used for transport. It was not only the fear of plague that deterred him, for he also saw the inviting target presented to the Russian Black Sea fleet which, if it had moved, might have made a terrible shambles of the unmanageable mass of ships.

In spite of all obstacles, the unwieldy fleet of some five hundred vessels of all types—sail, steam, barges under tow, and what have you—was shepherded in a great arc across the Black Sea to the Crimea. The landings commenced on the fourteenth of September. Even here there was confusion, as the original landing orders had called for disembarkation at a point not far north of Sebastopol. En route, however, Lord Raglan had overruled the reconnaissance surveys made of the Crimean coast and, for fear of Russian opposition to the landing, had selected a new point some thirty miles to the north near the town of Eupatoria. It is true that there was a better beach at that point, but the allied armies had then to face the barrier of three rivers flowing from east to west.

Notwithstanding this tactically dangerous change of orders, the landings were accomplished in good order and with an efficiency remarkable under the circumstances. About twenty-five thousand English, an equal number of French, and some eight thousand Turkish troops were put ashore in three days, together with horse and artillery. A Russian field army under the command of the quondam diplomatist, Prince Menshikov, issued forth from Sebastopol to meet them, and the first major battle of the war was fought at the River Alma on the twentieth of September. A bloody day-long battle ended in a sound defeat for the Russians, even though they had the advantage of defensive positions along the higher southerly bank of the Alma. In the latter part of the day Menshikov broke off from the fight and withdrew his forces.

At this point another tragic element was added. Intelligence reports indicated that Prince Menshikov, instead of falling back toward the defenses of Sebastopol, had pulled away to the northeast, toward the center of the Peninsula. Sebastopol

was not guarded by permanent fortifications on the north side
and lay open to an assault. Menshikov's retreat testified to
his belief that he could not hold the base in the face of a
determined attack, but unaccountably the allies rested on
their arms while the leaders pondered the next move. St.
Arnaud was dying and Raglan hesitated to assume an over-all
command. When he did finally make a decision, it was
illogical in the extreme. Instead of following up the initial
victory, he moved the army in a wide sweep around the city
and decided to invest the bastion from the southern side.
Even then Menshikov did not move, convinced that an assault
from this quarter could not be effectively resisted. The western allies did not attack, however, but began to construct
siege lines paralleling the southern defences of the city. The
siege was to last for almost a whole year and was to involve
the useless slaughter of thousands upon thousands of men on
both sides.

When the Russians, to their own amazement, perceived
the intentions of their foe, they began to make feints from
the interior and to send reinforcements back into the city.
One of these feints was made in some force and resulted
in the small battle of Balaclava, dubiously glorified by the
inane charge of the Light Brigade. It was followed on the
fifth of November by the murderous, fog-covered Battle of
Inkerman, and that was the last open field battle of the war.
Both armies retired to their lines and siege warfare began.
The allies were exposed on the rocky heights while the

Russians were protected by more permanent fortifications in Sebastopol.

On November 14, a tremendous hurricane lashed the southern Crimea and almost entirely destroyed the pitiful accumulation of supplies available to the besiegers, as well as sinking most of the supply ships anchored in the harbor of Balaclava or en route to that port. Clad in the summer uniforms in which they went to Bulgaria, without huts or tents, without even a supply of natural firewood in the area, the allied soldiers were left to face their greatest enemies, winter and disease.

In Constantinople, meanwhile, the aging Ambassador was fighting his own battles. The Embassy was the acting commissariat for the army. The Ambassador himself had to function as military and political liaison officer with the Turks. He had to battle growing French intrigue which was contriving to replace British influence at the Porte with French predominance. Furthermore, he had to plead with his own government and with the French to forcibly restrain Athens from sabotaging whatever war effort the Porte might effectively make, for revolts by Orthodox nationalities had broken out all over the Balkans, instigated by the Russians and openly abetted by the government of King Otho in Athens.

When the wretched survivors of plague and fever bid fair to overwhelm the inadequate army medical facilities around Constantinople, everyone looked to Lord Stratford de Redcliffe for a miraculous solution. He had already secured the Turkish barracks at Scutari for a base hospital, as well as many other buildings, but when the battlefield wounded were added to the typhus, dysentery, and cholera victims, the situation become chaotic. When the magnitude of the mismanagement finally dawned upon the English public, it was Lord Stratford de Redcliffe who bore the brunt of blame for what the army and home government had failed to provide for their men.

Newspapers railed at the British Embassy with total disregard for facts and circumstances. Miss Florence Nightingale, too, with equal disregard for reality, added her recriminations to the unjust attacks, even though she and her ladies had been the beneficiaries of much of his personal efforts. For all her good intentions, and in spite of all her great work, the heroine of the nursing services was an imperious woman who brooked no competition. When other groups of women, independent of her jurisdiction, arrived to lend their help, she would tolerate none of their "interference" and was quite prepared to see them sent away from Constantinople despite the crying need for their services. It was the Elchi who stepped in and quietly secured buildings from the Turks where other less publicized hospitals were organized and where other groups labored just as heroically to alleviate the suffering of the soldiers.[2]

The grossest of these charges were subsequently laid to rest and their injustice revealed later on, but at the time they threw a tremendous cloud over Canning's world. The London

politicians were content to let him be the scapegoat for all
that had gone wrong, and his future relations with his home
government were never restored to their rightful position.
The Porte, too, took advantage of his apparent downfall and
resisted his continuing efforts to implement the Tanzimat
and the goals of Gulhane. The opportunity for effecting
reform was golden, but under the circumstances it could not
be grasped.

The most herculean efforts were made by all concerned to
bring order out of chaos, but they were too late, and a whole
British army disintegrated during the winter of 1854-55. The
charge was made in Parliament in January that of the fifty-
four thousand British troops that went out in '54, a bare
fourteen thousand remained in the trenches before Sebastopol.
The Cabinet could not gainsay the evidence, and the Aberdeen ministry resigned in February. After several attempts to
find leadership more suitable to herself, the Queen was forced,
finally, to send for Palmerston, and he became the new
Prime Minister on February 8, 1855.

The advent of Palmerston was the symbol of a new order
of things, but it was months before the necessary corrections
could be made. Meanwhile the war continued on its tragic
course. Nicholas I died in March, Lord Raglan succumbed
to dysentery in June. Even civilians like the administrator of
the *Times* Fund, Mr. Stowe, fell victim to disease.

It was midsummer of 1855 before Britain had finished with
muddling through and had finally forged a respectable army

and supplied it with effective weapons for siege warfare. The weight of new levies and new weapons finally carried the field, and Sebastopol fell on the night of September 8-9 after a terrible price had been paid.

The fall of Sebastopol should have been, in Canning's opinion—and most of the Cabinet agreed with him—merely a prelude to a vigorous prosecution of the war to the end of bringing Russia to her knees. Only in that way, it was thought, could an effective and enduring peace be secured; and to accept anything less was to betray those who had fallen. But Napoleon III had his military glory, and the strain of the war was telling on France. He made it quite clear to London that he was anxious to conclude a peace with the new Czar of Russia, Alexander II, and that if England chose to pursue the war she might have to fight on alone. The Allied armies, therefore, did not follow after the retreating Russian forces but remained in Sebastopol methodically wrecking the remaining installations, and a virtual armistice came into effect. No real measures were taken to assist the Turks who were giving way to the Russians in the Caucasus, and the Russians, thereby, were able to balance the loss of Sebastopol with important gains elsewhere.[3] In short, Russia was not yet reduced to the straits considered necessary to throttle her as a disturber of the East.

The posture assumed by Canning was not motivated by a desire for crushing humiliation for its own sake. But since a price had already been paid he thought it only logical that the peace to be secured should be permanent. He felt that a Russia contained behind a chain of independent buffer states was a necessity. So he hoped that the peace to come would erect a chain of states beginning with a restored Poland, and including Serbia, Montenegro, and the Danubian principalities, along with some permanent arrangement in the Caucasus. These provisions together with an effective pacification of the Black Sea he felt were essential. As for the Ottoman Empire, the long-sought reform was to come first, to be followed by a sincere admission of the Porte to the councils of Europe on an equal footing with the other great powers.

He had been for such an arrangement consistently, especially after the war had begun. But the terms of peace being bruited about in the European capitals in the fall of 1855 fell far short of what he considered minimum guarantees. Indeed, they were little more severe than the Four Points of the second Vienna Note rejected by Russia in August of 1854, after Russia had evacuated the principalities. These points were advanced by Austria with the approval of the allies and included abolition of the Russian protectorates in Serbia and the principalities, the free navigation of the Danube, the closing of the Straits to ships of war in time of peace and restrictions on Russian naval power in the Black Sea, and, finally, the substitution of a collective European guarantee for the Porte's Christian subjects in place of any exclusive Russian privilege. In February of 1855, with Lord Russell sitting in Vienna as plenipotentiary for the Palmerston Cabinet, these same terms were again offered to Russia but again were rejected.

Now, with Sebastopol finally conquered, with a vigorous military machine at England's disposal, all was about to be thrown away by an ineffective peace. Canning's influence was on the decline at this time, however, both at home and at the Porte. He could not forestall the convening of the Conference of Paris nor could he do much about the terms of peace, for he was neither invited to attend the conference nor consulted about its provisions.

The Treaty of Paris was concluded in March of 1856, and ratified by the signatories in April of the same year.[4] Territorily, no change was effected, as all such arrangements reverted to the *status quo ante bellum*. The Sublime Porte, according to Article VII, was "admitted to participate in the advantages of the public law and system of Europe," and its integrity was guaranteed by the powers. The Black Sea was neutralized and both Turkey and Russia were forbidden to maintain "arsenals" on its littoral. The Straits were closed to foreign warships in time of peace and the Straits Convention of 1841 was reaffirmed. Serbia was removed from Russian protection and placed under a joint guarantee of the signatory powers (England, France, Russia, Turkey, Austria, Prussia, and Sardinia). The Danubian principalities were to be similarly guaranteed, but their constitution was left in abeyance pending further discussions and a plebiscite among the inhabitants to determine whether they were to be united into one domain or were to continue as two separate states. As for the protection of the Christian subjects of the Porte—the basic and enduring "question"—that was thought to be taken care of by Article IX of the Treaty.

Article IX referred to the only matter in which Lord Stratford had a direct part in the peace. He had secured, in February of 1856, a new *hattihumayun*[5] which reaffirmed the reforms of Gulhane, and theoretically solved the question. But, in taking note of their satisfaction with this decree, the signatory powers went on to declare specifically: "It is clearly understood that it cannot, in any case, give to the said Powers the right to interfere, either collectively or separately, in the relations of His Majesty the Sultan with his subjects, nor in the internal administration of his Empire." To anyone who knew the Turkish mentality such self-exclusion on the part of the European powers was tantamount to signing a death warrant for the Tanzimat. Reform, Canning knew, was dead for the foreseeable future.

The organization of the Danubian principalities into the separate state of Rumania was not finalized during his tenure of active service, but he was strongly opposed to the idea of uniting the two provinces. In this instance it seems evident that he did not examine the issues impartially, for neither union nor separateness was a matter of great moment, certainly not as important as maintaining a Franco-British accord with regard to the East. Canning seems to have been against union because it was a French idea more than for any other reason. He saw union as a symbol of French rather than British ascendancy and, at the age of seventy, he regarded it as another defeat. True, he was able to forestall it for the time being, but it came about shortly thereafter anyway.

Canning's pique at the French was understandable. Ever since the alliance of 1854 between England and France had united the two countries in war, the French had been working to destroy the position and influence of the British Ambassador in Constantinople. All during 1856 and 1857 there had been a tug of war between opposing factions at the Porte. The pro-British faction, represented by Reshid Pasha, to whom the Elchi looked as the best hope of internal reform despite his disappointment with the Turkish minister, was engaged in a continuing exchange of ministries with the French faction, led by the younger Ali and Fuad Pashas.

The British government also treated its Ambassador rather shoddily, even to the point of sending his obvious successor to the Porte in a separate capacity, thus detracting from the Ambassador's prestige. It was unfortunate that his long and valuable career was allowed to close in shadows of this kind, but he can be forgiven for trying to the last to achieve a goal that he had pursued ever since 1842.

When Lord Palmerston, whom Stratford felt had been personally loyal to him during all these trials and who had publicly defended him in Parliamentary debate, suffered a Parliamentary censure in February of 1858 and resigned from

office, Canning submitted his resignation as Ambassador to
the Porte. His resignation was accepted by Lord Derby,
although he was reappointed so that he could go back and
take proper leave of the Sultan and the host of friends he had
at the Golden Horn. (Canning had been home on leave when
the Palmerston Cabinet fell.) It was a strained situation, for
his successor was already resident at the Embassy, and the
Elchi was enjoined to take a ceremonious leave of the Sultan
and to come away. He was not to interfere with any of the
ordinary matters of the Embassy.

Reshid had died before this final departure of the Elchi,
and Abudul Medjid was but a shadow of his former self.
The Sultan was destined to die within three years, and it
must have seemed to Canning that all his hopes were dying
as well. To the Sultan and to Ali Pasha he upheld the ideals
of the new Hatti-Humayun, but he must have seen the
emptiness of his words. Time was to prove him right about
so many things, but defeat surrounded his last days in
Constantinople.

On October 19, 1858, Lord Stratford laid the cornerstone
in the foundation of the Memorial Church which stands on
Pera Hill to the memory of the British dead in the Crimea.
Then he boarded a frigate and departed from Constantinople
forever.

1. The reader who wishes to pursue a detailed account of the military
history of the Crimean War has ample material at his disposal. Alexander
Kinglake's voluminous history, *The Invasion of the Crimea*, is, of course,

a most detailed account. Kinglake was a friend of the family of Lord Raglan and wrote in answer to critical accounts of the British command, especially those of the famous correspondent of the London *Times*, W. H. Russell. One should, then, also peruse Russell's *The British Expedition to the Crimea* (rev. ed.; London: G. Routledge and Co., 1958) for a balance.

Either of these works will consume a considerable amount of time, but there are two contemporary works which have summarized (with the usual disadvantages of summarization) the campaign. One is Cecil Woodham-Smith's *The Reason Why* (New York; McGraw-Hill, 1953), which, as its title implies, focuses its attention on the Battle of Balaclava, and to that extent is somewhat particularized. More general in its account of the military campaign is Gibb's *The Crimean Blunder* (New York: Henry Holt, 1960). Gibb's short description of the historical background of the war is, however, most unreliable.

I have also found interesting sidelights in George Palmer Evelyn, *A Diary of the Crimea*, ed. Cyril Falls (London, 1954). Evelyn, a descendant of the famous diarist John Evelyn, was an Englishman who held a commission in the Turkish army and saw much service in the war.

Finally, there was a "Brady" of the Crimea, the photographer Roger Fenton, and a number of his fine photographs together with his letters were published in an edition by Helmut and Alison Gernsheim entitled *Roger Fenton: Photographer of the Crimean War* (London: Secker and Warburg, 1954).

2. Cf. Lane-Poole, *op. cit.*, II, 374 ff., for a discussion of the medical problems at Constantinople.

3. The situation in the Caucasus was going badly for the Turks. Again Lord Stratford was attacked for failing to see that the British liaison officer there did not get better supplies and reinforcements. I have passed over this in the text because it was a military problem rather than a diplomatic one, and because the Elchi was completely vindicated in Parliament by Lord Palmerston and in a subsequent Blue Book. The only censure laid against the Ambassador was that he failed to answer some unimportant letters from the officer, General Williams, a year previous to the campaign in question.

4. Cf. Hurewitz, *op. cit.*, I, 153-56.

5. *Ibid.*, pp. 149-53.

XXVII

THE last two years of Viscount Stratford de Redcliffe's official diplomatic service were clouded over by the confusion born of war, misunderstanding, and bitter personality clashes between himself and other participants in the great drama. Largely they mark a period of anticlimax, for his great work in diplomacy ended in January of 1854 with the entrance of the allied fleets into the Black Sea. From that moment on he, no less than all the others, was carried along in the vortex of war, and the forces unleashed were beyond the control of a single individual or even of a single nation.

The scope of this present work is limited to an assessment of Stratford Canning's major diplomatic accomplishments and therefore is not concerned with anticlimactic details. Nevertheless, something should be said about the aftereffects of the Peace of Paris. If it is true that Canning's misgivings over the terms of the peace and the many arrangements dictated by it were colored to a great extent by personal bitterness and disappointment, it is also true that these doubts were not solely motivated by these factors. He was to live to see the questionable Treaty unilaterally abrogated by Russia in 1870[1] when the western European powers were enmeshed in the uncertainties of the Franco-Prussian War. He was still alive in 1876 when Russian aggression was once more directed at the Ottoman Empire, again under the pretext of succoring Balkan Orthodoxy. He saw the European powers refuse to sanction the harsh terms imposed by Russia on the Turks in the Treaty of San Stefano which ended that war. He saw the Congress of Berlin convened to modify that Treaty and to discuss the age-old question of Ottoman reform and the integrity of the Ottoman Empire.[2] All these things might have been effectively disposed of by a stronger peace settlement in 1856 and history supported the core of his reservations on the terms of the Peace of Paris.

The "might-have-been's," therefore, are inextricably interwoven in the pattern of conclusions to be drawn from a study of Stratford Canning's diplomatic labors. To attempt such an assessment assuredly exposes the practitioner to arguments based on probabilities and improbabilities. To avoid meaningful conclusions on those grounds, however, would seem to reduce the study of history to an art of abstraction without lessons for future generations.

From 1842 to the close of his diplomatic career in 1858, Stratford Canning was motivated by two major, closely connected goals. The first was the preservation of the Ottoman

Empire, which he saw as necessary for the welfare of the millions living within its social structure as well as for the peace of Europe. Had there been effective internal reform after the Decree of Gulhane, or even after the Peace of Paris in 1856, the pretexts for outside interference would have disappeared. Because the powers of Europe bypassed successive opportunities to demand real reform in Turkey, the Eastern question remained as a factor disruptive of European peace. There is little to be gained from debating the question of who or what was the prime mover in the movement for internal reform. What is important is that Stratford Canning perceived the fundamental necessity of reform and became, certainly, the chief and most persevering European exponent of reform. He never claimed for himself the title of "Reformer of Turkey" mistakenly given to him by contemporary admirers. Indeed, he had all but lost hope of seeing effective reform accomplished under the Ottoman framework. This is why, in 1876, when he was still able to rise in the House of Lords and was still a prolific contributor to learned reviews, he failed to advocate a new British intervention on behalf of the Turk. He felt that they had made no effort to help themselves. The reforms he supported, although they were initiated and promulgated by successive sultans, were never really implemented until the whole Ottoman structure was torn asunder by the revolution of Kemal Ataturk after the First World War. Reform, however, was hindered not only by the internal barriers of immemorial custom *(adet)* but by outside interference as well. To impose reform upon un-

willing religious fanatics, the sultans, even had they been
most sincere in their professed ideals, needed undisturbed
peace and freedom from aggression. To protect them from
external aggression had been his second goal.

Historically, in his lifetime, the greatest single external
threat to the Ottoman Empire was the pressure of Russian
expansionism. For this fact Stratford Canning cannot be
blamed. He was no more anti-Russian than he would have
been anti-Austrian had the accidents of history substituted
one threat for the other. The Russian drive was there; it
was undeniable, whatever may have motivated it. It may
have been economic, it may have been political, it may have
been a mystical, neo-Byzantine messianism, or a mixture of
all three, but it was there. It might change its direction and
its emphasis temporarily, as it did after Adrianople, but it
never wholly desisted or disappeared. The Russian drive
used the internal corruption of Turkey, it used the threat
of Mehemet Ali and the Egyptians, it used the dispute of
the Holy Places, but they were all means for establishing
Russian rule and hegemony. The relentless pressure continued after his career ended and after his life came to a
close. So Leon Dennen could write in 1945: "For the
moment one thing seems obvious: The Crimean War between
Britain and Russia, to paraphrase Georges Clemenceau, has
not ended; it has merely changed its form." [3]

As for the Crimean War itself, undoubtedly it was the
climax of Canning's diplomatic career. Not that he sought
war, but he knew the Russian drive must be thwarted. He

had been instrumental in thwarting the Czar before that, and without major war. He had been able to block Russian aims during the Greek Revolution and during the refugee crisis, and his viewpoint had been adopted by Palmerston in the final years of the Turco-Egyptian struggle. All these potential conflicts terminated without major war because he had the benefit of strong support at home. In 1853-54, this strength was non-existent. The failure of the Aberdeen government to adopt a clear, forthright policy has been sufficiently mentioned, and because of this there was no over-all European unity against Russia. Had the original diplomatic unity effected by Canning after the Menshikov ultimatum was delivered to the Turks been preserved and carried over to a martial unity there is every reason to believe that war would have been averted. Despite Napoleon III's dreams of glory, and Nicholas' conviction of his "divine mission," collective security *for peace* might have been a fact in 1853 instead of being an ideal still eluding mankind today.

1. See Hurewitz, *op. cit.*, I, 173-74.
2. *Ibid.*, pp. 189-91.
3. Dennen, *op. cit.*, pp. 14-15.

EPILOGUE

VISCOUNT STRATFORD DE REDCLIFFE returned to England in 1859 and began a life of "honourable retirement." In no sense, however, was it a withdrawal from the world of men, for he exercised his privilege of speaking out in the House of Lords whenever he felt the need to comment on questions of the day. Though his preoccupation was naturally with matters of foreign policy, his views on domestic issues were no less explicitly stated.

As time went on the high points of his service stood out in bold relief, and the wisdom of his basic views was attested time and again. The bitterness and misunderstanding of the war years receded, and he came to be looked upon as a Nestor on foreign affairs. When he was past ninety years of age, he wrote a perceptive series of papers which were published under the title of *The Eastern Question*. He last addressed the House of Lords in 1873, speaking vigorously on the Turco-Persian boundary issue. He was then in his eighty-seventh year of life.

The respect that grew with the years was marked in 1869 by bestowal of the Garter, and, as a prominent figure of the day observed, it was a rare instance of the high honor being given as recognition of service to the state rather than to a party.

In the late seventies, when his growing physical infirmities made the cherished visits to Lords impossible, he moved to his country home at Frant in the Kentish country of Tunbridge Wells. There, on August 14, 1880, he passed away serenely. He was buried simply, in the village churchyard, to the accompaniment of a simple hymn sung by the village children.

The public tributes to him were many and came from all sides. The Dean of Westminster, Dr. Stanley, paid perhaps the greatest tribute when he testified to what the Ambassador meant to individual men:

> In his incorruptible integrity, in his magnificent liberality, in his unshaken firmness, no one could hear his influence spoken of by Christian or Musulman, Protestant or Catholic, Greek or Turk, without feeling that in him each man knew that there was a terror to evildoers which no one could confront with impunity, a refuge for the destitute and oppressed which none could seek in vain.[1]

Four years later the first statue ever placed in Westminster

Abbey in honor of a diplomatist was unveiled to the memory
of Stratford Canning. It bears the everlasting tribute composed by Lord Tennyson:

> Thou third Great Canning stand among our best
> And noblest, now thy long day's work hath ceased;
> Here silent in our Minster of the West
> Who wert the voice of England in the East.

1. Quoted in Malcolm-Smith, *op. cit.*, p. 341.

BIBLIOGRAPHY

ADAMS, JOHN QUINCY. *The Diary of John Quincy Adams 1794–1845*, ed. ALLAN NEVINS. New York, London, and Toronto: Longmans, Green & Co., 1929.

ARNOLD, SIR T. W. *The Caliphate*. Oxford: Clarendon Press, 1924.

BAILEY, F. E. *British Policy and the Turkish Reform Movement*. Cambridge, Mass.: Harvard University Press, 1942.

CANNING, STRATFORD. *The Eastern Question*. London: John Murray, 1881.

CHURCHILL, WINSTON. *A History of the English-Speaking Peoples*. 4 vols. New York: Dodd, Mead & Co., 1956–58.

CLIFFORD, HENRY. *Henry Clifford, V. C. His Letters and Sketches from the Crimea*, ed. CUTHBERT FITZHERBERT. London: Michael Joseph Ltd., 1956.

CRAWLEY, C. W. *The Question of Greek Independence*. London: Cambridge University Press, 1930.

DENNEN, LEON. *Trouble Zone*. New York: Ziff-Davis, 1945.

EVELYN, GEORGE PALMER. *A Diary of the Crimea,* ed. CYRIL FALLS. London: Duckworth, 1954.

FFRENCH, YVONNE. *The Great Exhibition.* London: Harvill Press, 1950.

FISHER, SYDNEY N. *The Middle East: A History.* New York: Alfred Knopf, 1959.

GERNSHEIM, HELMUT and ALISON (eds.). *Roger Fenton, Photographer of the Crimean War.* London: Secker & Warburg, 1954.

GIBB, H. A. R. *Studies on the Civilization of Islam,* ed. STANFORD J. SHAW and WILLIAM R. POLK. Boston: Beacon Press, 1962.

GIBB, PETER. *Crimean Blunder.* New York: Henry Holt, 1960.

GUEDELLA, PHILLIP. *Palmerston.* New York: G. P. Putnam's Sons, 1927.

HUREWITZ, J. C. *Diplomacy in the Near and Middle East.* 2 vols. Princeton, N. J.: Van Nostrand, 1956.

KINGLAKE, A. W. *The Invasion of the Crimea.* 6 vols. New York: Harper & Bros., 1864.

LAMB, HAROLD. *Constantinople—Birth of an Empire.* New York: Alfred Knopf, 1957.

———. *Suleiman the Magnificent.* New York: Doubleday, 1951.

LANE–POOLE, STANLEY. *The Life of the Rt. Hon. Stratford Canning.* 2 vols. London: Longmans, Green & Co., 1888.

LAYARD, SIR AUSTEN HENRY. *Autobiography and Letters,* ed. WILLIAM N. BRUCE. London: Murray, 1903.

LOW, SIR SIDNEY, and SANDERS, LLOYD C. *The History of England during the Reign of Victoria (1837–1901). (The Political*

History of England, ed. WILLIAM HUNT and R. L. POOLE, Vol. XII.) London and New York: Longmans, Green & Co., 1911.

MALCOLM–SMITH, E. F. *The Life of Stratford Canning.* London: Ernest Benn, Ltd., 1933.

RUNCIMAN, STEVEN. *Byzantine Civilization.* London: St. Martin's Press, 1933.

RUSSELL, WILLIAM H. *The British Expedition to the Crimea* (rev. ed.). London: Routledge, 1858.

SMITH, W. C. *Islam in Modern History.* Princeton, N. J.: Princeton University Press, 1957.

TEMPERLEY, H. W. V. *England and the Near East: The Crimea.* London: Longmans, Green & Co., 1936.

TEMPERLEY, H. W. V., and PENSON, J. H. *A Century of Diplomatic Blue Books 1814–1914.* London: Cambridge University Press, 1938.

TOYNBEE, ARNOLD J. *A Study of History.* 12 vols. London: Oxford University Press, 1934–59.

TYRRELL, HENRY. *The History of the Present War with Russia.* 3 vols. London and New York: London Printing & Publishing Co., [ca. 1855–57].

VERNADSKY, GEORGE. *A History of Russia* (3d rev. ed.). New Haven: Yale University Press, 1944.

WOODHAM SMITH, CECIL. *The Reason Why.* New York: McGraw Hill, 1953.

YALE, WILLIAM. *The Near East.* Ann Arbor: University of Michigan Press, 1958.

INDEX

Abdul Aziz, 223

Abdul Medjid II, 153, 157, 158, 160, 161, 172, 180, 188, 203, 256, 294; confidence in Stratford's power to aid, 295; proclaims Russian occupation of Danubian principalities a "casus belli," 327; Stratford's final leavetaking, 358

Aberdeen, Earl of (George Gordon), 119, 149, 163, 169, 181, 246, 253, 270, 275, 306, 323, 332; becomes Prime Minister, 239; censures Stratford and rejects Greek boundary decision of Poros Conference, 124; delineates new boundary, 127; relations with Czar Nicholas I, 240; and Seymour Correspondence, 285; support of cabinet wavers, 322; war reverses defeat ministry of, 352

Act of Occupation, 210

Adair, Sir Robert, 21, 27, 32, 50, 51, 55; as Minister to the Porte, 14; mission to Constantinople, 18; Stratford secretary to, 14

Adams, John Quincey, 78; Stratford's relations with, 78, 80

Addington, Henry U., 73, 83, 145

Adet, 362

Adrianople, 128, 162

Adrianople, Treaty of, 129; recognition of semi-autonomy of Danubian principalities in, 204

Aegean Islands: Allied squadrons in, 111; piracy in, 41, 109; Stratford confers with Greek nationalist leaders, 100

Afif Bey, 238

Akkerman, 105; Treaty of, 109

Albert, Prince, 225

Alexander, Eliza Charlotte, 98, 99

Alexander I, 9, 17, 52, 55, 58, 61, 86, 91, 95; death of, 101

Alexander II, 353

Ali Pasha, 203, 256, 293, 297, 316, 357

Ali Pasha, of Janina, 40

Alison, Charles, 162, 188, 249, 319, 320

Alma, Battle of, 348

Anglican church, 182

Apostasy controversy, 162-72; and Turkish reform, 176

Arta-Volo line, 123; established by Protocol of September, 1831, 131; Turkish agreement to, 137

Austerlitz, Battle of, 16

Austria, 9, 16, 51, 85, 198; and apostasy controversy, 165; asks extradition of Kossuth, 212; final diplomacy left to, 335; military co-operation offered to England and France, 323, 336; mobilizes, 330; Stratford visits during Holy Places crisis, 251; Seymour questions possibility of Russian agreement with, 283; warns Russia against war in Danubian area, 329; *see also* Metternich; Vienna, Conference of; Buol-Schauenstein, Karl Ferdinand

Bagot, Sir Charles, 74, 90, 91

Balaclava, Battle of, 349

Balkans, 86, 121; *see also* Montenegro

Barbary Powers, 40

Barraguay d'Hilliers, General, 341

Bashi-Bazouks, 340

Bath, Grand Cross of, bestowed on Stratford, 125

Beresina, Battle of, 61

Berlin, Congress of, 361

Bernadotte, 52

Besika Bay, Anglo-French fleet movements in, 323

Black Sea, 121; Allied fleet movements in, 331, 333; Czar interdicts Turkish commerce in, 331; Western powers forbid Russian operations in, 333

Bourbons, the, 66, 200

Bourqueney, Baron, 164

Brunnow, Baron, 209, 239, 240, 326

Bucharest, Treaty of, 61, 104

Buol-Schauenstein, Karl Ferdinand, 251, 318; declares unity with England and France, 308; summons Conference of Vienna, 308

Buyuklu Oglu Mustapha, 44, 55

Byron, Lord (George Gordon), 87

Caliphate, relation to Ottoman Sultanate, 39, 47

Cambridge, Stratford admitted to King's College, 8

Canning, Charles, 69, 73

Canning, George, 64, 65, 69, 72, 73, 79, 87, 88, 89, 91, 104, 109; abandoned to care of Stratford's parents, 5; becomes Foreign Secretary, 9; dispatches fleet to Copenhagen, 11; duel with Castlereagh and resignation, 27-28; early Turkish policy of, 50; enters Stratford in Eton, 7; non-commitment policy of, 86; orders to Sir Edward Codrington on interposition, 111; Prime Minister, 110; sudden death of, 111

Canning, George, son of Stratford, 139, 186

Canning, Henry, 73

Canning, Stratford, father of
    Stratford, 5
Canning, William, 12
Canynges, Sir William, 4
Cape St. Vincent, Battle of, 16
Capodistrias, Count Agostino, 130
Capodistrias, Count John, 70; Presi-
    dent of Provisional Greek Govern-
    ment, 100, 119, 122, 129
Carlos, Don, 145
Carroll, Charles, 82
Castlereagh, Viscount Robert, 61,
    65, 66, 69, 73, 77, 79, 80; dis-
    pute with George Canning, 27;
    Foreign Minister, 60
Catholic Emancipation, 191
Caucasus, Russian successes in, 353
Chartist Movement, 200
Clarendon, Earl of (G.W.F. Vil-
    liers), 250, 251, 253, 274, 275,
    286, 304; approves Vienna Note,
    314; Foreign Secretary, 254; in-
    structs Stratford to urge Vienna
    Note upon Porte, 315; loses hope
    for peace, 322; orders Stratford to
    summon fleet, 326, 328
Clay, Henry, 82
Clemenceau, Georges, 368
Codrington, Sir Edward, 111-12
Concert of Ambassadors: in Con-
    stantinople, 298-99; support of,
    by respective governments, 305;
    and Vienna Conference, 310
Constantinople: Concert of Ambas-
    sadors in, 298-99; crisis in, after
    Navarino, 112-15; destruction of
    Janissaries in, 107; importance to
    England during Napoleonic era,
    37; Leiningen mission to, 241;

Menshikov mission to, 243; revolt
    of Janissaries in, 23; revolutionary
    threats in, viewed by French and
    Stratford, 325-27; Stratford's com-
    missary difficulties in, 350; Strat-
    ford's early surroundings in, 35;
    Stratford's resignation and final
    leave-taking, 358; Stratford's suc-
    cessive missions to, 14, 98, 132,
    149, 202, 246
Corn Laws, 192
Crete, 91, 124
Crimean War: analysis of causes
    leading to, 303; expedition to,
    347; fiasco of military operations
    in, 352; formal declaration by
    England and France of, 337;
    judgment of Dennen on, 363;
    military deficiencies of England
    in, 343, 345, 347; Stratford's
    Russian policy and, 363-64; Strat-
    ford's war aims in, 353-54

Danubian principalities, 40, 86, 129,
    203, 205, 239; Napoleonic in-
    trigue in, 17; Nicholas I suggests
    independence of, 284; Russian
    troops in, 306, 338; Treaty of
    Paris unites, with Rumania, 356
Dardanelles, Straits of: Anglo-
    French naval movements at
    approaches to, 324; British fleet
    ordered to environs of, 305;
    French fleet enters, 327; inviola-
    bility of, and Straits Convention
    of 1841, 154-55; Parker enters,
    219; Stratford's instructions and,
    247-48; Stratford summons Eng-
    lish fleet to, 330; Treaty of
    Hunkiar-Skelessi, 152
Dardanelles, Treaty of, 20, 23

Denmark, British mission to, 10

Dennen, Leon, 368

Diebitsch, General, 128

Disraeli, Benjamin, 192

Divan, 39, 53, 58, 106; *see also* Grand Council

Dragomen, the, 42

Drouyn de Lhuys, Edouard, 336

Dundas, Admiral, 325

Eastern Question, The, 365

Egypt, 40, 91; Nicholas I suggests English acquisition of, 284

"Elchi," definition of, 103

Eton, Stratford at, 6-7

Eupatoria, 348

Ferdinand, Emperor of Austria, 200

Ferdinand VII, 145

Foreign Office: offered to Stratford, 227; Stratford's first employment in, 9; *see also* Aberdeen, Earl of; Canning, George; Granville, Earl of; Malmesbury, Earl of; Palmerston, Viscount; Russell, Lord John; Wellesley, Marquis of

Fox, Charles, 6, 8

France: action in North Africa, 151; and Aegean piracy, 41, 45; and apostasy controversy, 164; and Holy Places dispute, 233, 238; effect of Revolution on English policy, 8; lands troops in the Morea, 112; Louis Napoleon and Second Republic, 199; Louis Napoleon and coup d'état, 233; naval movements in environs of Dardanelles, 252, 305-6, 324, 333; preparations for troop arrivals at Porte, 341; Stratford sees growth of influence at Porte, 341, 357; takes leadership of Western powers, 323

Francis Joseph, Emperor of Austria, 200, 242, 251

Franco-Prussian War, 361

Frant, Stratford's country home in Kent, 366

Frederick William IV, 197

Frere, Hookham, 6

Fuad Pasha, Turkish statesman, 218, 256, 357

Gallipoli, 347

Garter, Order of, bestowed on Stratford, 366

George III, 7, 34

George IV, 75; as Prince Regent, 34, 62

Ghalib Effendi, 55, 60

Ghent, Treaty of, 77

Giaour, 42

Gladstone, William, 323, 332

Goderich, Lord, 117

Gordon, Sir Robert, 125, 127

Gortchakoff, Prince, 327; rejects ultimatum of Omar Pasha, 330

Grand Army of Napoleon I, 60, 61

Grand Council of the Ottoman Empire: and the Divan, 39; insists on alterations to Vienna Note,

317; rejects Menshikov proposals, 298; rejects Vienna Note, 316; votes for war, 319; war party in, 307

Granville, Earl of (George Levenson Gower), 226, 227

Great Exhibition of 1851, 225, 227

Greece: and administration of Ottoman Empire, 40; England recognizes belligerent status of Provisional Government of, 88; English policy on Greek War, 92; independence recognized by Turkey, 129; limited independence approved by European powers, 122; mediation of Stratford in, 97, 100; Metternich's policy for, 87, 94; monarchical form of government in, 123; Otho's maladministration of, 198; outbreak of revolt in, 86; supports revolutionaries in European Turkey, 340; see also Aberdeen, Earl of; Adrianople; Canning, George; Ibrahim Pasha; Mehemet Ali Pasha; Nicholas I; Otho, Prince, of Bavaria; Poros, Conference and Convention of; Wellington Protocol

Grenville, Lord William, 9

Grey, Lord Charles, 129, 150

Grillion Club, 66

Gulhane, hatti-sherif of, 157, 158, 161, 183, 352

Hackney, Mr. Newcome's school at, 6

Halicarnassus, tomb of King Mausolus at, 188

Haliki Pasha, 22

Hamelin, Admiral, 325

Hamilton, Lady, 8

Harach, 180, 195, 223

Hatti-humayun of February, 1856, 356

Hay, John Drummond, 187

Holy Alliance, 79, 85, 86, 120

Holy Places, 242, 243, 247, 254, 257, 278; French overtures on, 233; Menshikov accepts Stratford's solution for, 290; Orthodox tradition and, 234; Stratford's policy on, 263-65; Stratford's solution for, 267

Hungary, 200, 205, 211

Hunkiar-Skelessi, Treaty of, 152, 153

Hydra, conference at, 101, 104

Ibrahim Pasha, 91, 134, 150, 151, 154

India, British communications with, 88

Industrial Revolution, 193

Inkermann, Battle of, 349

Islamic law: and apostasy controversy, 163, 168; and civil equality, 261; and millet system, 259; and reform, 155

Italinski, M., 55, 58

Janissaries, 21, 22, 92, 105, 106, 128, 156, 182; destruction of, 107

Jefferson, Thomas, 80

Jerusalem, 238

Jingoism, 334, 338

John VI, 145
Joseph I, 56

Kemal Ataturk, 362
Kinglake, A. W., 302-3
King's Lynn, 146
Konya, Battle of, 151
Koran, the, 165, 166, 167, 319
Kossuth, Louis, 212, 213, 219
Kustchuk-Kainardji, Treaty of, 242

La Cour, M. de, 266, 267, 325, 341; asks for passage of French fleet through Dardanelles, 326-27
Lane-Poole, Stanley, 57, 301-2, 342
Lavalette, M. de, 233, 236, 237, 266
Layard, Austen Henry, 187, 188, 189, 224, 249
Leiningen, Count C.S.V., 241, 248, 251
Leopold, Prince, of Saxe-Coburg, 124
Levant, the, 35, 37; British commerce in, 88
Lieven, Prince Christophe Andreievitch, 144
Liston, Robert, 62
London, Treaty of (1827), 110, 118, 120, 129; secret article of interposition, 111
London, Treaty of (1840), 153-54; *see also* Straits Convention
Lords, House of, Stratford in, 365
Louis XV, 234

Louis-Philippe, 199
Ludolf, Count, 54

Macaulay, Thomas Babington, 193
Madison, James, 80
Madrid, Stratford's mission to, 144
Mahmud II, 21, 54, 55, 58, 63, 102, 103, 108, 119, 133, 156, 177; destroys Janissaries, 105-7; dies, 153; employs Mehemet Ali in Greece, 91; pleads for British aid against Mehemet, 150; rejects Protocol of March, 1829, 128; supported by Russians, 151
Malmesbury, Earl of (James Harris), 228
Mamelukes, the, 40, 107
Maria Louisa, Princess, of Austria, 27
Marshall, John, 82
Maubourg, M., 56
Mavrocordatos, Prince Alexander, 100
Mehemet Ali Pasha, 102, 106, 136, 150, 157; aids Sultan in Greece, 91; invades Syria, 134; renews war with Sultan, 152; smashed by Anglo-Austrian forces, 154
Melbourne, Viscount (William Lamb), 147, 148
Memorandum on the Turco-Egyptian Question, 150
Menshikov, Prince Alexander Sergeievitch, 248, 251, 252, 254, 262, 263, 265, 267, 269, 290, 291; commander in the Crimea, 348-49; ignores protocol of Seraglio, 256, 297; leaves Constantinople,

299; mission to Constantinople, 243; rejects Stratford's analysis of Holy Places dispute, 293; reveals proposed treaty goal to Stratford, 270-71; ultimatum to Turks, 296

Merry, Anthony, 13

Metternich, Prince, 69, 89, 92, 108, 200; leader of Holy Alliance, 79; policy on Greek revolt, 86, 93-94, 101

Miguel, Dom, 145

Millet, definition of, 259

Mohamed Izzet Pasha, 160, 161

Moldavia, 17, 129, 204, 207; *see also* Danubian principalities

Monroe Doctrine, 79-80

Monroe, James, 78, 80

Montenegro, 241, 257, 293

Morea, 91, 101

Morier, David, 12, 35

Mustapha IV, 22

Mustapha Pasha, 297, 307

Napoleon I, 8, 10, 11, 17, 18, 27, 51, 57, 65, 67, 70

Napoleon III, 250, 252, 265; coup d'état, 232; elected emperor, 233; letter to Czar, 336; president of Second French Republic, 231; Stratford's visit to, 249; tires of war, 353

Napoli di Romania, naval action at, 46, 59

Navarino, Battle of, 112, 159, 205

Nelson, Admiral Lord Horatio, 8, 16

Nesselrode, Count Charles, 95, 97, 144, 239, 266, 279, 280, 287,

322, 337; rejects Turkish alterations to Vienna Note, 318; ultimatum to Reshid Pasha demanding protectorate, 305

Nesselrode Memorandum, 241, 275, 278; and Russian policy, 288-89

Neuchâtel, 197

Newcastle, Duke of (H. P. Clinton), 342

Nezib, Battle of, 153

Nicholas I, 101, 104, 118, 204, 207, 209, 218, 239, 242, 257, 275; change of Turkish policy 139; death of, 352; defends Sultan in struggle with Mehemet Ali, 151; hints agreement with Austria, 284; meets Francis Joseph at Olmutz, 322; reaction to French overtures on Holy Places, 235; reaction to Vienna Note, 311, 317; rejects Anglo-French demand to evacuate principalities, 335; rejects Stratford as ambassador, 143; suggestions for disposition of Ottoman Empire, 284; understanding of Aberdeen policy, 240; withdraws troops from principalities, 346; *see also* Seymour Correspondence; Nesselrode Memorandum

Nightingale, Florence, 351

Nineveh, Layard's diggings at, 188, 189

Nizam-Jedid, 33, 107, 182

Old Sarum, 125, 141, 143

Olmutz, Nicholas and Francis Joseph meet at, 322, 329

Omar Pasha, 327

Orthodox churches in Ottoman Empire, 181, 182; foreign intervention in behalf of, 258; leadership of Greek Patriarch of, 260; Russian tradition and, 204; Russia demands formal protectorate of, 243; Russian rights defended by Nesselrode, 318; Stratford's analysis of proposed protectorate of, 292; Stratford proposes European guarantee of privileges, 330

Otho, Prince, of Bavaria, 139, 198, 201; covert aid to Russia, 350

Ottenfels, Baron, 108

Ottoman Empire, 276; administration of, 39-40; objectives of Stratford's reform policy in, 149; obstacles to reform in, 155-60; Russo-Turkish War of 1876 in, 361; Stratford's policy for, 361-63; *see also* Abdul Medjid II; Grand Council; Mahmud II; Reshid Pasha

Palmerston, Viscount (H. J. Temple), 130, 132, 143, 145, 150, 152, 153, 192, 193, 196, 199, 206, 208, 211, 215, 217, 218, 219, 220, 222, 224, 225, 226, 322; Foreign Secretary, 130; Home Office in Aberdeen Ministry, 239; questions Stratford's thesis on Turco-Egyptian dispute, 151; resigns from Aberdeen Ministry, 332; resigns as Prime Minister, 357; reverses policy, 151; returns on own terms, 332; succeeds Aberdeen as Prime Minister, 352

Paris, Treaty of, 355; effect of Article IX on Turkish reform, 356; general effects of, 360; Russia abrogates, 361; Stratford's misgivings on, 356-57

Parker, Sir William, 215, 217, 219

Parliament, debates on Crimean operations, 352; Stratford and, 125, 141, 142

Patrick, Mehitabel, 5

Pedro, Dom, 145

Peel, Sir Robert, 147, 191, 192, 240; Prime Minister, 146, 148

Peninsula Campaign, 9

Pera, Christian suburb of Constantinople, 35

Peterloo riots, 103

Petersburg Conference, 89, 95-97, 101

Pisani, Frederick, 44, 163, 171, 249

Pisani, Stephen, 44, 254

Pitt, William, 8

Planta, Joseph, 12, 72

Poland, 52, 200

Poros, Conference and Convention of, 121, 123, 124, 127

Portland, Duke of (W. H. Cavendish Bentinck), 27

Portugal, succession crisis, 145

Protestantism in Ottoman Empire, 181, 182, 223

Protocol of March, 1829, 127, 129

Protocol of March, 1829, Annex to, 127, 128

Protocol of September, 1831, 131

Prussia, 9, 85; and apostasy controversy, 165; intent to co-operate ignored by England and France, 323; support of England and France, 336

Pruth River, 61, 204, 207

Radzivil, Prince Michael, 214, 215
Raglan, Lord (Fitzroy J. H. Somerset), 343, 346, 348, 352; strategy of, in Crimean War, 349
Raikes, Harriet, 72
Rauf Pasha, 162, 165
Rawlinson, Sir Henry, 187, 189
Rayah, 156, 180, 196, 340
Reform Bill, 143, 191
Reform in Turkey; see Apostasy controversy; Gulhane, hatti-sherif of; Hatti-humayun of February, 1856; Ottoman Empire; Reshid Pasha; Tanzimat
Reis Effendi, 40
Reshid Pasha, 158, 159, 162, 177, 178, 179, 184, 189, 190, 195, 202, 203, 206, 214, 223, 224, 297, 298, 299, 305, 307, 325, 330, 342, 357, 358; author of Gulhane Decree, 157; contacts Nicholas I secretly, 242; informs Stratford of Grand Council vote on Vienna Note, 316
Rifat Pasha, 162, 165, 166, 169, 172, 177, 178, 179, 203, 223, 257, 270, 290, 291, 297, 316; reveals full extent of Russian demands to Stratford, 263
Riza Pasha, 160, 162, 180, 183, 184, 190
Rose, Colonel Hugh, 252, 257
Rumania, 356
Rush, Richard, 92
Russell, Lord John, 192, 217, 225, 227, 246, 268, 274, 275, 280, 322
Russia, 16, 40; armed forces in Bulgaria, 53; and Danubian principalities, 54; declares war on

Turkey, 118; and Kossuth affair, 212; memorandum on Greece, 89, 90; offers Sultan alliance against France, 258; policy in apostasy controversy, 165; proclaims innocence to European powers, 329; relations with England and France broken, 333-34; Russo-Turkish War of 1876, 361; summary of Turkish policy, 363; ultimatum on Greece, 104; see also Alexander I; Menshikov, Prince Alexander Sergeievitch; Nesselrode, Count Charles; Nicholas I; Petersburg Conference; Seymour Correspondence; Vienna Note

Safti Pasha, 160, 183, 184
St. Arnaud, Marshal Jacques, 346, 349
St. Petersburg Journal, 275
Salamis, Bay of, French Fleet in, 252, 268
San Stefano, Treaty of, 361
Sarim Effendi, 160, 162
Schönbrunn, Treaty of, 27
Scutari, 343; military hospital at, 351
Sebastopol, siege of, 347, 348, 349, 352, 353
Selim III, 17, 22, 106, 182
Seraglio, the, 39
Seraskier, 39
Seymour, Sir Hamilton, 252, 266, 304, 324; messages to London, 248; Seymour Correspondence, 274-89

Sheik-ul-Islam: and apostasy controversy, 184; rejects Vienna Note, 316

Shekib Effendi, 179

Sheridan, Richard Brinsley, 6

Sierra Capriola, Duke of, 54, 58

Sinope, Battle of, 331; English reaction to, 332

Slave trade, and U. S.–British relations, 77

Slavery in Ottoman Empire, 223

Sonderbund, 196, 197

Spain: American colonies of, 79; British operations in, 19; Stratford's mission to, 144-45; Stratford refuses ambassadorship to, 145

Staël, Madame de, 66

Stanley, Arthur, 367

Stanley, Lord Edward G. S., 146, 187, 192, 275; approaches Stratford on future foreign secretaryship, 227; nominates Stratford to peerage, 229; Prime Minister, 228; reappoints Stratford ambassador to Porte for final leavetaking, 358

Stockbridge, 143

Straits Convention of 1841, 154, 324

Stratfords of Baltinglas, 4

Sublime Porte; see Constantinople; Grand Council; Ottoman Empire

Suleiman Nejib Effendi, 138

Suleiman the Magnificent, 21

Switzerland: Congress of Vienna and, 69; neutrality of, 71; pre-Napoleonic organization of, 67; religious strife in, 196-98; Stratford minister to, 66; Stratford's mission to, 196; Swiss Confederation under Bonaparte, 67; Swiss Federation, 71

Syria, 40, 150; invaded by Mehemet Ali Pasha, 134

Talleyrand, Charles, 69

Tanzimat, 157, 352

Temperley, H. W. V., 302

Tennyson, Lord Alfred, 367

Tilsit, Peace of, 17

Times (London), 253, 318, 352

Titov, M., 219

Tory party, 9, 64, 191, 192

Townley, Captain Charles, 218

Transylvania, 209

Tunbridge Wells, 366

Turkey; see Abdul Medjid II; Divan; Grand Council; Mahmud II; Ottoman Empire

Tyrell, Henry, 318

United States: Canadian boundaries of, 77, 80; foreign policy of, 76; Stratford's mission to, 73; Stratford's opinions on Congress of, 81; Stratford's travels in, 82

Varna, port of, 346

Victoria, Queen, 148, 239, 303

Vienna, Conference of: Buol initiates, 308, 309; derogates from Concert of Ambassadors, 310; endorses Stratford's Protocol of December, 1853, 333; reasons for failure of, 321, 324; submits

Vienna Note to Nicholas I for prior approval, 310; suppresses Turkish ultimatum, 310-11

Vienna, Congress of, 69, 70, 77, 85, 94, 193; contrast with Conference of Vienna, 321; Stratford officially accredited member of, 69

Vienna Note, 309; submitted to Nicholas I and Sultan, 310; see also Clarendon, Earl of; Grand Council; Nesselrode, Count Charles; Nicholas I; Reshid Pasha; Westmoreland, Earl of

Vogordies, Stefanaki, 135, 136, 137

Wagram, Battle of, 27

Wallachia, 17, 129, 203; see also Danubian principalities

Wanstead, 6

Washington, George, 76

Wellesley, Henry, 12, 187; ambassador to Paris, 226

Wellesley, Marquis of (Richard Colley), 35, 36, 57, 59, 60

Wellesley, Richard, 20, 32

Wellington, Duke of (Sir Arthur Wellesley), 9, 34, 61, 69, 70, 104, 194, 200, 240, 279; Prime Minister, 115; views on Annex to Protocol of March, 1829, 128

Wellington Protocol, 104, 105, 110

Westminster Abbey, 367

Westmoreland, Earl of (John Fane), 286; advises Stratford of Clarendon's approval of Vienna Note, 314

Whig party, 9, 191, 192

William IV, 143